CONSERVATIVE BAPTIST
THEOLOGICAL SEMINARY

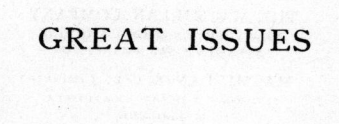

GREAT ISSUES

THE MACMILLAN COMPANY
NEW YORK · BOSTON · CHICAGO
ATLANTA · SAN FRANCISCO

MACMILLAN & CO., LIMITED
LONDON · BOMBAY · CALCUTTA
MELBOURNE

THE MACMILLAN CO. OF CANADA, LTD.
TORONTO

GREAT ISSUES

BY

ROBERT F. HORTON

AUTHOR OF "INSPIRATION AND THE BIBLE," "REVELATION
AND THE BIBLE," AND "VERBUM DEI"

New York
THE MACMILLAN COMPANY
1909

All rights reserved

COPYRIGHT, 1909,
BY THE MACMILLAN COMPANY.

Set up and electrotyped. Published December, 1909.

Norwood Press
J. S. Cushing Co. — Berwick & Smith Co.
Norwood, Mass., U.S.A.

CONTENTS

CHAPTER I

	PAGE
MYTHS	1

CHAPTER II

RELIGION 29

CHAPTER III

MORALITY 63

CHAPTER IV

POLITICS 92

CHAPTER V

SOCIALISM 124

CHAPTER VI

PHILOSOPHY 156

CHAPTER VII

SCIENCE 188

CHAPTER VIII

THEOLOGY 222

CHAPTER IX

LITERATURE 255

CHAPTER X

ART 286

CHAPTER XI

LIFE 319

CHAPTER XII

DEATH 351

INDEX 381

GREAT ISSUES

GREAT ISSUES

CHAPTER I

MYTHS

When Plato desired to utter some truth which lies deep in the mystery of being he was accustomed to glide into what he called a myth. Such myths, "truths embodied in a tale," are among the masterpieces of his style, or, one might say, of all literature. He uses the myth, not to avoid speaking truth, but in order to speak it. There was no other medium through which he could convey realities which belong, not to the phenomenal, but to the noumenal world. Well he knew the difficulty of dealing with that spiritual background of human life. Dialectic was no adequate instrument. Logic missed the mark. Science, if he had known the meaning of science in the modern sense, made no pretence to penetrate that region, or to report on it. And yet men wished to know, and he for one felt able to tell, much that lay thus beyond the confines of scientific inquiry or of logical discussion. This vague stuff of the soul and of life, these certainties which admitted of no proof, these dogmas which could never be formulated, he brought into the plane of common observation, if not of common understanding, by means of tales — the Greek word μῦθος, which in English takes the form of "myth" is only a tale — tales beautiful in form, sparkling with wit and wisdom; tales which, not affecting to be true, yet conveyed the deepest, the ultimate, the ineffable truth.

For example, the "Gorgias" ends with the myth of Minos, Rhadamanthus, and Æacus. "Listen," says Socrates to Callicles, "as story-tellers say, to a very pretty tale which I daresay that you may be disposed to regard as a fable only, but which, as I believe, is a true tale, for I mean to speak the truth." There the myth begins. Formerly men were judged in their bodies and clothes before death, with the result that the soul frequently reached the wrong destination. The judges were awed by the trappings, and also misled by the clothes which they themselves had on. Zeus therefore determined to make a change: "In the first place, I will deprive men of the foreknowledge of death, which they at present possess; that is a commission of which I have already entrusted the execution to Prometheus; in the second place, they shall be entirely stripped before they are judged, for they shall be judged when they are dead; and the judge, too, shall be naked — that is to say, dead: he with his naked soul shall pierce into the other naked soul, and they shall die suddenly, and be deprived of all their kindred, and leave their brave attire strewn upon the earth; con-

ducted in this manner the judgment will be just."
The three judges shall give judgment in the meadow
at the place where the three ways meet, out of which
the two roads lead, one to the islands of the blessed
and the other to Tartarus.

From the tale Socrates proceeds to draw inferences, precisely as a divine reasons from a passage of Scripture. The myth, indeed, is Scripture. "Death, if I am right, is in the first place the separation from one another of two things, soul and body, nothing else. And after they are separated they retain their several characteristics, which are much the same as in life; the body has the same nature and ways and affections, all clearly discernible; for example, he who by nature or training, or both, was a tall man while he was alive will remain as he was after he is dead, and the fat man will remain fat, and so on; and the dead man who in life had a fancy to have flowing hair will have flowing hair. And if he was marked with the whip and had the prints of the scourge or of wounds in him when he was alive, you might see the same in the dead body, and if his limbs were broken or misshapen when he was alive, the same appearance would be visible in the dead. . . . I should imagine that this is equally true of the soul, Callicles; when a man is stripped of the body all the natural or acquired affections of the soul are laid open to view. When they come to the judge, as those from Asia come to Rhadamanthus, he places them near him, and inspects them quite impartially, not knowing whose the soul is; perhaps he may lay hands on the soul of the Great King, or of some other king or potentate, who has no soundness in him, but his soul is marked with the whip and is full of the prints and scars of perjuries and crimes with which each action has stained him, and he is all crooked with falsehood and imposture, and has no straightness, because he has lived without truth. Him Rhadamanthus beholds, full of all deformity and disproportion, which is caused by licence and luxury and insolence and incontinence, and despatches him ignominiously to his prison, and there he undergoes the punishment which he deserves."

Some of the stained, distorted souls are curable; "they are improved, as in this world so also in another, by pain and suffering; for there is no other way in which they can be delivered from their evil." Others are incurable, but they serve as deterrents; "there they are hanging up as examples, in the prison-house of the world below, a spectacle and a warning to all unrighteous men who come thither."

On the other hand, the judge "looks with admiration on the soul of some just one who has lived in holiness and truth," and sends him to the islands of the blessed.

"Now I, Callicles," says Socrates, "am persuaded of the truth of these things, and I consider how I shall present my soul whole and undefiled before the judge in that day. Renouncing the honours at which the world aims, I desire only to know the truth, and to live as well as I can and, when the time comes, to die." And then he adds: "Perhaps this may appear to you to be only an old wife's tale, which you will contemn. And there might be reason in your contemning such tales, if by searching we could find out anything better or truer."

It would seem, then, that no discourtesy need be intended if a narrative or a piece of literature is described as mythical. Such a judgment might mean that it is only an old wife's tale, which can be told and heard, only for a child's pastime; but it may mean that in this way the truth is conveyed by and for the wisest and most mature of human minds, because the nature of the truth is such that it cannot be otherwise expressed, or even suggested, to hearer or reader. One, for example, who has not reflected on this fact might be inclined to dismiss the story of Adam and Eve as incredible because it is a myth or another who has not reflected might resent the charge that it is a myth as a disparagement. But suppose the matter in hand is such as cannot be conveyed in any better form than that of a myth, and suppose the myth brings home to men, even to-day, the most and best that we can know about human freedom, and sin, and redemption, in that case the firmest believer will welcome the myth. The question about the story is not, Is it true? but, Does it convey truth? The origin of evil is a problem which has never been solved. But men are engaged in a conflict with evil, sometimes suffering under defeat, sometimes rejoicing in the sense of victory. They ask eagerly the why and the wherefore. They feel the necessity of some interpretation in order to fight successfully. How does the myth of the Garden of Eden serve us? As history it would seem to break down. No reasoning can represent the sin of Adam as a sufficient cause of all human sin. Milton's heroic effort to tell the story of the fall,

"To justify the ways of God to man,"

does not convince the reason. The splendour of the poetry carries the mind away in another direction, and "Paradise Lost" becomes one of the transcendent creations of the human intellect. But no truer, no more reasonable, appears the suggestion that because an innocent and ignorant woman was persuaded by a subtle serpent to eat the fruit which was forbidden, the whole progeny of Adam, to the remotest generations, was involved in guilt which merits death and eternal pain. Milton still believed he was answering a theological problem by his argument. St. Augustine found no difficulty in the theory. We hesitate to say whether St. Paul believed it or meant it, for his mind was soaked in the rabbinical symbolism; and it is more than likely that he, like the best of the Rabbis, knew that the story of Paradise was a myth to be interpreted, and not a fact on which to build a doubtful scheme of human sin and redemption.

But whatever Milton or St. Augustine believed, we to-day can never, except under the coercion of a dogmatic authority which we are afraid to question, seriously hold that the sins of mankind are due to the sin of a primal parent; still less can we hold that the sin recorded is sufficient to account for the errors and the travails of the whole race.

So far as the story of Eden was mistaken for historical fact, and in that sense incorporated in theological dogma, we must welcome the assaults of doubt and infidelity which have poured ridicule upon it. Interpreted in that way, it not only fails to explain human sin, but it libels, and even caricatures, God. To say that we are born in sin because Eve transgressed in Paradise, and that God has condemned us on the ground of that transgression, is to confuse every judgment, moral and theological. How can the conscience work if it is led into the false position that the fault of a distant ancestor lies at its door? The first condition of a healthy working of the conscience is to feel the responsibility for what we have done or left undone ourselves, and to be assured that for this alone we are to give account. How can we understand or love or obey God if we are to suppose that the basis of His dealings with men is an injustice, an arbitrary decree which causes generations of helpless beings to spring out of one mother, all tainted, corrupted, enfeebled, by her distant, and not very heinous, sin? The God who sanctioned that doctrine of original sin was not, and could not be, benevolent, just, or moral. Men cannot attribute such a thought to God without seriously injuring themselves. They cannot set up arbitrary injustice on the throne of the universe as the object of devotion and worship without warping their own judgment and hardening their own heart.

But to sweep away the story of Eden on such theological grounds is as misguided as to retain it in that misapplied sense. Apart from dogmatic prepossession, any candid reader of Genesis to-day would recognize at once that the story is a myth, and must be used and interpreted as a myth. It cannot be said to claim attention on any other ground. The writer is as well aware of the nature of his story as Plato was in the myth at the end of the "Gorgias." When he connects knowledge and the opening of the eyes with the eating of a certain fruit, he avows that he is speaking in allegory. He is not so childish as to suppose that any vegetable product that ever grew on earth could generate our moral nature or endow us with eternal life. When the serpent talks the writer assumes, as Æsop did, that the reader will at once recognize the symbolical character of his story. When God and the serpent and the woman are represented in conversation the writer of that richly significant passage would be horrified if he thought that any one could be childish enough to take him literally. He, like Plato, weaves a myth, perhaps repeats an ancient story, breathing into it a truer and more spiritual meaning. He conveys the truth in a myth because he has no other vehicle in which to convey it. Have we to this day any other, or at least any better, vehicle in which to tell the meaning of man's moral conflict, its origin and its issue?

"There might be reason in our contemning such tales if by searching we could find out anything better or truer."

But let us take it as, what it is, a myth, and the story of Adam — or man — and of Eve — or life — becomes not only rich in meaning, but the best and the fullest truth that we have yet discovered on the subject of that mysterious disorder, or dislocation, in the relation between God and man, which it is the object of human life to overcome. The myth is told so faultlessly in Genesis iii. that it seems presumptuous to retell it. But in order to bring out its character and its truth it may serve a purpose to clothe it in slightly different dress, not better, but more in the fashion of our time. What is the meaning of our moral nature, and of the struggle, which goes on continually within us, between good and evil? Is the struggle intelligible? Has it an origin and an issue? We can partly trace our relation in it to our fellow-men, because the good is largely that which benefits them and the bad is almost wholly what injures them. But what is our relation in this lifelong struggle to powers beyond humanity? Are other intelligences concerned with our victory or defeat? Are we assaulted or aided by them? Is the whole situation — human life as a conflict, a moral development — of value or despicable? Is the interpretation optimistic or pessimistic? Is Leibnitz or is Nietzsche right? It is to these essential, important, and perennial questions that the myth gives an answer, the best answer that we have yet been able to obtain or to surmise.

There was, we suppose, at the beginning the beast-nature, the serpent, that degree of wisdom which comes to us as the crown of the brute creation. The moral nature was not yet; we lived the life of unconscious animals. But the serpent impels us to make trial of right and wrong. We are driven to the fateful beginnings of the moral life. An instinct in us tells us that in this way alone we come into conscious relation with God. When the woman dared to eat the fateful fruit, and to become the mother of a race engaged in the moral struggle, the myth suggests that she violated the will of God. Did God design for men the unmoral lives of the lower creatures — that sinless, thoughtless rhythm between life and death which Walt Whitman admired in the brutes? Did He wish men, too, not to mourn for their sins or sigh with regrets and aspirations? Here is the limitation of the myth, or rather the insoluble riddle of the stuff which the myth is trying to present. God meant man to have the knowledge of good and evil; He meant him to develop a moral life. And yet, this is the mystery of life, we enter upon that higher existence by the discovery of evil rather than of good. Good emerges first as the victory over evil. It is by an act of disobedience, not by an act of obedience, that we begin our genuinely human existence.

Here the myth, however mysterious, is more accurate than the most careful analysis which ethics can offer.

Consequently, the moral life begins in shame and the sense of nakedness. God comes upon us, in infancy, and always, as the voice walking in the garden in the cool of the day. It is an accusation and a judgment. Instinctively we try to shift the blame to the woman, and she to the serpent. But conscience disallows the excuses. The guilt is distributed, none escapes his share.

So far the myth presents in picturesque swiftness of detail the mystery of our moral life and relates it to God. The conscience is explained as the voice of God in the soul. The Fall is the assertion of the soul's independence of God. But the truth is carried on into the explanation of human life and of its issue. As moral beings we shall gain the goal only by toil and conflict. There is no return to the earthly Paradise of *un*moral innocence. "The flame of a sword which turns every way" forbids that easy, but useless, solution of the problem of human life. Man, every man, enters upon a career of achievement. The serpent in him is condemned to subordination and defeat. Birth is to be difficult and sorrowful. The man that is born of the woman is to work. In the sweat of his brow his earthly life is to be lived and his destiny is to be worked out. This is all good. The subjugated serpent, the painful joys of motherhood, the strenuous work for man, this is the lot of humanity when at last it has entered upon its moral conflict. Nor is Adam or Eve removed from the thoughtful care of God; He made for them "coats of skin and clothed them."

Thus the myth interprets human life, the life we are called upon to live in the knowledge of good and evil. What more can be said than is here said once for all? No investigation of our moral nature carries us farther back; and any theory which leaves God out fails to carry us as far. The decisions of the conscience, the struggle for right against wrong, the suffusion of the human life of pain and toil with the thought of a moral conflict, and of a goal to reach, are only justified in the last resort by faith in God, who ordains and watches the whole. The essential truth is carried home, embodied in this tale. As history it would be confusing and misleading; as a myth it is inspired, it is divine, the thought of God communicated to the intelligence of man.

Sometimes the myth is not so much the expression of the ineffable, which baffles other modes of communication, as the description of a large and general truth in a compressed or individualized tale. For example, the mediæval mode of delineating the relation of Judaism to Christianity, the life and destiny of the Jewish people, and their actual place in the society of the time, is to construct, perhaps unconsciously, the myth of the Wandering Jew. We could not for a moment think of such a person living on from age to age, appearing in countries near and distant. Treated literally, it is an idle tale. But as a myth it is truth. Even the article in the "Encyclopædia Britannica" on the Jews is not more instructive than this symbolic story which Matthew Paris copied from the chronicles of St. Albans. In the year 1228 "a certain Archbishop of Armenia Major came on a pilgrimage to England to see the relics of the saints and visit the sacred places in the kingdom, as he had done in others; he also produced letters of recommendation from his holiness the Pope to the religious men and prelates of the churches." He went to St. Albans and remained some days to rest himself. In conversation with the brothers he was asked if he had seen or heard anything of Joseph who had been living when our Lord suffered and was still alive. A knight in the retinue of the Archbishop replied in French: "My lord well knows that man, and a little before he took his way to the Western countries the said Joseph ate at the table of my lord the Archbishop in Armenia, and he had often seen and held converse with him." What had passed between Christ and the same Joseph was this: When the Jews were dragging Jesus forth from the judgment-hall, "Cartaphilus, a porter in Pilate's service, as Jesus was going out of the door, impiously struck Him on the back with his hand, and said in mockery, 'Go quicker, Jesus, go quicker; why do you loiter?' And Jesus, looking back on him with a severe countenance, said to him, 'I am going and you will wait for My return.' And, according as our Lord said, this Cartaphilus is still awaiting His return. At the time of our Lord's suffering he was thirty years old, and when he attains the age of a hundred years he always returns to the same age as he was when our Lord suffered. After Christ's death, when the Catholic faith gained ground, this Cartaphilus was baptized by Ananias (who also baptized the Apostle Paul), and was called Joseph. . . . He is a man of holy conversation and religious; a man of few words and circumspect in his behaviour; for he does not speak at all unless when questioned by the bishops and religious men, and then he tells of the events of old times. . . . And all he relates without smiling or levity of conversation, as one who is well practised in sorrow and the fear of God, always looking forward with fear to the coming of Jesus Christ, lest at the Last Judgment he should find Him in anger whom, when on His way to death, he had provoked to just vengeance. Numbers came to him from different parts of the world, enjoying his society and conversation; and to them, if they were men of authority, he explained all doubts on the matters on which he was questioned. He refuses all gifts that are offered to him, being content with slight food and clothing.

He places his hope of salvation on the fact that he sinned through ignorance, for the Lord when suffering prayed for His enemies in these words, 'Father, forgive them, for they know not what they do.'"

The legend assumes many forms in the process of time, as the reader may see, if he chooses, in Mr. Baring-Gould's "Curious Myths of the Middle Ages," but seldom or never does it depart from essential veracity. It follows with careful accuracy, under the form of a single wanderer, the fate of that wandering race out of which Christ came, and which is to wait for His return. It shows how this race on its converted side became the apostle of Christianity, and on its unconverted side must continue always the most remarkable, though unwilling, testimony to the Christian verities.

A fact so wide and fluctuating as the history of the Jews, a people without a country, yet always retaining a spiritual nationality, a people appearing in all Christian countries, yet not Christian, playing a remarkable part, in persecution or in liberty, producing men of the most varied and surprising genius [1] — such a fact is hard to record in its shifting and scattered details. But that fact is, for practical purposes, sufficiently characterized and stamped

---

[1] Mr. Zangwill's "Children of the Ghetto" sets in a brilliant light the types of men that Judaism produces. Dr. Schechter's "Studies in Judaism" (A. & C. Black) adds to the store which the novelist has given us.

upon the popular mind by the legend of the Wandering Jew.

Half a century ago Christendom was greatly disturbed by Strauss' "Life of Christ." The argument of the book transformed the fact on which Christianity was supposed to rest into a myth. The solid foundation of religion seemed to crumble away. The book was so serious, so reasonable, so plausible, that for a time the thinking world regarded the story of Christ as a mythical creation of a credulous company of enthusiasts. And in the opinion of many Christianity was *ipso facto* dissolved. The echoes of Strauss' revolutionary theory are still heard among the less informed opponents of the Christian faith; but the careful discussion of the theory has resulted in its almost complete rejection. A myth takes time to grow, and it demands certain conditions in the minds of those among whom it grows. A myth is not formed about contemporary persons and events, nor does it grow up in an active and aggressive movement of thought. Renan, in his oration on Lesseps, made a fine apostrophe which well embodies this truth: "You were born," he exclaimed, "to pierce isthmuses, and in earlier times you would have become a myth." That is the point: a person must lie in a distant past to become mythical; and the story must shape itself in a long lapse of time, passing from mouth to mouth among naïve and uncritical people. The myth, in a word, has its natural history, and we are not entitled to demand a miracle for its production. On investigation Strauss' theory of the origin of the Christian religion did not stand the test. The myth, if myth it was, had sprung up in the minds of men, like Paul, who were actually contemporaries of Jesus. There was no mist of distance in which the figure could assume mythical proportions. When Paul referred to the resurrection he spoke of numbers of persons still living who had seen the risen Christ. And even if there had been longer time, if, which is impossible, the New Testament literature could all be moved into the second century, and a good hundred years could be interposed between the presumed life and the construction of the story, still the ceaseless activity and strenuous onrush which founded the Churches and shaped the thought of the early Christian community do not afford the conditions in which a myth can grow. Granted that legends might accumulate around the name of Jesus, as they undoubtedly did, yet the central fact, the Person, could not be a myth. But the question of interest in the present connection is whether the thought of fifty years ago was right in assuming that the Christian religion would have melted away, or ought to have melted away, if Strauss' view had been confirmed.

Let us suppose for a moment that the Gospel narrative was mythical, and that Jesus Himself was a creation of the mythopœic faculty which resides in human nature. We will assume, as Strauss did, that the figure and the events were constructed, with a free poetic licence, out of the stories and forecasts of the Old Testament or the current facts and fancies of the time. It will sound to some an absurd, and to others an impious, assumption. But let us exercise forbearance and make it. There never was a Jesus; the words in His mouth and the deeds which came from His hands are merely the creation of the popular imagination. The death and resurrection are not facts, but ideas clothed in the vivid colours of a story, "truth embodied in a tale."

Nothing, of course, is more certain than that Christianity, as a historic religion, actually grew out of this supposed myth. Was it not justified in growing out of it? Did not the myth afford a sufficient seed of truth to produce a religion, and a true religion? Let us look at it for a moment. First of all there are the moral teachings put into the mouth of Jesus, the ideas and suggestions, for example, of the Sermon on the Mount. This body of teaching, as Wendt has exhaustively shown, is so coherent, so convincing, so essentially true, that it stands by its own weight; it requires no further evidence. The central principle makes the spring of all morality love to God and to man. Morality is distinguished from external ceremonies and obligations; it is sought and found in the inward state of the soul. The type of character commended is gentle, patient, merciful, pure, beneficent. This morality is identified with religion.

Secondly, God is presented as a pure and holy Spirit, siding with, approving of, the right morality — demanding it, indeed, as the only acceptable service or worship which man can render to Him. Attention is directed to the Spirit of God that witnesses in the human heart to God, and prayer is enjoined, real and heartfelt prayer, as the means by which God and man communicate.

Lastly, the character and conduct of Jesus are drawn to illustrate these teachings. He is such an One as the teaching commends. He embodies the precepts in Himself. He lives just such a life as one would live who believed that God is such as He taught. In Him religion ceases to be connected with a cultus, or a ritual, a temple, a holy place, a system, an organization of priests; it becomes a life, an inward life, expressing itself in holy activities — a brave, self-sacrificing life, moving without hesitation to the death incurred by its fidelity. Thus the death assumes a special significance; it is the death which faultless benevolence and beneficence and obedience to God incur at the hands of men, even of men religious in the older and darker meaning of the word "religion." The resurrection is added as God's protest against the mistake of men; for such an one it was not possible that death should be the final issue.

This is the outline of what is embodied in this presumed myth. The myth, therefore, conveys a body of truth, ethical and religious, which is of priceless moment to mankind. Would it be right or reasonable to forfeit that truth because it had reached us in a mythical form? Would it not rather be the duty of mankind to take the truth, and to live on it, to work it out in life and conduct, thanking God who had conveyed it to them in such a way, and honouring with perpetual wonder and reverence those unknown benefactors who had constructed, for the good of the race, this myth of the true morality and the true religion?

But, as is now generally agreed, the mythical explanation of the Gospels cannot stand. With the progress of inquiry the historic fact of Christ settles back again more firmly on its foundation. We no longer attach a superstitious infallibility to the documents. No one now asks us to believe that the gospel narratives were guaranteed against error or supernaturally sifted from all admixture of legend. But just in proportion as a free historic light plays about the sources the conviction grows that the sources are essentially historic. Jesus of Nazareth lived and died. We do not know all about Him, nor anything that approaches to all, as the closing words of the Fourth Gospel admit. But the Gospels are the *memorabilia* of a real person. They are in all probability the notes of the earliest apostolic preaching, which were written down in order to be preserved when the Apostles themselves were passing away. The earliest testimonies of Papias and of the Muratorian Fragment may be absolutely correct; for tradition is more and more recognized to be rooted in truth; that is to say, Mark's Gospel represents the account of Jesus which Peter was accustomed to give, Matthew's includes the recollections of the teaching of Jesus which that member of the apostolic group recorded, Luke's is a compilation of the various records which were in use during the ministry of Paul, and the Fourth Gospel is a careful and artistic digest of the teaching which the beloved disciple was accustomed to give in Ephesus to the generation following.

In the ordinary sense of the word, therefore, the Gospels are not mythical, but historical; they are not an attempt to clothe an idea in a concrete creation of the imagination, but the honest and sufficient picture of a Person who appears on the plane of history, the record of such details of His life and teaching as were in the memory of His contemporaries when a new generation succeeded.

And yet there is a sense in which this fact of Christ, this historic fact, may be treated as a myth. This is the vast and honourable usage of the word "myth." It is the myth in Plato's sense, the human medium through which high and difficult matters, which evade logic and definition, may be conveyed to the soul.

Granting that the narrative of the Gospels is the genuine record of what happened, and that the New Testament writings correctly interpret the events, is not the whole unique phenomenon of the origin of the Christian religion a figure, a picture, a tale, in which is bodied forth the thought of the Infinite for man? Does it not then for the first time begin to be intelligible when it seems to be a symbol of a Reality which lies behind, a Reality which is not easily conveyed to our human minds, a Reality, which, for anything we know, could not otherwise have been expressed at all?

St. Paul was conscious of this when he tried, perhaps not with complete success, to draw a parallel between the first man, Adam, and the second Adam, the Lord from heaven. The reader of Romans is aware that the logic halts, that the terms of the antithesis are imperfectly expressed, that the argument *à fortiori* does not seem quite cogent. But for us who understand more clearly what the story of Adam is it becomes possible to see in St. Paul's argument a richer meaning. The first Adam and the Fall is a tale which endeavours to set forth the nature of human sin, and does it with considerable success. The second Adam is a fact in the history of humanity which declares human redemption. It is a fact which, as it were by symbol, shows the bearings of life, the inner nature of man, the goal to which we move.

In the person of Christ man is presented occupying his proper relation to God. Perhaps the ultimate reason why the fact of Christ is established as real and not a free creation of the fancy is that it does not seem conceivable that any skill could have invented a personality so exactly expressing this right relation between God and man. Every trait is exhibited unconsciously. It does not appear that either evangelists or apostles were able to sum up in abstract terms either that relation or the personality of Jesus. All they could do was to delineate Him and to direct attention to Him. When the Church in the age of the Councils endeavoured to express the relation in exact psychological terms, she produced a jargon of language, a variety of warring opinions, and ultimately a paradox of definition, which so far from improving on the fact of Christ only obscures it. Nestorian, Apollinarian, Eutychian, Monophysite, Monothelite, Sabellian; the shameful scenes at the Council of Ephesus; the unwholesome gride of dogmatic formulæ, then and since — these are the futile results of attempting to improve on the bare, but sufficient, simplicity of the fact of Christ. All that can wholesomely be said is: Study the gospel narrative honestly and earnestly, and thus learn in the person of Jesus what the relation between God and man ought to be.

In the same phenomenon the thought of God for man appears. Theology attempts to develop the truth which is given there once for all. We are loath to say that the efforts of theology have failed. But theology is most successful when it is able to carry the mind back to the original revelation in the gospel, and to endow that revelation with its first freshness and surprise. Sometimes after strenuous study and profound thought the student, if he be sincere and unbiassed, is brought, as it were suddenly and unexpectedly, face to face with the idea of God which gives colour and meaning to the New Testament. He lights upon that ancient Paradise, from which man is not expelled; there is a rustle of the leaves in the cool of the evening, and the waters lapse with a tinkling melody. The light is visionary and the heart is hushed. And there

"Visibly through the garden walketh God."

God is not in the image of man, but with deep gratitude the seeker who has surprised the Divinity recognizes that man is in the image of God, and by virtue of that characteristic is able to apprehend Him.

"Were not the eye itself a sun,
No sun for it could ever shine;
By God the heart could not be won
Were not the heart itself divine." [1]

There is no form, no voice. Now more than ever He is spirit, dwelling in light which no man can approach unto. The vision is not as of Apollo or of the Athene of Phidias, but as of the image which floated always in the mind of Jesus. God is the original will that produced the universe; matter in its countless forms and mysterious energies is the expression of the will; life is imparted by the same will; consciousness is the pulse of that will within

[1] Plotinus, "Enneads," i. 6.

the limits of a human soul. God is wisdom and strength, and He loves. The Creation is the outcome of a brooding tenderness. The moral nature within is the revelation of the Being that produced all things. The good is God; the evil is what He tolerates as a means of realizing the higher and the permanent good. In a word, this seeker with kindling eyes has come upon his Father, the Father of him and of all men, the creative, brooding love, which makes for perfection and unity and infinite progress. Yes, he has come, perhaps through geology, perhaps through theology, back to the truth of Jesus, the revelation which shone in the tale of the gospel. He has come with the experience of the centuries, with the beatings of the human heart of generations, with the discoveries of science, with the suggestions of poetry and of art, back to God, to the God revealed in Jesus Christ, the God who loves and forgives, who seeks and saves, the God who does not shrink from the cross nor despise the shame in the task of the redemption of man. The truth of God told in the tale, the historic fact of Christianity, the truth which made Christendom, the idea of progress, the hope of eternity, that truth is verifying itself in the whole history of man, and is the prophecy of the future. The highest religion is drawn out of it, the only practicable philosophy rests on it; practical politics must be determined by it; art will fail as it leaves it; science is ever confirming it.

That "truth embodied in a tale" is not only a tale,

but a truth. Its vitality is inexhaustible. The manifestation of an infinite God is infinite. Nay, not only is the story of Christ the effort of the invisible God to put into an accessible form His thought of love for the world, but the world itself, the whole mysterious cosmos of phenomena, is a myth of the unseen. It is a tale that is told, from the electron upwards and onwards to the highest thought which has worked in the brain of man, a tale which no man has yet told in its entirety nor understood in its fulness —

"A tale divine of high and passionate thought
To its own music chanted."

For no one can meditate on the whole — the formation of the sun and the planets in the incalculable "backward and abysm of time," on the exquisite beauty of earth and sky and sea, as the pictured dwelling-place of beings drawing thoughtful breath, on the deep significance of man's religions, on the pathos of the moral struggles, and the nameless heroisms of men and women from the beginning until now — without the awed sense that in this way, in this mighty drawn-out myth, there is a revelation going on, a revelation of that which cannot be more explicitly told to our limited intelligence, the revelation of God:

"A fire mist and a planet,
A crystal and a cell,

MYTHS

A jellyfish and a Saurian,
    And caves where cave men dwell;
Then a sense of love and duty
    And a face turned from the clod:
Some call it Evolution,
    And others call it God.

A haze on the far horizon,
    An infinite tender sky,
The living gold of the corn-fields,
    And the lark soaring up on high;
The bright procession of flowers
    From primrose to golden-rod:
Some call it Summer and Nature,
    And others say it is God.

The echo of ancient chanting,
    The gleam of altar-flames;
The stones of a hundred temples
    Graven with sacred names;
Man's patient quest for the secret
    In soul, in star, in sod:
Some deem it superstition
    And others believe it is God.

A picket frozen on duty,
    A mother starved for her brood,
Socrates drinking the hemlock,
    And Jesus on the rood;
The millions who, humble and nameless,
    The straight, hard path have trod:
Some call it consecration,
    And others feel it is God.

Like the tide on crescent sea beach,
    When the moon is new and thin,

They come, our soul's deep yearnings,
　Welling and surging in,
They come from the mystic ocean
　Whose rim no foot has trod:
Some hold it idle dreaming,
　We know that it is God."

— Professor Carruth.

CHAPTER II

RELIGION

"WHEN I speak of religion," says Parson Thwackum, "I mean the Christian religion; and when I say Christian religion I mean the Protestant religion; and when I say Protestant religion I mean the Church of England." Most men, until they have reflected, mean by religion their own tenets and practices, and are liable to refuse the name to other tenets and practices, which may yet be equally religious.

The easiest and simplest method of determining the right religion is to adopt, and to swear by, that which is established in the country to which you belong. It is a good way to preferment. Indeed, it is good for everything in you, with the possible exception of character.

When in 1788 a deputation waited on Lord Chancellor Thurlow to obtain his support for the repeal of the Test and Corporation Act he listened civilly, and then said, "Gentlemen, I'm against you. I am for the Established Church. Not that I have any more regard for the Established Church than for any other Church, but because *it is* established. And if you can get your religion established I'll be for that too." A principle of such simplicity and advantage must commend itself to a large proportion of any community. But, notwithstanding the simplicity and advantage, it represents but a low degree of religion. It favours prejudice, intolerance, and that type of character which was admirably hit off in Addison's essay on the Tory foxhunter. This typical gentleman uttered a panegyric to Mr. Spectator on his spaniel: "But I found the most remarkable adventure of his life was that he had once like to have worried a dissenting teacher. The master could hardly sit on his horse for laughing all the while he was giving me the particulars of this story, which I found had mightily endeared his dog to him, and, as he himself told me, had made him a great favourite among all the honest gentlemen of the country." As they rode on the way, "Where do you intend to inn to-night?" asks the squire. "I can help you to a very good landlord if you will go along with me. He is a lusty, jolly fellow, that lives well, at least three yards in the girth, and the best Church of England man upon the road." Then the narrative proceeds: "The landlord had swelled his body to a prodigious size, and worked up his complexion to a standing crimson by his zeal for the prosperity of the Church, which he expressed every hour of the day, as his customers dropped in, by repeated bumpers. He had not time to go to church himself, but, as my friend told me in my ear, had headed a mob at the pulling down of two or three meeting-houses. While supper was preparing he enlarged upon the happiness of the neighbouring shire. 'For,' says he, 'there is scarce a Presbyterian in the whole country except the bishop.' In short, I found by his discourse that he had learned a great deal of politics, but not one word of religion, from the parson of his parish; and, indeed, that he had scarce any other notion of religion but that it consisted in hating Presbyterians. I had a remarkable instance of his notions in this particular. Upon seeing a poor, decrepit old woman pass under the window where he sat he desired me to take notice of her, and afterwards informed me that she was generally reputed a witch by the country people, but that, for his part, he was apt to believe she was a Presbyterian."

But if a State establishment of religion tends to produce this ignorant kind of prejudice, and a religious temper which is of all things the most irreligious, the same infirmity is found in every system, or Church, or sect, in which the idea is encouraged that it is the exclusive possessor of the truth. The Moslem scorns the Christian infidel as the Jew once scorned the Gentile. The Orthodox Russian, though a saint, like Ivan of Cronstadt, regards with loathing the Dissenters from the Orthodox Church. The Roman Catholic will not even pray with those who are outside his fold. The size of the Roman Communion tends to hide the corrosive influence of this exclusive spirit. But the Catholic regards the rest of the Christian world as the Tory fox-hunter regarded the Presbyterians. His religious spirit intrinsically is the same as that of the narrowest sectarian, who, after banning all the other sects of Christendom, quarrels with the members of his own sect, and finally finds that there is scarce a man within the country that he can "break bread with." [1]

The sectarian spirit, in Islam or Romanism, in an Established Church or in a minute and powerless sect, is the disease of religion, the antithesis of it, in many cases the destruction of it. As was once said about the narrowest form of what is called Brethrenism, "it skims off the cream of the Churches, and turns it sour."

Religion is a universal phenomenon. It is the *differentia* of man: for man might be defined in creation as "the religious animal." If men are without religion, they are so far forth not human. It is this universality which should be first impressed

---

[1] A friend of mine had a brother who came to visit him for a Sunday at Eastbourne. "Well, George," he said, on Sunday, "will you come to church with me?" "No," he replied, "there is a brother a few miles out with whom I shall break bread." In the evening George returned. "Well, how did you get on?" was the genial inquiry. "Pretty well," was the doubtful reply, "but the Brother, as he sat down, said to me: 'Now I wish you to understand, that though you break bread with me, I do not break bread with you.'"

This is the same spirit as was shown by Cardinal Manning and some other Roman clergy, whom we met in Christian conference in the Jerusalem Chamber. We all had to withdraw into the unlighted chancel of the Abbey for the opening prayer, because the Roman Catholics would not pray with us.

on the mind. Before any question is raised about particular religions and the relative truth of our own, the point is to be secured that man from the earliest records we possess of him in the Palæolithic Age is religious. Religion, like other things terrestrial, develops. It may be in a backward or an advanced stage. The ideas and practices may be relatively good or bad. But it is not given to man to be absolutely irreligious; it is only given to him to choose between the better or the worse, between the true or the false in religion.

Not to weary the reader with many definitions of religion, let us be content with M. Albert Réville's: "Religion is the determination of human life by the sentiment of a bond uniting the human mind to that mysterious Mind whose domination of the world and of itself it recognizes, and to whom it delights in feeling itself united." Man may interpret that mysterious Mind as fetich, as a tawdry doll, as a human being, as an unknown force, as the personal God, sole and supreme, of Mohammed, or as the Father of Jesus Christ. But the savage, the Sicilian peasant, the Positivist, the Spencerian, the Moslem or Jew or Unitarian, or the orthodox Christian, are, each in his own way, religious.

It may, however, be said that there are always men, and now an amazing number, who care and think nothing of that mysterious Mind, and have no desire to be united with it. In this sense surely there are many who are non-religious. That is very doubtful. Many live without much thought, but directly they think — and all must some time or other think — they stumble into religion. Thus M. Guyau, with modern France before him, wrote a book entitled "The Non-religion of the Future"; the object of the book is to show how Catholicism in France is dying and Protestantism is impossible. All religious dogmas are discussed and dismissed. But does the writer succeed in getting rid of religion or in proving that the future will be irreligious? Far from it. He finds that: "Materialism leaves us, as other systems do, in the presence of that ultimate mystery which all religions have symbolized in their myths, and which metaphysics will always be obliged to recognize, and poetry to express, by the instrumentality of images.

"By the seaside stood a great upright mountain that pierced the sky like an arrow-head, and the waves beat upon its base. In the morning when the first light of the sun touched the ancient rocks they shivered, and a voice rose from the grey stones and mingled with the sound made by the blue sea; and mountain and wave conversed together. The sea said: 'The heavens have been mirrored in my shifting waves a million years, and in all that time have held as high aloof from me and stood as motionless.' And the mountain said: 'I have climbed towards the heavens a million years, and they are still as high above me as ever.' One day a ray of sun fell smiling upon the brow of the mountain, and the mountain questioned it on the distant heavens from which it came. The ray was about to reply, but was reflected suddenly from the mountain to the sea, and from a scintillating wave back to the heavens from which it came. And the ray is still *en route* across the Infinite, toward the Nebulæ of Meia in the Pleiades, which were so long invisible, or toward some point farther still, and has not yet replied."[1]

This does not sound much like getting rid of the material of religion. And, indeed, M. Guyau ends by justifying the religious sentiment as ultra-scientific but not anti-scientific, and by adopting or approving the philosophical hypothesis of moral idealism, as it "affords unusual scope for the religious sentiment, freed from its mysticism and transcendence." The book closes with an eager argument, as if wrung from the heart of the writer, for the immortality of the soul: "A man of science was one day holding a handful of wheat that had been found in the tomb of an Egyptian mummy. 'Five thousand years without sight of the sun. Unhappy grains of wheat, as sterile as death, of which they have so long been the companions; never shall their tall stalks bow beneath the wind on the banks of the Nile. Never? What do I know of life or of death?' As an experiment simply, without much hope of success, the man of science sowed the grains of wheat that he had recovered from the tomb, and the wheat of the

[1] "The Non-Religion of the Future," by Marie Jean Guyau, p. 492.

Pharaohs received the caress of the sun, of the air, and came up green through the soil of Egypt and bowed beneath the wind on the banks of the sacred and inexhaustible flood of the Nile. And shall human thought, and the higher life which stirs in us like the germ in the seed, and love that seems to sleep for ever in the tomb, not have this reawakening in some unforeseen springtime, and not be brought face to face with eternity, which seems at present to be buried once and for all in darkness? What is death, after all, in the universe but a lesser degree of vital heat, a more or less transitory lowness of temperature? Death cannot be powerful enough to hold life and its perpetual youth in check and to prevent the infinite activity of thought and of desire."

Thus it may be suggested that they who count on the disappearance of religion reckon without their host. The impatient rejection of current religious ideas and dogmas is often mistaken for the repudiation of religion. The iconoclasts, however, are breaking, not the reality, but the images. We see around us old religious ideas dying, sometimes with a pathetic beauty of their own; for, as Lecky says, "religious ideas die like the sun; their last rays, possessing but little heat, are expended in giving beauty." But this passing of the forms is far from implying the loss of the reality. A religion can be superseded, but religion is immortal. As Tyler [1] forcibly says: "Unless a religion can hold its place *in the front of*

[1] "Anthropology," ch. xiv.

science and morals, it may only gradually in the course of ages lose its place in the nation, but all the power of statecraft and all the wealth of temples will not save it from eventually yielding to a belief that takes in higher knowledge and teaches better life."

We may deplore the decay of a religion, but we must not fall into the error of thinking that religion can cease. Human life and its relation to the Cosmos compel a desire to determine the relation between man and God, and maintain in the heart of man an irrepressible desire for union with God. No one was ever more impatient with the current formulæ, more scornful of the delusion that the plan of the universe was "your Nine-and-Thirty Articles," than Carlyle. His diatribe against Hebrew old clothes sounded like the knell of the religion of his time. But what a mistake would it be to charge Carlyle with indifference to religion! His voice rolls like thunder and rattles with heaven's own artillery against the deluded men who suppose that they have got rid of religion.

"Enlightened philosophies, like Molière doctors, will tell you: 'Enthusiasms, self-sacrifice, heaven, hell, and such like: yes, all that was true enough for old, stupid times; all that used to be true, but we have changed all that — *nous avons changé tout cela!*' Well, if the heart be got round now into the right side and the liver into the left; if man have no heroism in him deeper than the wish to eat, and in his soul there dwell now no Infinite of hope and awe, and no divine silence can become imperative because it is not Sinai thunder, and no tie will bind it, if it be not that of Tyburn gallows-ropes, then verily you have changed all that, and for it and for you and for me behold the abyss and nameless annihilation is ready. So scandalous a beggarly universe deserves, indeed, nothing else; I cannot say I would save it from annihilation. Vacuum and the serene blue will be much handsomer; easier, too, for all of us. I, for one, decline living as a patent-digester. Patent-digester, spinning-mule, Mayfair clothes-horse, many thanks, but your Chaosships will have the goodness to excuse me." [1]

We may then, perhaps, conclude that religion is universal as humanity, that it is not disposed of, nor will ever be. Good or bad, true or false, religious ideas and beliefs will possess the mind of man, and religious rites, or abstention from rites, will seek to express the ideas and beliefs. We are bound to religion as we are bound to the earth on which we live; we can escape it at best but temporarily as an aeronaut can mount for a time by gas or the machinery of wings. But while it is not given to us to escape the earth or religion, we have much choice left us. We can live in morasses and malarial bogs, or on mountain heights. We can herd in dirty slums, religiously speaking, or breathe the fresh air of heaven. We can, with the sluggard, yawn, and expect our harvest — of weeds and thistles; or we

[1] "Past and Present," bk. iii. ch. ix.

can with diligence cultivate our plot, and produce grain by which a man can live, and fruit of the trees which are for the healing of the nations.

Within the infrangible walls of destiny so much liberty is ours, and this obvious obligation lies upon us: We are on the one hand bound to find and practise the truest and best religion that is open to us, and on the other hand bound to regard all religions, however poor and imperfect, with respect, never permitting our religion to separate us from men, but always seeing in our religion the instrument for drawing all together in the unity of God.

It is certainly one of the quaintest delusions of the human mind to suppose that religious life, goodness, godliness are confined to a particular form of faith or cultus. The latitudinarian doctrine that "the religion of all good men is the same" comes far nearer to the truth of fact. The devout Buddhist Lama, the Mohammedan Sufi, the mediæval mystic, William Law, John Wesley, Charles Gordon are curiously alike. Seneca and Paul are not only contemporary but spiritually related.[1] It is rightly reckoned one of the ironies of history that Marcus Aurelius persecuted those of his subjects who were nearest to his own spirit, and, though unconsciously, conformed most perfectly to his doctrine. Christianity is not so sharply marked off from the religions of the world as dogma and exclusiveness lead us to think. Christ in this respect does not agree with some of

[1] Lightfoot, "Commentary on Philippians."

His most devoted followers. In the gospel there are two people who draw forth His admiration by their faith, One of them is a Roman centurion, the other a Syro-Phœnician woman (Matt. viii. 10, xv. 28). And in the Fourth Gospel, notwithstanding the impetuous temper of John, who once would have called down fire from heaven on a Samaritan village, Jesus appears as drawing together in one the children of God that were scattered abroad, and uniting the numerous folds of humanity in one ideal flock.

But if it may appear too latitudinarian to say that the religion of all good men is the same, there can be no hesitation in admitting that the religion of all genuine Christians is the same, to whatever age or Church they may belong. Let us by way of illustration set side by side the picture of a pious merchant in the period of the Renaissance and the strongly contrasted picture of Russian Nonconformists in our own time, and let us ask ourselves whether the difference or the similarity is the more striking.

In the latter part of the fifteenth century, when the corruptions of the Church seemed to threaten its dissolution unless a Reformation should come, when Cæsar Borgia was living the scandalous life at Rome which made Alexander VI. the grossest outrage on Christianity that history records, Giovanni Rucellai was living his life of industry and beneficence at Florence. He employed Leon Battista Alberti to finish the marble façade of Sta. Maria Novella, and also to build the Oratorio S. Sepulchro, in imitation of the holy Sepulchre at Jerusalem. These monuments in themselves might betoken nothing but the superstition of the Middle Ages, which sought to atone to God for the breach of His laws by building churches in His honour. But, happily for us, Rucellai wrote in his later years a journal, which was published by his sons Pandolfo and Bernardo in grateful recognition that their father was the pride and glory of the Rucellai family which he had adorned. Here is a passage from the journal: "I thank the Lord that He made me a reasonable and immortal being in a land where the true, the Christian, faith prevails, near to Rome, which is the centre of this faith; in Italy, the noblest and worthiest part of the Christian world; in Tuscany, one of the noblest provinces of Italy; in the city of Florence, to which is given the praise of fairest not only in Christendom but in the world. I thank Him that He has granted me a long life with perfect bodily health, so that I do not remember in the course of sixty years a month in which I was kept to the house; for health is the highest earthly grace. I thank Him that He has vouchsafed me success in my business, so that I have risen from the small things with which I began to riches and general esteem, while I have not only acquired with honour, but given proportionately, which is a greater gain than acquisition. I thank Him that He appointed for my earthly life a time which by universal consent must be called the happiest for Florence, the time of the illustrious citizen Cosmo de' Medici, whose fame in the whole world finds no equal, a time of ten years' peace and undisturbed tranquillity, the blessings of which have appeared the sweeter for the heavy troubles and sorrows which previous times had to bear. I thank Him for a worthy mother, who at my father's death when I was just nineteen rejected all proposals for a second marriage, and lived only for her children, to their great comfort, also for a not less worthy wife, whose love to me was combined with devoted care for household and family, who was spared to me for long years, and whose death was the most sorrowful loss which could or can befall me. While I survey all these countless graces and blessings, I detach myself now in my old age from everything earthly, in order to praise Thee the Lord and living Source of all, and from my innermost soul to thank Thee." [1]

No one will hesitate to recognize in this thankful and contented piety the best type of religion, which is to be found better in the world than in a cloister, in a merchant than in a prince. The tendency to look for the types of Christianity in the clergy or in the extravagances of ascetic renunciation has obscured the prevalence of true religion, which is essentially for common nature's daily food.

But if the Florentine merchant of the fifteenth century presents the picture of religion, let the pic-

[1] "Geschichte der Päpste," Dritter Band, p. 14, by Ludwig Pastor.

ture which Prince Kropotkin gives of his old nurse, Vasilisa, remind us how the same essentially religious qualities appear in poor Russian peasants, under the ban of the Church for their dissent.

"Her family was one of the poorest; besides her husband she had only a small boy to help her, and a girl, my foster-sister, who became later on a preacher and a 'virgin' in the Nonconformist sect to which they belonged. There was no bound to her joy when I came to see her. Cream, eggs, apples, and honey were all that she could offer; but the way in which she offered them, in bright wooden plates, after having covered the table with a fine snow-white linen tablecloth of her own making (with the Russian Nonconformists absolute cleanliness is a matter of religion), and the fond words with which she addressed me, treating me as her own son, left the warmest feelings in my heart. I must say the same of the nurses of my elder brothers, Nicholas and Alexander, who belonged to prominent families of two other Nonconformist sects in Nikólskoye. Few know what treasuries of goodness can be found in the hearts of Russian peasants, even after centuries of the most cruel oppression, which might well have embittered them." [1]

No Church has any monopoly of religion; no sect, however narrow, can claim the monopoly which is denied to the most exclusive Churches. The recognition of this fact, which is forced on every mind that

[1] "Memoirs of a Revolutionist," by P. Kropotkin, p. 42.

candidly inquires, is the first step towards a real catholicity. The attempt to secure a unity of thought, or of culture, by coercion, political or ecclesiastical, has only irreligious issues. Conformity can be produced by compulsion, but agreement cannot. The differences between human minds are radical and ineffaceable. In the Roman Church, for example, ever haunted by memories of its origin in the Imperial unity of Rome, and employing every weapon, carnal and spiritual, to maintain her corporate unity under an infallible autocracy, differences and antagonisms reveal themselves which are fiercer than the quarrels of rival sects outside her borders. Franciscans and Dominicans began with antagonism to the older Orders, and proceeded to antagonism to each other. Jesuits and Jansenists maintained a bitter feud; Pascal, victorious in dialectic, was crushed by the weight of the opposing legions. The Jesuits conquered, but only to become the scandal of the Church which they saved, and the main argument against the conversion of the world to the system of casuistry and intrigue with which they have managed to identify their Church.

In the middle nineteenth century there were two great converts from the English Church to Rome; their portraits are side by side in the National Portrait Gallery, and their names will always live in the religious history of England. Were these two distinguished converts at one in the unity of the One Church to which they had both fled? The memoirs of their lives record the curious fact that they were not. The natural antagonism of their temperaments survived the unifying process of their conversion.

While religion is one there cannot be one Church or one creed without that kind of coercion, physical or mental, which is injurious to religion itself. The only unity which is worth anything is a unity which can be found in the absolute liberty to differ and under the countless forms which the differences assume. The lower types of religion exact uniformity; they make exclusive claims; they deny that anything outside themselves is or can be truly religious. But the higher the type of religion the wider is its outlook, the more comprehensive is its sympathy, the more ready is it to recognize its own truths, obscured, it may be, under the forms of other systems; acknowledging the unity of man and the unity of religion in the fullest sense of the word, it keeps in touch with all and tends to draw the lower thought up to its higher level. It realizes the unity in which it believes by believing it. Its catholicity is its universalism; it finds that God is One and God is the Father; consequently all men, wandering or foregathered, in darkness or in light, are brothers; all religions are the sincere, if blind, effort to find the Father and the oneness.

The justification of Christianity, and its claim to be the best and truest religion known to the world, must rise and fall with its universality. If it gathers together in one, if it breaks down the middle walls of partition, if it can substantiate its message to man as man, to the world as a world, it is thereby proved to be the best and the truest. If it fails in this respect, it cannot keep its place at the head of the morals or the science of advancing humanity, and nothing can hinder it from a destined decay. If it is exclusive and damnatory, if it seriously maintains that the vast majority of the human race are reserved for an eternity of penal fires in the world to come, it sinks to the level of other religions; and already there is in sight a larger and a better faith burning in the hearts of men.

The present writer distinguishes between the Christian religion and its embodiment in the Churches and creeds with which we are familiar. He is prepared to admit that these are capable of amendment, or even of advantageous annihilation; but Christianity, as it emerges from the crucible of modern thought and experience, seems to him to be not only the best we know, but the best that can be known. Let the patient reader follow him for a moment in the defence of this position.

There is in Churches and religious organizations the same tendency to decay as in other human institutions. The scheme of Providence does not guarantee any immunity, on the ground that these devices are originally intended to embody and to promote religion.[1] In the first instance, the Church, or the

[1] "A religion gains nothing by time, but only loses," says Harnack, "Dogmengeschichte," li. 447.

order, or the sect is purified by its passion and kept efficient by its onward movement. The ardour cools, the onrush ceases; things settle down; presently there is decorum, decency, tradition, and then decay. When the decay is far advanced the Church, or society, once the embodiment of a religious truth, becomes not only ineffective, but even a positive hindrance to religion. The stronger the organization, the more tenacious of power and influence, so much the more injurious and corrupting it becomes. Civilization may be arrested, science may be checked, thought may be sterilized, whole nations may be destroyed, by such an organization, which still bears the name of religion, but has become merely a vast political engine, preserving by superstition, or intrigue, or power the influence and authority of its priesthood.

The holy well, Lenzem, at Mecca, into which the moon once fell, which pilgrims drink or use for their ablutions, the waters of which are sent to Mohammedan princes throughout the world, was, some years ago, analyzed by Dr. Frankland at South Kensington. The water was found to be sewage, seven times more concentrated than London sewage, containing 579 grains of solid matter per gallon. It had, in a word, become the cholera centre of Arabia.[1]

That is the fate of many holy wells. When Italy and Spain and France in turn suppressed the monastic orders; when even the Pope suppressed the

[1] *Spectator*, September 10, 1881.

Order of Jesuits; when the Reformation broke over Europe in the sixteenth century; when Francis and Dominic came propping the tottering Church in the thirteenth; when Wyclif and the Lollards woke England out of the dogmatic slumber of centuries; when Augustine directed the distracted times in which he lived to the City of God; when Christ came and Jerusalem fell; when the prophets of Israel inveighed against the corrupt cultus; when Moses framed the Law for his people in the midst of the surrounding corruption — far back as the eye can carry the thought in the earliest history of man, the everlasting spirit of religion has been breaking away from the forms, the institutions, the corporations, guilds, Churches, which once embodied and then choked it, to reassert its living power and to seek fresh and more suitable embodiments for new times and conditions.

The stronger a Church is the more dangerous it is, for in its decay it will more powerfully infect the world. And it is one of the most striking evidences of Christ's religion, the first mark which destines it for permanence and universality, that, in its purity, it has no priesthood and no organizations. "My kingdom is not of this world," says the Founder. He does not ordain priests, but only messengers of the evangel (*i.e.*, Apostles). He does not frame an organization, but only the gathering of two or three in His name, with His spiritual presence in the midst.

As Christianity is, in its origin, perfectly free of

organization, and as the organizations which have in the course of time sprung up are merely the attempt made, necessarily made, from age to age, to embody the eternal spirit, all Churches may decay, become obsolete, prove springs of corruption, holy wells of infection, and their doom may be sealed, and yet Christianity remains what it was at the beginning, is now, and ever shall be — a historical fact, a religious idea, the truth about man and God, a power, the only power in the world, which works steadily for the salvation of men.

Let us endeavour to see clearly what this religion is, which is embodied in Churches, travestied in Churches, often strangled in Churches; let us insist on distinguishing it, as a vital factor in history and in men, from the humiliating story of ecclesiastical institutions which is frequently mistaken for Christianity. Christendom to-day presents an extraordinary spectacle. The Catholic Church is discredited in Catholic countries, and flourishes only in Protestant countries by virtue of the very liberty which she has herself consistently denied. There is hardly a country in Europe in which the strength and manhood of the people are not arrayed against Catholicism. The Orthodox Church of Russia has betrayed her country to her ruin; the hope of regeneration is entirely divorced from that stereotyped and sterile expression of the Christian religion; one solitary Protestant, Count Leo Tolstoi, carries more weight in the living world of to-day than the whole body of Eastern Orthodoxy. In Protestant countries the Churches are very largely neglected. The buildings, though far too few for the population, are generally half empty. Being weaker and more divided than Catholicism, and not aiming at political domination, they do not excite the same dread or antipathy; but they are neglected and despised and left to decay.

But only the most careless observer thinks that Christianity is weakened or decaying. Christendom is more clearly defined than ever as the progressive part of humanity. It is marked off from ancient systems like Confucianism or Buddhism, and from systems more recent than itself, Mohammedanism or Positivism, by the possession of a vital power, which extends its borders, enlarges its life, and leads it, by an irresistible destiny, to dominate the world.

The Churches seem to be dying, but Christianity is living. Every day it asserts itself more clearly as the best which the human race knows, or even can know. What, then, is this living and irrepressible spirit, which, driven from Churches, takes possession of the world; which, while working in all minds, and through all channels of human activity, has the potency and promise of universal empire? That is a question which every serious mind will like to answer. It is, first of all, what has been happily called the Fact of Christ.[1] The person of Jesus Christ is Christianity. In that person there is an

[1] "The Fact of Christ," by P. Carnegie Simpson. Hodder & Stoughton.

ideal for humanity, which neither experience nor theory can better. In the judgment of the gravest sceptics, after the most impartial inquiry, there is no way of attaining a good life, or of judging what a good life is, so effectual as to determine to act in such a way as would win the approval of Jesus of Nazareth. The character presented to us as the norm of humanity is one that contains the noble ingredients which have always been recognized as indispensable, viz., courage, wisdom, justice, and temperance; but certain qualities which were new, or at least unrecognized as parts of the perfect man — these are purity, love, forgiveness, and humility. The character of man is ideally rounded and completed. What a man should be swims into human ken, not by the theorizing elaborations of the moralist, but in the artlessly-drawn presentation of an actual person.

Christianity is simply Christ. It is this Person presented to the intelligence and conscience of mankind, for each to accept and believe in.

The Person, however, is not sufficiently described when His characteristics are delineated. His offer of Himself to men is part of His person. His redemptive power for, and over, men is also part of His person. The image of God reflected in His consciousness is part of His person. The promise and power of spiritual continuance after His death, and of active operation in human life to "the end of the world," is part of His person.

Thus we obtain as the essence of Christianity the fact of Christ, a Person who is, in the first place, the ideal Character, presented to mankind for following and imitation; in the second place, a living and eternal power accessible in the Spirit to the spirit of every man, a power to change and save every soul that receives Him; and in the third place, a mirror in which the Infinite and Eternal Being that made the world and man is sufficiently reflected.

God as reflected in the human being of Christ appears in a light which man had not up to that time conceived, nor since has man obtained any clearer or better conception. The Infinite and Eternal Being is Spirit; He stands in relation to men as a Father; He loves them and cares for them. He is holy Spirit, identical with the good, antagonistic to the evil, in the world and men. He has holy designs of love for men. Christ is the declaration and the agency of these designs.

Apart from all Churches, which are merely the human efforts, made age after age, to grasp and to embody this religion; before the Churches were, and even should the Churches cease to exist — here is the best that we know in the way of religion. And as the truth it is indefeasible and irresistible. When it is understood, separated from the accretions and corruptions, the ambitions and the claims of interested persons, and the corrupt illusions of our own minds, it immediately commends itself to men:

This must be the key to the mystery of life, the light of eternity falling on the dim tract of time.

And it may be called not only the best we know, but the best that can be known, because after some generations of the freest and most vigorous inquiry, after a century of amazing progress in science, and in full view of all attempts to improve upon this truth, or even to make suggestion of an improvement, nothing better emerges, nothing more probable or more certain. Comte's religion, the only serious attempt of the nineteenth century to provide a substitute for Christianity, is no improvement even in idea. His *Grand Être* is not in any intelligible sense a God; his roll of human saints presents no better ideal, and a far weaker incentive to imitation, than the lone person of Christ. A visitor to the temple of Positivism, after half a century of propaganda, found, in place of the Christian doctrine of three Persons and One God, three persons present and no God.

The other great attempt of the nineteenth century to find a substitute for religion in a philosophy, the synthetic system of Herbert Spencer, was already, before the great master was dead, falling into decay. The conclusion to which his speculations pointed was that we are in presence of an Infinite and Eternal Energy from which all things proceed.[1] This is an absolute certainty. But Spencer persisted in the idea that this mysterious being is unknown.

[1] "Ecclesiastical Institutions," ed. 1885, p. 843.

And his attempt to found a system of ethics on the theory that the human mind is an automaton, the product of the evolutionary forces which made the universe, led thought back to the confusion in which the earliest Greek philosophers were involved. The one assured fact of knowledge, personality, remained unreal; that is to say, not only God, but man, is unknown.

How can this cumbersome and contradictory system, which leaves all that is best in man and in life unexplained, except that it is resolved into what is lower, be an improvement upon the fact of Christ and the truth of the Christian religion?

If we are to consider Haeckel's monism another attempt to find a better way, we have only to study Dr. Ballard's "Haeckel's Monism False" to see how this later gospel is not only no improvement, but a tissue of absurdities and contradictions, and that when Haeckel strays out of his province, which is that of biological inquiry, into the realm of philosophy and religion, he is weak as another man.

The simple truth of Christianity holds the field because man can find nothing better. Men turn to it, sometimes after years of careless and godless indifference, sometimes after long excursions into modern speculation and the medley of other religious systems, with that cry which was uttered at the beginning: "Lord, to whom shall we go? for Thou hast the words of eternal life." Within the Churches and outside of them the best men and women are moulding their lives on the fact of Christ; and it is that which constitutes the strength of Christendom; that is the salt of the earth and the light of the world. Everywhere there are "holy and humble men of heart" who in their secret chamber commune with God in Christ, and in their daily life walk with God; their life is hid with Christ in God, but the effects of it work in the world as its salvation. Not all the blindness, ignorance, prejudice, self-seeking, and uncharitableness of Churches can alter the reality of this secret and persistent working. Christ is in the world, and is conquering the world, by the method which He Himself announced, when He said that His kingdom would not come with observation. They who are in the secret recognize Him working everywhere. His visionary form moves in and out among the haunts of men, overshadows parliaments and governments, visits the hearts of kings. Through political and social movements, led sometimes by men who do not recognize Him, He works. In poems and pictures and other forms of art, even in the drama and the playhouse, He appears.

The kind of unity which He desired He has achieved; it is the spiritual unity of men and nations under the utmost variety of forms, and creeds, and organizations. From all parts of the earth to-day eyes are turned towards Him; more and more men are able to distinguish between Him and the Churches, between His reputed vicegerent and His own living, ubiquitous presence. He is fulfilling His design of gathering together in one the children of God that are scattered abroad. Eventually humanity will be one in Him.

Appendix to Chapter II

The following extracts from a *Journal Intime* may shed some light on that inner life which is everywhere being lived to-day, by persons entirely unsuspected and unknown:

"Let us get at the things we do most surely believe. Let us look into our own hearts and write. Not for human eyes, but as between God and the soul, let us set down the points which are settled and beyond dispute: Jesus Christ is the supreme revelation of God. Within the circle of His being lies all that we can know of God. Apart from Him we have only metaphysical and inferential knowledge of the Infinite and Eternal Energy, too vague to be personal, too abstract to be practical."

"It is in the study and contemplation of Jesus Christ that I discover my sin. With my eye on Him, I know that I am sinful; if I do not feel it, I am the more sure of it, for the callousness is an aggravation."

"But in the close approach to Him, as He was in the Gospel narrative, as He is in the Spirit — for Christ is above all a Presence always at hand to the soul — I am impressed with the certainty that forgiveness is brought to my sin, and complete restoration to my moral and spiritual nature. This is clear in experience, but only at times, and partially, lucid to the intellect. This broad fact stands out like a rugged mountain-range, softened in the morning and the evening lights, outlined against the saffron sky, bathed with purple and crimson dyes in moments of magical transformation, but hard to climb or to penetrate. There are times when the whole range is covered with dense and thunderous clouds. For days together the mountains recede and are invisible. This is the rugged fact of Christianity: that Christ is the propitiation for sin, the propitiation set forth, not by man, but by God; that in Him God passes judgment on sin, and yet forgives; that all who believe in Him are forgiven; that the pardon works deliverance; that as the soul dwells more and more trustfully in this reality of reconciliation with God in Christ, the example of Christ becomes more and more imitable, and the word of Christ more and more authoritative, more and more sin ceases to have dominion."

"Here is a certainty of experience. From this central core everything else is developed: the knowledge of God, the love of man, the guide for conduct, the commission of life, the hope in death, the belief in the future world. These things are not as certain as the central experience, but they are connected with it by an organic tie. They fall like inevitable conclusions from an admitted premiss. This one thing I know, that whereas I was blind now I see. But these other things I believe because they grow naturally out of what I know. Life must be a progressive inliving into the fact of Christ, an *imitatio Christi*, not from without but from within."

"Plotinus describes the religious life as φυγὴ μόνου πρός μόνον, the retreat of the solitary to the solitary. I perceive the truth of this, and yet it does not satisfy me. As a nomad in the boundless universe I have suffered, and yearned for companionship. To Thee, O God, have I fled, and found that I was not alone. But the coming to Christ has brought me into a large and jocund company. Thou art no longer a distant solitary, but a persuasive sympathy, and a consoling society. I find I am in relation with all. In the arid place is the sound of abundant waters. The wilderness rejoices and blossoms as the rose."

"The true contrast is not between selfishness and altruism, for altruism may itself be selfish, but between selfishness and God. The mind of the flesh is still selfish even in the performance of unselfish work. The mind of the spirit, on the other hand, is a harmony with the All, and is therefore peace and joy. In place of the self is God, God who is in, and unites, all. The atheist self has vanished."

"Why then shouldst thou delay to make the true choice and take thy place with God and in the universe? Here is the Way, the Truth, the Life. Why stop short? Enter the Way, believe the Truth, live the Life."

*　　*　　*　　*　　*

"How long wilt thou persist, O my soul, in making demands, especially here, where thou hast no rights except such as are forfeit? And why wilt thou talk ever of humility and yet refuse to be humble? Once thou demandedst success and reputation; shaken from so presumptuous and vain a request, thou askedst at least for enjoyment or comfort; perceiving at length that this was, except intermittently, impossible in a world of change, thou yet preferredst a petition for subsistence, for the privilege of serving and being useful. O most vain soul, is not this the greatest demand of all? What inherent claim hast thou to subsistence? And to serve and be useful is the richest boon on earth. Wilt thou not therefore attain a true humility, and demand nothing of thy God except a complete contentment with His ways?"

"Why this avidity of joy in our hearts? Clearly there is a true joy to be attained. But it cannot be that which men commonly desire. We covet joys which are fires within, with brief pleasurable warmth and leaping flames, followed by consuming pain and dead ashes. But One promised us His joy, which is the genial and unfailing warmth upon the hearth of God. But what kind of joy was His? The joy of renunciation and of the Cross."

"'They would not receive Him because His face was set to go to Jerusalem.' We cannot accustom ourselves to this necessity, that if our face is in that direction the world will not receive us. Thus, setting our face resolutely, we still inwardly expect admiration, and the solicitation of men's desire. We are still surprised at their indifference. We go forward, but we look back. We are so far Christian that we do not seek the world; we are not so far Christian that we give up expecting that the world will seek us. Hence this constant disappointment and fretfulness, this suspicion that we are unappreciated or hardly dealt with. The Samaritans did not receive Jesus; the Jews crucified Him."

"After many protests of renunciation, there remains still the inward renunciation to be made. We forego for a time, with implicit hope that presently ample amends will be made. We consent to be nothing to-day, that we may, even by this foregoing, be much to-morrow. This means that there is yet a corner to be turned in the inward life. Not to-day nor to-morrow expect or desire to be anything. Self is the boulder in the way which must be passed and left behind; its very memory must be distasteful."

"How is it that we continue to expect, as if there were always something behind? Is it not ignoble to be cheated in this way by the illusions of life? There is nothing behind. The scenes and the moving wings of the stage are all. Life does not contain the completeness that it suggests. The soul is meant to be wistful. Forbear to rummage in the back parts of the stage among the sordid properties and in the cavernous emptiness. The hunger in thy heart is satisfied only in God; and God is here and now. There is nothing more than this omnipresent Presence, this eternal Now."

"Frequently it happens that the way is bared, and all objects of beauty and interest disappear. Also, by an illusion, the sense of a goal withers in the heart, and there seems to be no scope: even humblest service appears rejected. These are the times for sheer faith, and for the discovery of the reality within.

'When to thy ship in tempest hell appears,
And every spectre mutters up more dire
To snatch control
And loose to madness the deep-kennelled fears,
Then to the helm, O soul!'"

"Now what is this strange sweetness which breaks upon the soul when renunciation is made — *l'ineffable joie du renoncement de joie?* Certainly it was intended. The way through the desert, honestly chosen and faithfully pursued, has suddenly plunged down into a flowery dell, where the waters are cool and the fruit is luscious and the birds sing."

* * * * *

"We are feverishly anxious that the estimation in which the world holds us should be equal to our desert. Ought we not rather to be preoccupied with the desire to *be* better than we are esteemed? Thus the world's low estimate would be a consolation, as a lessened reproach of our poor advance."

"Were it not well, O foolish heart, to seek definitely not to be known, to court the obscurity of a hidden life? What hindrance is like publicity? What check is like the loosened praise of men? A life hidden with Christ in God is the true life. Let after generations discover thee, when it no more concerns thee; let them light on traces of a shy soul that dwelt intimately with God, and take heart for a like inwardness. But thou art happy if it is said of thee: 'Of his generation, who among them considered him?'"

"For, of a truth, O God, thou regardest those whom men ignore. Thou art One that hidest Thyself, and lovest hidden souls."

* * * * *

"When, O my soul, wilt thou begin to see in Sorrow thy Preceptress? Is it necessary to have sat in her school for a lifetime, and to be by now well-nigh out of her hands, before thou wilt perceive her solitary ways? At least here at the midpoint of life recognize that thou hast learnt thy wholesomest lessons at her feet, and that her face is beautiful as the dew-washed evening star."

"Unhappy are they who see pure truth, for they must declare it; and no one wants it or will receive it. Truth accommodated to error is the article demanded in the world's mart. Inevitably therefore they who come to bear witness of the truth proceed to Calvary. For wickedness and truth-loving alike the world provides a cross; for it does not distinguish between them."

* * * * *

"When Prince Charles of Roumania ascended his throne, on the declaration of independence in May, 1877, the crown was made out of the iron of a Turkish gun captured by his troops at Grivitza; in the arsenal Roumanians worked all day, foreigners excluded, to prepare the crown for the King's brow. There is another King whose crown is wrought of the engines which have been brought by His enemies against Him. But the coronation is not yet."

* * * * *

"You say that evolution is shaped by environment; you say that the universe has been evolved. What, then, was the environment of the universe, or if it had no environment, how was it evolved?

"Always there is something fatally lacking in every attempt to account for things. Certainly there must be an environment of the universe if evolution is its law. How should Personality emerge from the undesigned collision of impersonal forces? How should matter produce spirit? The venture of Faith is therefore also the necessity of Reason: in the beginning God created."

CHAPTER III

MORALITY

MR. COULTON'S vivid picture of mediæval life, derived largely from the chronicle of Salimbene, raises a most interesting question. The period it covers is that between St. Francis and Savonarola, those three centuries, the thirteenth, fourteenth, and fifteenth, which are, if any, the age of faith. To say that this period was not an age of morality is to use the figure of speech known as *litotes*. The evidence of wickedness, especially among the clergy, is given, happily for the general reader, in Latin. No purpose can be served by presenting these revolting details to the eyes of the public. Yet the general conclusion is one which the public is entitled to know. Indeed, no more salutary lesson is to be learnt, for religious teachers and for the rising generation, than the connection between morality and religion which here receives copious illustration.

There is a loose assumption underlying most modern criticism of Churches, that religion and morality are identical. But in reality no two things are in their beginnings wider apart. So far from being identical, their identification is a slow and arduous achievement. To accomplish that identification is the main purpose of human evolution. That Christianity identifies them is its main distinction. It is the first religion which explicitly and frankly makes the two inseparable. That is the strongest line of defence, its chief claim on the adhesion and the gratitude of mankind. A book like Mr. Coulton's reminds us how slowly the Christian idea made its way, against what overwhelming obstacles it had to contend, and how often in the history of the Church it almost vanished out of sight.

If religion and morality are not yet brought together in practice, if the divorce is still flagrant, if ethical societies are formed for the purpose of carrying out the morality which the Churches neglect, if infidelity finds its weapons with which to fight religion in the immorality of religious persons and institutions, there is less cause for astonishment and discouragement than at first sight appears. The one great and constant and irrefragable fact to the good is, that Christianity does identify religion and morality, and therefore affords the most powerful engine in the world for making religion moral. That at any rate is a *fait accompli*. Here is a vast major premiss which, before Christ came, was wanting. It stands, however bad the minor premiss of practice may be, however illegitimate the conclusion drawn from the premisses may seem. Here is a statement of Mr. Carnegie Simpson's, which in its crisp distinctness affords us a good starting-point for the argument:

"In the civilization of the Roman Empire — a civilization in some respects more elaborate than ours — religion was something absolutely apart from morality. The priests and augurs of ancient Greece and Rome never for one moment regarded it as any part of their duty to exhort or help men to a purer life. Alike public life and private were steeped in a heartlessness of cruelty and an abandonment of vice such as we can hardly realize; but the pagan religion made no protest, for, on the contrary, its mysteries often screened and its ministers sanctioned the grossest iniquities. It is this entire divorce between religion and morality in the ancient world which supplies the explanation, as Mr. Lecky has pointed out, of the apparently strange circumstance that the classical philosophical moralists pay so little attention to the appearance of Christianity. One would suppose that that religion, as a mere system of ethics, apart from any theological beliefs, would have commanded the notice of all serious men. But so we can imagine the philosophers who were in earnest about moral things saying: Is this not a religion? and what has a religion to do with the matter of moral life? Thus argued, and most naturally, such men as Plutarch, or Seneca, or Epictetus, or M. Aurelius, and thus before the eyes of these great moralists emerged what was to be the supreme moral phenomenon of history, and they gave it hardly a glance." [1]

If this sounds a paradox to the reader, it is only because the fundamental idea of Christianity, viz., that religion and morality are identical, has so permeated the modern mind, that it is assumed even by sceptics in their criticism of the Churches. If ecclesiastical history presents everywhere the most painful discord between religion and morality, that is only a reminder that Christianity is not identical with the Church, or at any rate that the Church is only struggling to realize the Christian ideal. The failures at which we are about to glance do not disprove Christianity, they only show that Churches and Christians are not yet Christian.

Suppose we establish it as our first principle, not open to serious debate, that the distinctive feature of Christianity is the identification of religion and morality. Without as yet determining what the religion is, or what the morality is, let it be granted that the two are one. Morality cannot admit a religion which violates it; religion cannot sanction immorality. The religious truth has its counterpart in the moral life; the moral life is the test and the evidence of the religion. There is no divorce, but an indissoluble union. This is the Christian doctrine, or philosophy, or revelation. This is Christianity. To this, no doubt, the Law and the Prophets were working up, slowly, and not

[1] "The Fact of Christ," p. 54.

without many backwashes; to this, no doubt, the great minds of all ages pointed — Buddha, Confucius, Plato; all the religions of the world were visited with occasional twinges of conscience, and inasmuch as they were held by men who also had a moral nature, ever and anon the sigh went up that the two might be one — "Oh, might the margins meet again!"

Some haunting, vanishing reminiscence of a Golden Age caused a vague discomfort: How can the august Ought in the conscience be separated from the august Varuna, or Zeus, on the throne of the Universe?

But the achievement of Christianity was, that religion was presented as an ideal morality, and, embodied in the person and character of Jesus, was identified with God. Ceremonial terms, like "sanctification" and "holiness," "profane" and "unclean," were either dropped or transformed. There was only one term retained — "goodness." God is good, and man must be good too. Christ came to be good, and to make men good. There at last shone out the lucid truth of things. That is essentially the one all-embracing revelation.

It need not surprise us that the truth was not immediately grasped. How could it have been? It had to be grasped by men, by thinkers, by races, that were obsessed with alien notions, with ancient custom, with stains in the blood. All the persons who embraced the gospel were persons brought up in the alienation of religion and morality; the pagan view of things was strong in them. We are startled with the outcrop of rabbinical Judaism in Paul; still more startling is the outcrop of the extra-Judaic paganism in Justin Martyr, Irenæus, or Origen. The revelation of Christ was before their eyes and in their ears, but the ideas and practices of paganism were in their hearts, formed their subliminal consciousness, coloured all the doctrines which they accepted. "J. B." in his fascinating optimism takes the view that the departure from religion which we see in the modern world is really the surrender of the old paganism which was incorporated with religion. As compulsion is withdrawn, and we are all at liberty to think, we give up the traditions, the survivals, the accretions. We go back to Christianity; we look Christ in the face.

It can hardly therefore be matter for surprise that the ages of faith were also the dark ages, that the true Christianity was working its way through great obstacles, against the deadweight of surviving paganism.

With this preliminary explanation we may look at Mr. Coulton's facts, and learn from them.

"The 'Chronicle of Meaux' was written at the Cistercian abbey of that name in Yorkshire, by Abbot Thomas, of Burton, at the end of the fourteenth century. On p. 89 of Vol. III. he speaks of Pope Clement VI.,[1] who instituted the fifty years'

[1] Pope from 1342 to 1352, A.D.

jubilee, and against whom the Cistercians as a body had certainly no grudge. The chronicler goes on: 'Now this same Pope Clement VI. had been lecherous beyond measure his whole life long. For every night at vespertide he was wont, after the cardinals' audience, to hold a public audience of all matrons and honourable women who wished to come. At last some men, speaking ill of him on this account, began to stand by the palace doors and secretly to number the women who went in and who came out. And when they had done this for many days, there was ever one lacking at their egress from the number of those who had entered in. When therefore many scandals and obloquies arose on this account, the confessor of the Lord Pope warned him frequently to desist from such conduct, and to live chastely and more cautiously. But he ever made the same answer: "Thus have we been wont to do when we were young, and what we now do we do by counsel of our physicians." But when the Pope was aware that his brethren the cardinals and his auditors and the rest of the Court murmured and spake ill of him on this account, one day he brought in his bosom a little black book wherein he had the names written of his divers predecessors in the Papal chair who were lecherous and incontinent; and he showed by the facts therein recorded that these had better ruled the Church, and done more good, than the other continent popes. Moreover on the same day he raised to the cardinalate one of his sons, a boy of sixteen, who was afterwards Pope Gregory XI. This Clement VI. was succeeded by Innocent VI., who like his predecessor Clement, promoted his own sons and brethren and nephews to cardinals and bishops, so that scarce any were left in the sacred college who were not of his kin or of the aforesaid Clement's. The chronicler's account is, no doubt, exaggerated, in parts at least; but the significance of the story lies in the fact that it was believed and recorded for posterity by a man in Abbot Burton's position. Hardly less significant is the praise occasionally bestowed on popes of exceptional virtue. Peter of Herenthals thinks it worth while to note that Gregory XI. 'died a virgin in mind and body as some have asserted'; and similarly Wadding is proud to record of Salimbene's Nicholas III., 'he kept perpetual virginity.'"

Indeed, the scandal sometimes forced even the laity to interfere. In 1340 the King of France felt bound to complain publicly to the Pope, who had legitimized "three brothers born of a detestable union — that is to say, of a bishop in pontifical dignity, degree, or order, and an unmarried woman. The word in the original being *Pontifex*, it is possible that the father may have been one of the Pope's predecessors, several of whom were notoriously unchaste." [1]

The singular thing is that not Rome, but the

[1] "From St. Francis to Dante," Coulton, p. 426.

MORALITY

Papal court, was, in the ages of faith, the scene of this moral depravity. Avignon became as Rome when the Pope resided there. Constance was as Avignon when the Council met there. "Petrarch has still harder words for Avignon" — Mr. Coulton has just quoted a visitor to Rome who describes the city as one continuous brothel — "during the years of the Pope's abode there; and its common nickname of 'the sinful city,' finds its way even into English parliamentary documents of the time. Exactly the same complaint was made against the city of Constance during the sitting of the Great Council in the next century. The iniquities of the city of Rome itself have always been proverbial; both Boccaccio and Benvenuto da Imola refer to them as notorious, and they are silently admitted even by Father Ryder in his reply to Littledale's 'Plain Reasons.'"[1]

Sometimes the popes have been better than the bishops. For example, at the Council of Lyons the good Gregory X. roundly asserted that the prelates were "the cause of the ruin of the whole world." By exerting his full power he forced the prince-bishop Henry of Liège to resign. This great prelate had two abbesses and a nun among his concubines; and he boasted of having had fourteen children in twenty-two months.

Of course this inner corruption implied outer corruption too. The ages of faith, as they have

[1] Coulton, *loc. cit.* p. 283.

been called, were unutterably miserable. "Italy," says Mr. Coulton, "remained for generation after generation in a state of anarchy and misery which among our own annals can be paralleled only in Stephen's reign, when men said that God and his saints slept. Yet the sad facts must be faced; for it was from this violent ferment that noble minds like St. Francis and Dante took much of that special flavour which appeals so strongly to the modern literary mind. Here, as on many other points, Salimbene's evidence is all the more valuable that he himself was neither saint nor poet, but a clever, observant, sympathetic man with nothing heroic in his composition." [1]

Here, then, we have the extraordinary anomaly, that the religion which in its inception was identical with morality became in the age before the Reformation not only divorced from it, but wedded to immorality of the grossest type. The religion developed along the lines of an imperial political organization. The supreme ruler of the system was a sovereign, a king of kings, God's vicegerent on earth, designated "Our Lord God the Pope." [2] This exalted and absolute representative of Christ, the Founder of the religion, might be, and often was, immoral, without impairing his authority or shaking the faith of the Church. Good Churchmen, like Abbot Burton, would admit the immorality without

[1] Coulton, *op. cit.* p. 132.
[2] "Corpus Juris Canonici" (Extrav. Johannis xxii. Tit. xiv.).

questioning the religious authority of the head of the Church. Nay, to this day more than half of nominal Christendom is of the same opinion. The loyal Roman Catholic can read the story of Clement VI., or of Alexander VI., and maintain that such men were the Vicars of Christ. The Roman Catholic admits in the very centre of his spiritual life the separation between religion and morality. The Church, with Clement VI. at its head, with a Curia such as is described by Petrarch, producing the misery and anarchy of Italy in the age described by Mr. Coulton, is yet the "holy" Catholic Church. Holiness does not mean goodness. The Holy Father does not mean necessarily a good man. Though the priest be morally corrupt he is still able by his word to "create his Creator," or by another word to absolve the penitent.

It is not altogether astonishing that in the ethical revival which is visiting the modern world men who are reverent to ethical ideals should break away from the Church. The Church which claims the title of Holy, Catholic, and Apostolic has made the same divorce between religion and morality which occurs in the other religions of the world. The religious claim is other than ethical. The vicegerents of God need not be good, and therefore, it would follow, the God whom they represent need not be good. If Catholicism is identical with Christianity it can be no cause for astonishment that men with ethical ideals should turn away from Christianity. A Church which regards Clement VI. as the vicegerent of God — the Vicar for Christ on the earth — which demands for such a representative the reverence and obedience which are due to Christ, must encounter the uncompromising resistance of all who identify religion and morality. If we have reason to believe that such an identification is the distinctive feature of Christianity, we are forced to the conclusion that this Church is not Christian. It is a mistake to renounce Christianity because ethical truth requires us to renounce the Church. The Reformation was a desperate, blind effort to reassert the major premiss of Christianity. Get beneath the cross currents of the surface, and you find that the deep, irresistible tide of the movement flows from an outraged conscience. Everything else is temporary and incidental. The political intrigues, revolts, and aspirations which attempted to exploit the Reformation must be distinguished from the Reformation itself. Even the limitations and passions and ancient prejudices of the Reformers themselves must be put aside. Whether we regard Wicklif the morning star, or Luther the meridian light, of the movement, we ought not to miss the simplicity and sincerity of the motive.

Here was the discovery, shall we say in Scripture, or in the deep inner testimony of the human spirit itself in the evolution of time? that the all-important factor of human life is goodness, and that the religion which for a thousand years had dominated and moulded Europe was not good and did not make men good. If the Imperial Court of the religion is also the centre of moral corruption, of unscrupulous intrigue, of amazing avarice, ambition, and obscurantism, the religion stands condemned.

In that great moral uprising Europe would have broken with Christianity altogether but for one thing. There was a book — like that book brought to Josiah from the recesses of the Temple, six centuries before Christ — hidden away in the dusty libraries of the Church, a venerated Law-book, but unstudied and practically unknown. This Book was unearthed. By the recent discovery of printing it could be circulated. By the labours of scholars like Erasmus and Œcolampadius it could be given to the world in the vernacular. It was this Book which saved the situation. It had the authority of antiquity; it was admitted by all the Fathers of the Church to be the sole guide for doctrine and practice. Practically unknown as it was, it was carefully preserved. Obscured as it was by tradition, its pristine value and meaning were still treasured.

Not only the scholar, but the plain man, could see two things in this book: first, that its condemnation of the Church was no less clear than the voice of his own conscience; the whole system which presented itself as Christianity was refuted by the Book which was presumably its authority; its popular doctrines, rites, practices, objects of devotion, conception of God, ideals of life, were unknown, and implicitly repudiated, in that Book. Secondly, the Book showed the original message of Christianity, and behold, it was that identification of religion and morality for which the conscience was crying out!

It became apparent, and has remained apparent ever since, that to repudiate the Church is not to break with Christianity; it may, on the contrary, be to go back to it. It is Christianity itself which united religion and morality, and justified the better instinct that makes morality the criterion of religion.

If Protestantism is a failure, as Dr. Newman Smyth [1] implies that it is in America, and as it would seem to be from the decay of Protestant Churches on the Continent, the alternative is not a return to Catholicism, but a return to Christianity. Protestantism may have failed to settle a final creed, or to establish Church institutions, it may have failed in its cultus and in its organization, but in one thing it has completely succeeded: it has made the return to Catholicism impossible for progressive nations and for fearless lovers of truth. If it has not successfully presented the truth of Christianity, it has at any rate demonstrated that the truth of Christianity is very different from Catholic truth; and it has made an impression on the thinking part of Europe, which can never be removed, that Christianity means the identification of religion and morality. The idea

[1] *Cf.* "Passing Protestantism and Coming Catholicism," by Newman Smyth (Scribners).

that Clement VI., with his systematic lechery, could by any possibility be the vicegerent of Christ on earth has passed away forever from Christendom. No dogmatic assertion, no terrors of ecclesiastical censure, will ever convince that growing part of the modern world which has attained its freedom, or alter that instinctive major premiss which is written in the conscience. To the assertion that the Pope was the Vicar of Christ it is now a sufficient answer: "But he was not good." This Protestantism has done once for all. Catholicism has no future unless it alters its fundamental dogma. The moral sense of the world, since Luther, has become stronger than the Church. But a return to Christianity is possible because of the Book. The place of morality in the Bible is singular and most interesting. There is no exact parallel in any other religion or literature. The Bible does not confuse morality with religion, but from first to last it maintains the indissoluble union. In the Bible the religion grows, and the morality grows, but the tie between them is so close that they grow together. Confucius has a strong morality, but it has no connection with religion; Mohammed has a strong religion, but it has only the weakest connection with morality.[1] But the Bible presents this very peculiar phenomenon:

[1] Whenever the devout life, with its spiritual aspirations and fervent longings, touches the scheme of Moslem theology, it must bend and break. For it, within Islam, there is no place, the enormous handicap of the dogmatic system is too great" ("The Religious Attitude in Islam," by Professor Macdonald, p. 301).

the religious ideas from the first involve morality, and the morality makes no pretence to any existence independent of religion. The morality of the New Testament is not that of the Old, nor is the religion of the New Testament that of the Old; but the connection between religion and morality is the same in both. In the Old as in the New the morality is enforced by the religious sanction; in the New as in the Old the religion is ethical. In each case God is the highest goodness known; in each case obedience to God means being good. When new ideas of God evolve, or when new commands of God are given, the clearer knowledge of God is always a raising of the standard of morality, and likeness to God in an ethical sense is insisted on as the main demand of the religion.

For example, no passage takes us to the heart of the Jewish Law more rapidly than the summary of the ceremonial and social regulations at the end of Leviticus. Amid much that has become obsolete with the evolution of moral ideas, one principle stands out clearly; it is that of social justice. "Ye shall not wrong one another." The time has not come for extending the principle to other nations or to humanity; but for those who are members of the one community the duty of justice and even of love is uncompromising. That is the sum total of morality. No one is to do to another what he would not have done to himself. That is the doctrine of Confucius; it is also the law of Moses. But the distinction of the law of Moses is in the sanction. If the Confucianist questions the Law, and asks, "But why must I treat my neighbour in this way?" Confucius has no answer to give unless it be the prudential one: "You must treat your neighbour in this way in order that he may treat you in this way." But if, by power or influence, you see how you can make your neighbour treat you well without your treating him well, the sanction is gone. The sanction of the law of Moses, on the other hand, lies in the nature and the rule of God: "Ye shall not wrong one another; but thou shalt fear thy God; for I am the Lord your God."[1] This is a fundamental difference. It is God, the final Authority and unquestioned Ruler of men, who requires this treatment of one's neighbour. It is from no prudential hope of getting good from others that you must do good to them. The duty rests on the nature and the will of God. The good one does to others from a prudential motive is hardly "good" in the ethical sense at all. It becomes good only when it is done with the good motive. And the good motive is only furnished by the religious idea that goodness is God, the Object of worship, the Sovereign to whom obedience is due.

In the New Testament this principle becomes both deeper and stronger. The goodness in the Divine nature receives a fuller illustration, and the sanction contained in it to induce goodness in men is both clearer and more cogent.

[1] Lev. xxv. 17.

There is a little conjunction in the Epistle to Titus, a "for" which, as a pivot, carries more on it than, perhaps, any conjunction in the written words of men. It is found in Titus ii. 11. The life of a strict and lofty morality is enjoined in a few golden directions; it is sanctioned by the revelation of God that has been made in Christ, the grace of it, the promise of it. Here in the most concentrated form the Christian connection between religion and morality is expressed. We are required to be good, and the nature of the required goodness is defined by the fact that God wishes to make us good, and has actively intervened in the affairs of men in order to effect His purpose. Possibly any ancient writer could have summarized what ought to be the character of the several ages and grades of humanity. In that respect the New Testament does not greatly differ from Seneca or Epictetus. In that respect the evolution of moral ideas may have carried us to-day farther than the writer of this passage. Mankind has always felt that aged men ought to be temperate, grave, sober-minded, exhibiting love and patience. For aged women there is no greater glory than to be reverent in demeanour, refraining from slander and wine, handing down to their daughters the noble tradition of domestic order and fidelity. To make the home is still admittedly the first duty of women. But at this point we are already pushed farther than any writer (however inspired) of the first century could be. We take into account the women who will never be wives, and conceive an ideal of public service for them which gives them their proper place and privileges in the commonwealth. We still demand that they should be chaste, but not necessarily that they should be "workers at home." As to those who are married we still desire them to be kind, but we should not lay stress on "being in subjection to their own husbands." Increasingly the married relation must come under the great principle, "By love *serve one another*." For young men all ethical codes can agree that the master-virtue is what the Greeks call $\sigma\omega\phi\rho\sigma\sigma\acute{\upsilon}\nu\eta$ — that is, not the intellectual wisdom which makes a philosopher, but that judgment, balance, and sobriety which form the indispensable condition of effectiveness in life. Richard Feverel's heedlessness is flanked by the sterile wit of the Wise Youth; each is equally remote from the wisdom which is covered by the word "soberminded." Good works, right opinions, incorruptibility, dignity, true and strong speech, these are admittedly the virtues of manhood, the radiant manifestations of the right moral conditions. Passing to the directions for servants, we are again conscious of the immense forward thrust of our ethical ideals. Servants, in the sense of this passage, *i.e.*, slaves, no longer exist in Christendom — at least, in Protestant Christendom.[1] But for the milder rela-

[1] The practical slavery in Angola, and especially in S. Thomé and Principe, forbids us to say that no Christian power tolerates slavery.

tion of employer and employed, it is impossible to state more effectively the ethical idea of service to an employer — "not gainsaying, not purloining, but showing all good fidelity." Liberty is essential to a complete morality; but the liberty of a good servant may be just as genuine as the liberty of a master or of a king. For liberty is not emancipation from duty to others, but rather the opportunity to render that service effectively. The master is bound by his obligation to the State, and even to his servant; the king is bound by his duty to the laws and to his people. It has, therefore, always been perceived that a servant may ethically be as complete and as noble as any one else. And there is no fairer example of a true and even great character than one who by respect, by honesty, and by fidelity identifies himself with the interests of a master or a family. Very suitably this type of moral life is regarded in a special degree as "adorning the doctrine of God our Saviour in all things."

But now we come to the point. This moral life, briefly but sufficiently sketched for all ages and degrees, hinges upon the religious truth of the Christian revelation. This is the force of the potent *for*. The manifestation of Christ is presented as the motive and sanction for all details of good and heroic conduct. Let a child's remark light up the position. She was a very little girl; two pieces of cake were brought in for the two children, herself and her brother; she, after a moment's pause, selected the smaller. Evening came and the child's prayers. That little choice had filled the child's mind during the day, and now she offered an explanation to her mother. "Do you know why I took the little piece?" "Why?" "'Cos I remembered Jesus died." That is the secret of Christian morality, as it is expressed in this passage, and as it has worked out ever since the passage was written.

"*For* the grace of God hath appeared bringing salvation to all men, instructing us to the intent that, denying ungodliness and worldly lusts, we should live soberly and righteously and godly in this present world, looking for the blessed hope and appearing of the glory of our great God and Saviour, Jesus Christ; who gave Himself for us, that He might redeem us from all iniquity, and purify unto Himself a people for His own possession, zealous of good works."

The return to Christianity is not impossible, nay to the eye of faith it seems as good as certain. So great an idea, an idea so foreign to man in his primitive state, as the intimate identification of morality and religion, could hardly take possession of mankind at a bound. Some millennia of human evolution occurred before the idea was conceived. We are able in the Bible to trace at least a thousand years of the germination of the idea. In Christ it was above the surface of the soil, but, theoretically secure, it has pushed for nigh two millennia more against the superincumbent obstacles. The old Paganism, and even the old Judaism, were strong. The whole Roman Empire attempted to crush it, or rather crushed, in attempting to exploit, it. The Pontifex Maximus of the Roman Empire is still the Pope. The prelates and priests of Christendom still exercise their functions in the similitude of the older order. Innumerable traditions, superstitions, and conventions prevent men from recognizing the identity of morality and religion which in Christ was once for all established. In Protestantism the Church twitched one arm free from her ancient bondage. It was liberation, but not yet emancipation. Emancipation yet lies in the future. It will come, because it is implied in the Christian truth, it is even explicit in the Christian documents. The world is to discover that Christian morality is inseparable from the Christian religion, and that Christianity is the revelation of a perfect goodness in God for the purpose of producing perfect goodness in men. "Ye shall be perfect as your Father in heaven is perfect."

Sometimes we light upon a character which gives large hints of perfection, and even offers reminiscences of Christ, a character singularly unlike the ideal of ancient morals, unlike Plato's philosopher hiding from the blast of reality under the wall of idealism, unlike Aristotle's picture of the magnanimous man, strong, self-centred, self-conscious, dignified, unlike even the pensive stoicism of M. Aurelius. This Christian character, embodiment of the Christian morality, product of the Christian revelation, being unique in human experience, the fine flower of millennial evolution, affords a hope of what is yet to be. Such, some day, all men will be.

It was my lot to know one such man. He endeared himself to all who knew him, and undesignedly won a reputation wide as the English-speaking race, and lasting, we may surmise, as that of all saints. This was Henry Drummond, of whom more than one averred that to be with him was to receive a singular impression of what manner of man Christ Himself might have been in the days of His flesh. If that is too strong a mode of speech, it is at least no exaggeration to say that, as his character was produced by an intimacy with Christ, so it was one which Christ would have fully approved. We could easily imagine Christ saying of him: "This is My beloved brother, in whom I am well pleased." Happily his books remain behind to show that things spoken of him in love and gratitude are not impossible. "Natural Law in the Spiritual World" flashed like a meteor across the sky in the eighties. Every one read it. It had the vogue which a novel of Miss Corelli's would have in our day. The attempt to trace the same principle at work in the physical and in the religious spheres was condemned as unorthodox, but it was not shown to be untrue. The germ of thought then sown has developed. We are more and more inclined to seek for such a monistic interpretation of the universe. But the breach with orthodoxy in the interests of faith was characteristic of Drummond as it was of his Lord. There comes back to me a memorable episode in Harvard fifteen years ago. The secretaries of the Y.M.C.A.'s from all over the United States were met to confer, and the distinguished visitor was there to answer their questions. One secretary from the West, a champion of orthodoxy, seeking encouragement and countenance for his conflict with unbelief, rose and said: "Professor Drummond, I should like to ask you what you would say if a man came to you and said that he did not believe everything that is stated in the Bible?" The quiet, cultured voice, and still more the smiling face and restful eyes, replied, "I should say that I agree with him." It was as if a bombshell had exploded in the room. No further explanation was given. It was just like those pregnant, far-reaching words of Jesus, which can never be forgotten and can never cease to operate.

Strange to say, the brochure "The Greatest Thing in the World" was also condemned by the orthodoxy of the time. To count Love the greatest thing in the world shocked religious people, to whom love was secondary. But it could not be denied that the writer had Christ on his side, and even Paul and the other Apostles. Perhaps no book ever had a wider or more effective circulation. If we may compare it with the dogma of papal infallibility which had been propounded by an Ecumenical Council fourteen years before, we may say that, while the influence of the brochure was almost as wide as the dogma, it differed from the dogma in this: that the dogma was the death-blow of Roman Catholicism, and the brochure was the herald of Christian Catholicism.

I am not attempting to appraise the works of Henry Drummond, I am only drawing the portrait of the man; but it is impossible to pass by that scientific work, which was also a poem, that expansion of 1 Corinthians xiii. in terms of modern science, and the fullest knowledge we have as yet gained of man and of the universe, "The Ascent of Man." Here the world saw what gain there is in having its men of science Christian. Haeckel can give the facts of evolution, but he is totally unable to interpret them. He handles the riddle of the universe on the plea of solving it; but he leaves it not only insoluble, but disheartening. He borders on pessimism. The universe, as he sees it, has no reason for existence, and no goal, beyond the transitory sensations of existing organisms. Drummond does not discover the facts, he only knows them as discovered; but he interprets them. Running through the whole evolutionary process he finds Love. Darwin dwelt on the struggle for existence as the determining factor in organic evolution. Drummond dwelt on the equally indisputable fact, the struggle for the life of others. Was not mother-love, emerging in even the lowest organisms, and rising in the highest to realms of religion and eternity, as constant and incontestable a phenomenon of world-experience?

Working on this line, the man of science, who is also the seer, sees the universe as not unintelligible nor aimless. Love is creation's final law. The whole process is interpreted, science repeats in her own way the assertion of theology that God is Love. It becomes probable even from the constitution of things and from the evolution of all life, that each man's life is his chance of learning love, what love is, and how it came to be.

But to return to the writer of the books. He drew around him the young manhood of Edinburgh. The students were at home with him. From him Christianity came without offence, and was established, because it was accurately exemplified in his person. In London he spoke to audiences of the wealthy and cultivated. The same convincing power attended his words.

One of his peculiarities was to dress with the utmost nicety; no man of fashion would have felt ashamed to walk with him in the Mall. I do not know whether he saw a symbolic meaning in the seamless coat which Jesus wore. But it was as native to him to bear distinction in dress and demeanour as it was impossible that the Divine characteristics of Christ should be hid. The tall, erect figure, faultlessly dressed, the light hair, thrown back, the deep-set burning eyes, the sensitive, refined features, the quiet manner, the musical voice, the easy flow of beautiful language, the picturesqueness of thought, the sense of truth, the subdued emotion, made a personality that arrested and enchained attention. One involuntarily said, "Such should all men be." I remember that there was in him a surprising serenity. He worked hard, he had an overwhelming burden of engagements, he was in ever-growing demand. But he was never in a hurry. He seemed to have full leisure for you. He was equally ready to hear and to speak. The feeling he gave you was that, though he was for the moment walking and living in time, he came out of eternity. He had the bearing and the manners of that unhasting life.

No man in so brief a life ever impressed the world more widely or effected more. Great multitudes followed him and found in him their leader and teacher. But he gave you no sense of effort: it was not as if he did anything, but rather as if God was working in him to will and to do of His good pleasure. As Ian Maclaren said: "From first to last he was guided by an inner light which never led him astray, and in the afterglow his whole life is a simple and perfect harmony."[1] Another friend, who knew him well, Dr. Robertson Nicoll, confirms the impression which was made on me, and sheds further light on the character. In the memorial sketch occur these words: "He wrote brightly and swiftly, and would have made an excellent journalist. But everything he published was elaborated with the most scrupulous care. I have never seen manuscripts

[1] "The Ideal Life," p. 36.

so carefully revised as his. All he did was apparently done with ease, but there was immense labour behind it. Although in orders, he used neither the title nor the dress that go with them, but preferred to regard himself as a layman. He had a deep sense of the value of the Church and its work, but I think was not himself connected with any Church, and never attended public worship unless he tho ght the preacher had some lesson for him. He seemed to be invariably in good spirits an invariably disengaged. He was always ready for any and every office of friendship. It should be said that though few men were more criticised or misconceived, he himself never wrote an unkind word about any one, never retaliated, never bore malice, and could do full justice to the abilities and character of his opponents. I have just heard that he exerted himself privately to secure an appointment for one of his most trenchant critics, and was successful." [1]

Here is the finished picture of a Christian; here are gleams and outlines, appearing not altogether fitfully and disconnectedly, of the character of Jesus Himself. No treatise on ethics could convey so completely what a Christian character is as this concrete example of a Christian man. In one thing alone does the copy fall short of the original. It was given to Drummond to live for men. This he did with a good will. One might even say that in a bright and sunny sense he gave himself for us. But

[1] "The Ideal Life," p. 18.

the redemptive death of Jesus he was not able to imitate. Many a martyr for truth or in the mission-field has been permitted to imitate more closely that redemptive death. It is not an exaggeration to say, for instance, that Livingstone by his death at Ilala has redeemed the dark continent. Men who fell far short of Drummond's ideal character have in their deaths been allowed to reproduce, in a limited and human degree, the work of Christ's Cross. Drummond lived the life, and taught it by living it. He was one who involuntarily suggested Christ. And yet the manner of his death was in harmony with the life and the general impression that he made. With Dr. Nicoll's words I will close this adumbration of the character which illustrates the identity of religion and morality:

"The end came suddenly, from failure of the heart. Those with him received only a few hours' warning of his critical condition. It was not like death. He lay on his couch in the drawing-room, and passed away in his sleep, with the sun shining in and the birds singing at the open window. . . . It recalled what he himself said of a friend's death: putting by the well-worn tools without a sigh, and expecting elsewhere better work to do."

CHAPTER IV

POLITICS

THE word "politics" is so ambiguous and covers so many varying notions that it may be prudent to offer a definition of it, in order to save the reader the vexation of not knowing what is the subject of discussion. The term is here used in this sense: *the application of a man's religion to the life of the State.* It may be objected that such a definition begs the question in some of the issues which will be raised. Perhaps it does. It may seem to imply that if a man has no religion he can have no politics, which certainly would seem to be a paradox. But it must be remembered that, according to the present writer's view, every one must have a religion; every one must have some idea of the Power to which we owe our existence, must have some mental attitude towards the Power, and must shape the conduct of life accordingly. This view we have of the Power behind and above things, our attitude towards It — or Him — and the conduct which results therefrom, is our religion. Now, according to the definition, politics is the application of this religious principle in us to the life of the State. I am not pleased with this definition because it is my own, but because, whatever may be said against it, it is pregnant and leads to results. With the reader's permission, therefore, I will spend a little time on its defence.

Aristotle wrote his "Politics" as the necessary sequel to his "Ethics." The ethical life which he delineated could only be lived in a *polis* (πόλις) or State. The political organism not only resulted from the ethical principles, but was in its turn the essential condition of their working. Jowett passes on Aristotle the criticism that he did not sufficiently distinguish between ethics and politics. With the modern mind, on the other hand, the difficulty is to connect the two. In some modern States politics would seem to be the negative of ethics. And even in the best of modern States many persons would seriously maintain that a man can be morally good and have nothing to do with politics at all. But Aristotle defined man as "a political animal," not remembering that several species of insects, such as ants and bees, would come under the same definition. His good man was before all things the citizen of a good State; the good man's goodness was largely the excellence of his life as a citizen.

Now, our definition affirms the same relation between religion and politics that Aristotle maintained between ethics and politics. Aristotle would not quarrel with the contention, for with him, as with modern ethical societies, ethics takes the place of religion. Of this truth God is a witness to us, for

He is happy in His own nature. In like manner the State which is happiest is morally best and wisest; and the courage, justice, and wisdom of a State are the same qualities which make a brave, just, and wise man.[1] For Aristotle ethics is religion. We have maintained that ethics and religion are perfectly distinct, and yet must be indissolubly united; we do not, therefore, part company with Aristotle in claiming that politics is the application of religion to the life of the State; for us ethics can only be applied to the State as an inseparable part of religion. If our religion is noble and worthy, our politics will profit by its nobility and worth; if our religion is base, merely materialistic and sensual, selfish and practically godless, our political ideals and activities must be of the same kind.

It will be observed that we do not here mean by religion the Christian or any other particular religion. The term is used in the widest sense. Whatever our religion may be, Theism or Atheism, Christianity or Buddhism, Gnosticism or Agnosticism, our politics is the application of this religion to the life of the State. Our most general and most fundamental ideas of life, our idea of the Being that is responsible for our being, our sense of relation with that *Grand Être*, our practical conduct resulting from the relation, must colour all our action as citizens of the country to which we belong. If we are Christians, our politics must be Christian. If we are atheists,

[1] Arist. Pol. vii. 1, 2.

our politics must be atheistic. Our view of the State, our sense of duty to it, our action in it, must be determined by our religion, such as it is.

Now, let it not be deemed scholastic and affected to appeal in these enlightened times to the authority of Aristotle. If that authority has been abused in the arid discussions of mediæval theology, it is not therefore impaired. His is the view which antedates the age of specialists. He sees things in their connection, and never forgets that they are essentially connected. He "anticipates by his great power of reflection the lessons which the experience of ages has taught the modern world," says Jowett; and perhaps he anticipates by the same power some things which the modern world has yet to learn. When, therefore, he establishes the indissoluble connection between ethics and politics, or when he defines man as a political animal, our wise course is to accept the principles, and only to modify them by those enlargements of knowledge and insight which have resulted from the development of two thousand years. By ethics we now must mean that wedded pair of religion and ethics which God has at length joined together so that no man may put them asunder. And by a "political animal" we must mean an animal who is rational and religious, an individual as well as the unit of a community, a personality as well as the member of a State. Religion and personality are ideas which have acquired a new and a deeper meaning since the days of Aristotle, and by this new and deeper meaning we modify the dicta of the "master of those who know."

If, then, our dogmatic definition of politics may be allowed, let us proceed with the discussion. The first point is to establish the duty incumbent on every man — and in this connection man includes woman [1] — to play a political part. The second point is to discuss the political principles which should be accepted by all, and those on which a legitimate difference of opinion may exist.

Finally, an attempt must be made to sketch in the concrete the ideal politician; for in politics example tells more than abstract reasoning.

> "Grau, theurer freund, ist all Theorie
> Und grun des Lebens goldnerbaum."

1. It must be admitted that both in ancient philosophy and in modern religion some countenance can be found for those who decide to recede from the conflicts and disappointments of political activity. Plato's philosopher is seen cowering under the wall for protection from the rude storm of practical life. He decides frankly for the speculative as against the practical. When by good fortune his principles were carried out in an actual State the result was a tyranny. On such an experience the thinker may claim an exemption from political duty. He may

[1] In the early Acts which gave the franchise to men the Latin word *homo* meant "human being," man or woman. Accordingly, in Plantagenet days women had the vote.

let the storm of contested elections pass by him unheeded, as Hegel quietly completed his great philosophical work at Jena while the battle which shook the world was raging at its gates; he may abjure the newspapers in favour of the established realities of literature and science. But be it observed, in the modern State at least, this desertion is ignoble; it is not the less selfishness because the self served is the higher and ideal self.

One of the noblest men whom it has been my lot to know was Thomas Hill Green. He was a philosopher, a Hegelian, who by his power of abstract reasoning exercised a kind of spell over the more thoughtful minds in Oxford in the early eighties. Shy and reserved by nature, he might well have excused himself, as university people in Oxford usually do, from the strife and turmoil of affairs. But by the inner principle of his ethics and of his religion — for him the two were strictly identified — he was driven to throw himself, not only into the politics of the State, but even into the municipal politics of the city. It was an instructive spectacle to see the man, whose every lineament and deep-set eyes confessed the thinker and the recluse, coming as a simple citizen into the council, among tradesmen and others, whose readier speech and familiarity with business gave them an apparent superiority over the scholar and the philosopher. But owing largely to this fulfilment of an irksome duty, his philosophy, remote and abstract as it seemed, acquired hands and feet; it gripped men, and it carried them forward. Unlike the philosophies of cloistered schools, it was the making of men, of leaders, in economics, in the State, and in the Church. No one had less natural adaptation for political life, but the very effort which it demanded of him made him the man he was. Platonic in philosophy, he was as a citizen Aristotelian.

Not only has philosophy sometimes encouraged political abstention, but again and again religion, and even a nominal Christianity, has fostered the same cloistral indolence. Very early the cold shadow of monasticism was cast by Buddhism upon the Christian world. The anchorite withdrew from men; the cœnobite withdrew from the world in company with others. But each of them renounced the part of the citizen, and interpreted the application of religion to politics as a duty to keep out of politics altogether. On the plea of saving their own souls — for the monastic life never, except incidentally, had any nobler motive than self-preservation — they left the wicked world to perish. They ignored politics, until, with growing wealth and power, they meddled with the State, to buttress their own privileges. Possibly no single cause has done more to prevent the Christianizing of the State, and, from a Christian point of view, the salvation of the world, than this wholesale desertion, this grand refusal made by generation after generation of the pious. The "religious," as they are called by

Catholics, are they who have left the world, they who decline the duty of citizens and make it their boast that they are dead to this world and alive only to the world beyond.

It is the intrinsic cowardice and the blind delusions of this choice which have combined to make conventual establishments a gangrene in the State. The great Catholic countries, Italy, France, and even Spain, have been compelled in self-defence to abolish or to reduce these establishments. The dissolution of the monasteries is everywhere the signal for recovery from the sleeping-sickness of mediævalism; the recrudescence of conventual institutions is the sure sign of disease and decay. Men and women educated by monks and nuns can hardly be good citizens; the disease of the great delusion and the great refusal is infiltrated into the scholar from the teacher.

The Reformation, at least for a time, saved Europe from this deep-seated disease. "No life is more worldly than a Christian's," said Luther. The Christian is in the world, as Christ was in the world, to save it. He is here to follow Christ. No one by following Christ can arrive at seclusion from life. He went by all the crowded ways of healing and teaching, through all the activities of beneficence, not to a cloister, but to a cross. Oddly enough, one of the vagaries of the recluse has been to think that he could imitate Christ by having himself nailed to a cross. But to go from the morbid fancies of the cell to the self-immolation of crucifixion is not to follow Christ. He reached the cross by His public life and service, and especially by an ethical collision with the usurping authority of the Government of His day. To follow Christ would, for the monk, be to leave the cloister, to throw himself into the life and service of his time, and by such self-forgetting toil to face the crucifixion which, it may be, awaits every one who loves men unto death.

The disease of monasticism, however, is not cured by the Reformation. Even amongst the ultramontanes of Protestantism the idea perpetually recurs that spirituality is gained only by renouncing all political duties. There are zealots who hold it a sin to vote at an election, or even to read a paper. Under the illusion that the world is the realm and property of the devil, they will take no part in its management. This abstention may be more respectable than that of many who decline political duty from sheer indolence and frivolity; but it is more to be regretted, for while the frivolous and ignorant do in a sense serve their country by keeping their hands off the sacred ark of her covenant, these serious abstainers are precisely the people who, if they would bring their ethical earnestness and their religious conviction to bear upon the practical questions of legislation and government, might do more than any others to reform abuses and to ennoble the community. It were worth while, therefore, to take all pains to convert and to win them.

In a Greek State it was, Aristotle tells us, often a law that if a *stasis*, or revolution, occurred, every one must take sides on pain of banishment. The wisdom of Aristotle here again comes to our aid. On political issues it is the duty of every one to understand and to take sides. The first thing is not to decide which side ought to be taken, but to decide to take one side or the other, convinced that abstention is treachery to the community.

Irresolute minds may object that it is difficult to decide which view or party is right, and may excuse themselves from political claims by a conscientious indecision. But it must be remembered that the excuse is sophistical. It may not be possible to decide which party is right; but it is by the conflict of parties that the right is reached. To decline the combat and let the case go by default is to leave out an important element in the discovery of the right. Parliament is aptly described as a high court. Within its walls the case is stated; Government and Opposition are the counsel on either side. The nation occupies the tribunal and brings in the verdict. The citizen is not asked to be infallible, he is only required to do his best in the working of the machine by which the results are ground out. He is required not to shirk. The antagonism of parties is merely a device; it must not decide us. Truth is not in either side, but is the resultant of the conflicting forces. Thus there is only an apparent paradox in the common spectacle of two politicians, equally honest, equally religious, equally prayerful, taking opposite sides and tilting at each other with the ardour of conviction.

In the early days of the Home Rule fight the champions on either side, pitted against each other in unflinching antagonism, Mr. Gladstone, the author of the Home Rule Bill, and Colonel Saunderson, the leader of the Ulster Orangemen, were both intensely religious. Of each of them it is known that he never made a speech in the House without silently lifting up his heart to God for guidance and help. The one argued for Home Rule with a passion of pity for Ireland, with a wide knowledge of public affairs, with a command of the most copious and persuasive eloquence that ever led the House or fascinated the country. The other strove against Home Rule with an artillery of wit and invective, raillery and passion, which kept his hearers in laughter and his friends in confidence of victory from the beginning to the end. The tribunal has not yet decided on that conflict. The case is *sub judice*. But the conscientious and eager presentation of the arguments on both sides was the necessary preliminary. Neither champion could be blamed for his convictions. The only person to be blamed would be he who abstained altogether and would not take the trouble or responsibility of noticing, or seeking to staunch, the wound through which Ireland is bleeding to death.

The strong argument for political interest and

activity is at bottom humanitarian and even religious. The final judgment, so Christ has taught us, will go chiefly by the omission to minister to men, hungry, sick, and in prison. He will regard this neglect as shown towards Himself, and the punishment, the certain punishment, will fall upon the surprised delinquents. Now, in a modern State this ministry, in any large and adequate sense, is a matter of legislation and of the administration of the law. In a word, it is political.

A passage in Aristotle is a rebuke to much modern political indifferentism: "The true friend of the people should see that they be not too poor, for extreme poverty lowers the character of the democracy; measures also should be taken which will give them lasting prosperity; and as this is equally the interest of all classes, the proceeds of the public revenues should be accumulated and distributed among them, if possible, in such quantities as may enable them to purchase a little farm, or, at any rate, make a beginning in trade and husbandry. And if this benevolence cannot be extended to all, money should be distributed in turn according to tribes or other divisions, and in the meantime the rich should pay the fee for the attendance of the poor at the necessary assemblies, and should in return be excused from useless public services. By administering the State in this spirit the Carthaginians retain the affections of the people; their policy is from time to time to send some of them into their dependent towns, where they grow rich. It is also worthy of a generous and sensible nobility to divide the poor amongst them and give them the means of going to work. The example of the people of Tarentum is also well deserving of imitation, for, by sharing the use of their own property with the poor, they gain their goodwill." [1]

Here the father of political philosophy and political economy has anticipated the latest developments of social organization.

The treatment of the poor, the access to the land, the opportunity of earning the daily bread, the sanitary conditions on which the moral wellbeing of man depends, the correction and cure of crime, the education of the children, the commodities and enjoyments of life, the care of the sick, of the deficient, of the aged, depend upon the decisions of legislators and the efficiency of magistrates and public officers. When a man declines his responsibility for Parliament, for local government, for Poor Law administration, he incurs the punishment which our Lord denounced on those who do not these things to Him because they do them not to their fellow-men.

If the principles of land tenure make it impossible for the poor to work on the land; if the rights of property make the life of the poor in a great city like an inferno; if the administration of the Poor Law makes more poverty than it cures, and demoralizes those whom it relieves; if a prison system

[1] Arist. Pol. vi. 5.

hardens the criminal instead of reforming him; if the drink monopoly establishes a power of organized temptation which ruins hundreds of thousands; if defective education renders the young unfit for the task of life; if the bad educational machinery closes a career to the gifted and industrial child — who is to blame? Surely every one who does not use all his legitimate influence to reform the abuses and to institute a better order. Pity to men and duty to Christ alike require the member of a modern State to be political. It is no restless love of change which impels us to be always improving the machinery of State. Rather it is the obvious fact that a political organism is always developing; to neglect the task of repairing and readjusting the machine is to entail suffering and loss on millions. The policy of an unthinking Conservatism is cruelty; the policy of *laissez-faire* is equivalent to letting men run down the steep incline to destruction.

We do not pause to discuss the question who should have the franchise. Whatever may be the extent or limitations of the franchise, no intelligent person is precluded from political influence. A woman without the vote, if she gives time and thought to political questions, can do more than fifty men who vote mechanically, without knowledge. The world is swayed by personality, by the wisdom, the experience, the energy of those who think and speak, and combine and act. What is here contended is that every one, while demanding, if need be, greater political opportunities, is bound to use the opportunity which is already procured. No one must abstain. It is a manifest duty to understand political questions, so far as we can, to take our side to the best of our judgment, and to play our part to the best of our abilities. A Christian who shirks his political obligations is not only a traitor to the State, but he incurs the condemnation of his Lord, whose foreannounced judgment decisively condemns political abstention.

2. There are some political principles which in a Christian State at least should be axiomatic, and probably are. Whatever parties may exist they must be regulated by them. The difference occurs in the mode of carrying out the principles, not in the principles themselves. To obtain a grasp of these fundamental axioms of political philosophy would greatly serve us in choosing or in justifying our political party. Unless a man has settled such principles in his own mind he acts blindly in the struggles of party warfare.

Let us endeavour to lay down these admitted principles, and then we can examine more fruitfully the dogmas of political parties and the methods by which the parties propose to carry out the admitted principles.

The first axiom of politics is that the good of the whole community is to be the aim of all laws and of all government. This axiom was granted verbally in antiquity; but it was vitiated by one fatal flaw —

the Greek State rested on slave-labour. The slaves had no rights. Mechanics could not be citizens.[1] In Athens, for example, there were only twenty thousand citizens and four hundred thousand slaves. When the Greek, therefore, spoke of the good of the whole community, he meant only the good of the small minority who had political rights and were citizens. Happily in the modern world slavery has ceased; all persons are citizens. And the first principle of all legislation is that the good of all, of all ranks, sexes, and ages, should be sought.

It is highly important that this fundamental axiom should be secured and understood; for all men are easily warped by their selfish interests. Unless the first principle is fixed, a class will seek to legislate for itself and will justify its egotism by expecting other classes to legislate for themselves, if they can. In this way class legislation and class antagonism take the place of public spirit and patriotism. Most of the sufferings in every modern State are due to the neglect of this axiom, which yet theoretically all would accept.

No doubt there may be the widest difference of opinion about what is the good of the whole community, and here the divergent political parties have their justification. But there should be absolute agreement on this, that the object is not to secure the privileges of the few, but to serve the good of all, and never to base the happiness of a class on the suffering

[1] Arist. Pol. iii. 5.

or degradation of the rest. A Tory of the old school, no doubt, believed that it was for the good of all that they should abide in the station of life in which Providence had placed them. He thought that his own position as landlord was best for him and the labourer's position as labourer was best for him. With a certain religious fervour he would pray:

> "Let acts and manners, laws and systems die,
> But spare us still our old nobility."

He saw nothing but the fitness of the Divine order in the poor people drawn up on the village green, as the squire went to church, offering their litany:

> "God bless the squire and all his rich relations,
> And teach us poor folk to keep our stations."

This old dogma of a feudal aristocracy had its roots in history. It was justified by a time when the feudal lord was the protector and friend of his dependants, and every individual found his highest good in the maintenance of the feudal organization. The Tory principle seems to the modern mind inconsistent with the first political axiom; and probably it is defended now only by selfish interests which set the axiom at defiance. But it was in rude times, and in the early efforts to reach security of life and status, a genuine effort to serve the common good.

But the axiom operating more freely, and unquestioned, to-day is leading men of all parties to take a broader view. Even Toryism is merging into Tory-democracy. No politician can now confess that he is seeking only the welfare of a class. If he opposes a Licence Bill, it is not because he defends the drink interest, but because he is anxious for temperance. If he resists land legislation, it is not that he may keep intact his hundreds of thousands of acres, but that the poor man who has acquired three acres and a cow may not be disturbed in his possession.

The second axiom is that the wealth of a country consists in its manhood, and not in its property. The Greek was able to maintain this principle easily because he did not count the artisans as human. Slaves had no rights; they were only living tools, as tools were lifeless slaves. There was no difficulty, therefore, in recognizing the dignity and value of that small minority that constituted the citizenship. The democracy in Greece was the rule of the privileged few, precisely what in the modern world would be called an aristocracy.

But for us, with all the masses of the toilers recognized as men, claiming equality as men, the axiom is more difficult to grasp and to apply. Our failure to grasp and to apply it involves us in the admitted anomalies of heavy punishment inflicted for the stealing of a carrot and far lighter punishment inflicted for the beating of a wife, or of the astonishing neglect of the tramps who infest our streets and roads compared with the jealous protection of every minutest item of material wealth.

Ruskin was the modern master who drew this axiom out in its self-evident clearness. He has convinced the modern world. Economists now agree with him. Politicians speak and act as if the principle had never been questioned. The wealth of a nation is to be estimated by the number of healthy, moral, and happy human beings that compose it. The material wealth may conceivably be a hindrance to the things which make men really wealthy.

In the present condition of the United States there is a salutary lesson for the world. With boundless means of production and complete political liberty, with universal education, and the higher grades of education put within the reach of all, this great nation has as yet failed to produce happiness and wellbeing, simply because the old delusion that wealth consists in the abundance of possessions was carried over into the New World. Men live feverish lives accumulating, not to enjoy, but for the mania of accumulation. The masses of the workers are in an unstable condition, and by the fluctuations of trade are either overstrained or reduced to idleness and penury. The enormous national wealth is appropriated by the skilful men who can manipulate markets or monopolize industries. The trusts and the millionaires are entrenched in a position which the most enlightened President assails in vain.

What ought to be the best and happiest State in the world is not the object of admiration or desire.

Its politics are corrupt, the sport of interested self-seekers. Even the integrity of municipal administration is impossible to secure. In new cities, flanked with fertile prairies, there are the same slums that defile the cities of Europe. Religion and art are tainted by the commercial spirit. Prudential considerations arrest the growth of a native population, so that the State grows only by alien immigration. Every one is conscious of a kind of metallic deterioration. The coinage of humanity is fretted or debased. The countries of the Old World have certain ancient checks upon the unlimited pursuit of material wealth. The New World gave itself up, unbridled and unlimited, to that pursuit.[1]

The axiom, therefore, must be reasserted and refurbished. Manhood constitutes the wealth of a nation. The rights of property have their place, but the rights of man take precedence. Human nature, human wellbeing, human development, and education must be the first consideration of the statesman, the legislator, the voter, the politician, as well as of the preacher, the philosopher, and the publicist.

[1] I am constrained to say that a brief visit to the United States, and a happy sojourn in Hartford, Conn., enabled me to see the brighter side of American life. There is a chosen seed, a remnant, in that vast country. The spirit of the Pilgrim Fathers is not dead. And though the surging tides of immigration sweep in the alien ideas of European atheism, anarchy, and superstition, that mighty leaven of the early settlers works, and may, by the grace of God, leaven the whole lump.

There is a *third axiom* which, at least since the French Revolution, has been tacitly accepted by every one, and to it even the most antiquated Toryism does not now oppose a direct negative. It is the principle of the *carrière ouverte aux talens*. It is admitted that men are not equal, it is suspected that they never can be, it is doubted whether equality would be beneficial for the world. But no one now questions that every human being should have the opportunity of becoming all that he is capable of being. The invidious bars of birth and circumstance must be, as far as possible, broken, so that whatever faculty or power there may be in every individual may have its fair chance of developing for the good of the whole. Ancient forms, and the ossification of an old society, oppose the most formidable barriers to this natural claim of genius and ability. A wise social legislation aims, therefore, at a constant correction and readjustment.

Education, it is now admitted, must be universal, and graded in such a way that the poorest child can pass unimpeded, if he has the faculty, from the primary to the secondary school, and from the secondary school to the university or the technical college. Every one sees the cruelty of leaving gifted children condemned to the mill of monotonous labour, when they might become the leaders and inspirers of their kind. It is a familiar fact that genius usually emerges from the cottage rather than from the mansion, from the Ghetto rather than from the Pincian. A nation cannot, therefore, afford to lose its gifted sons and daughters who are born to penury and stinted opportunity. But is it not equally obvious that even ordinary children, who have no promise of distinction, must not be left to the cruelty of ignorance or vice in their parents, but must have their chance of training for life, their opportunity of making their way? Careless or needy parents take the boy from school and send him to a job which brings in a few shillings a week, instead of training him for a trade which will last a lifetime. Myriads of messengers, errand boys, newspaper sellers, and others are permanently unfitted for life by filling up the formative years of youth with labour which fits them for nothing, labour from which they are ousted so soon as they demand the wages of a man.

All parties in the State, all shades of political opinion, whatever may be the differing methods proposed for achieving the object, must agree that nothing presses more urgently, in the vast confusion of a modern community, than to secure this elementary justice for every child born within our shores.

A *fourth axiom*, the cardinal principle of democracy, is no longer now seriously questioned, viz., that the will of the people must be the ultimate authority in government and legislation. We have seen in the year of grace 1908 the amazing spectacle of a Sultan opening a constitutional Parliament. He drove through the crowded streets of Constantinople, in which for many years he had been afraid to appear, from the Yildiz Kiosk, across the Golden Horn, to the chamber close to St. Sophia, recalling the glory of the great Sultans and even the majesty of Constantine or Justinian. After thirty-two years, he had abandoned the crudity and monstrosity of absolutism, and came to rejoice that his people were at last prepared for constitutional government, which thirty years before was premature. And though the person of Abdul Hamid proved to be irreformable, that has not hindered the reform and the resuscitation of the Turkish people. This modern miracle is peculiarly salutary at a time when impatient doctrinaires, in Oxford cloisters, pour contempt on parliamentary government, and demand a bureaucracy or even an absolute monarchy.

It is not likely that the Western world will ever recede from the coign of vantage which it has reached. *Vox populi vox Dei*. The Divinity is widely diffused through humanity. No human being is without the Divine spark. No individuals, however good or great, can claim a monopoly. The wisest despot is not wise enough to perceive the highest good of millions. The most disinterested bureaucracy never succeeds in seeing beyond the machine of government and its efficiency into the human sentiments, passions, needs, and rights which constitute the life of a nation. Honesty, virtue, valour in a Government never atone for the lack of the one principle on which a Government can securely rest, the free consent of the whole people.

POLITICS

Doubtless, a whole people may appoint a dictator for a limited period, or may even trust absolutely a statesman or a Cabinet for a given purpose. But the security lies in the account which must be rendered to the people, and in the latent sense that the authority is delegated. No individual in a State is or can be supreme. Autocracy is weakness, secured by craft, maintained by force, perishing in panic and demoralization. There is only one autocrat, that is God. He expresses His will through the whole people. It is therefore the first principle of government, and the ultimate precept of religion, to obtain the most considerate, the most unbiassed, and the must unhindered expression of the people's will. This is the democracy which political prophets from the earliest ages desired to see. Its day has dawned. Towards it Europe has moved with a slow, unresting course. Its full realization is the problem of to-day and of the future.

"The word which waited so long to be spoken, behold, it is gone forth!
Lo, shooting of swift auroral gleams,
Thoughts hither and thither spreading, coherent.
Words, hark! babbling multitudinous,
Waves to and fro in the sunlight flowing, lisping —
Louder and louder lisping, into one consent waking." [1]

The *fifth axiom* which is now granted by the democratic conviction of Europe is one which finds

[1] "Towards Democracy," p. 139. Edward Carpenter.

the most formidable obstacles in the traditions and survivals of the evil ages that are gone. It is the principle of the *Jus Gentium*, though it has taken a far wider scope than was intended in Roman Law. The *Jus Gentium* was the code, imaginary rather than written, which applied to the relations of Rome with other States, the Common Law of the nations. When the Roman Empire vanished in the nations of modern Europe the principle survived. Like a germ it has pushed towards the light. No one now disputes it, though few see whereunto it will grow. Nations as units have their justification, but not as hostile units, only as units in the large body of humanity. Humanity is the unit. As God is one, man is one. Any sincere belief in God involves a belief in the solidarity of humanity.

Once the counties of England were warring kingdoms. England only emerged in their fusion under Edward the Elder. America had the advantage of starting with the fusion; her great war was to prevent division. The United States covers a continent. Each State is independent, but the United States is a nation.

Shall we call it a certain trend of evolution, or shall we regard it as the beckoning ideal, which we are called on to realize? There should be a United States of Europe; as the kingdoms of the Heptarchy became England, the States of Europe should become at last Europe.

Long ago, at the beginning of the nineteenth century, it was said, "There are no longer nations in Europe, but only parties." It seemed as if democracy bound the people together more than the idea of the nation to which the particular people belonged. Royalists were one, Ultramontanes were one, more than the English were one or the French were one. But one of the most curious movements of the nineteenth century was the creation and the strengthening of national ideals. Italy, which for centuries had been, as Metternich expressed it, "a geographical expression," became a nation. The innumerable German kingdoms and dukedoms became a nation. Even the conglomerate of Slavs and Czechs and Germans, gathered under the Crown of Francis Joseph, became a kind of nation. The national idea fostered the national consciousness, and set the nations on the path of military armaments, a rivalry of futile preparations for imaginary wars.

Europe, which once enjoyed the Pax Romana under a strong Emperor at Rome or even at Ravenna, has become an armed camp, wasting her strength and resources on soldiers that never fight and ships that are broken up and sold as old iron. The thing has become not a little ridiculous. The interlude in the world's progress has become a farce, a tragi-comedy.

The Hague Conference recalled Europe to its senses, just as the revolution in Russia and the protest in the Reichstag called to their senses the two autocrats whose vagaries maintain the unnatural militarism of Europe.

But the interlude will pass away as an evil dream. War, whether of arms or tariffs, cannot permanently be endured as the democracy triumphs. The peoples have no quarrel with one another. They are kept asunder by interested persons, a mere handful, who profit by their estrangement. Presently they will decline to fight with their brothers, and will demand for peaceful development the wealth which is at present wasted on armaments.

A distinguished journalist told me of his experience in the Greco-Turkish War. In the first battle he and the volunteers repulsed the Turks who were opposed to them. He saw the dead, and among them a grey-haired peasant with a bullet through his head. The innocent conscript had been commandeered and sent to fight the Greeks. What knew he or cared he for the war or the cause? The Englishman thought, "Perhaps it was my bullet that killed this poor old man." There on the battlefield he became a convinced opponent of militarism, a believer in peace.

Gradually, on the battlefield of the world, mankind is waking up; it sees the huge tragedy of its estrangement, the fair earth marred by the quarrels and misunderstandings of brothers. The high politics of the future will be peace.

It has happened in my time that one man illustrated all that has been said on politics. If for a moment since his death his fame and name have seemed to be eclipsed, there is no doubt that his figure will emerge and shine as a star in the receding past. For he raised the standard of politics in this country to a moral, and even a spiritual, height, which we cannot afford to surrender. William Ewart Gladstone was a man who might have been a theologian and a great ecclesiastic; he might have been a scholar and a great writer; he might have achieved success in any professional career. But he was led into politics, and he brought with him into that field all the qualities which would have made him great in any other. Coming generations will not be able to understand the spell which he exercised over his contemporaries. Never can I forget the May day in 1898, when a friend and I tried to read through our streaming tears the accounts which appeared, the speeches which were delivered in Parliament, the tributes which came from all over the world, at the time of his death. One of his colleagues has concluded a fine study of his career in this way: "There is a passage in the 'Odyssey' where the seer Theoclymenus says, in describing a vision of death, 'The sun has perished out of heaven.' To Englishmen Mr. Gladstone had been like a sun, which, sinking slowly, had grown larger as he sank and filled the sky with radiance even while he trembled on the verge of the horizon. There were men of ability and men of renown, but there was no one comparable to him in fame and power and honour. When he departed the light seemed to have died out of the sky." [1]

He showed us the glory and dignity of political life, and how its warfare may be carried on and accomplished. He was not a party man; but, filled with great ideals, he used, to attain them, the party which promised the best help; he made the party for the purpose. Brought up in a straitened political school, at home and at the university, he did not learn at Oxford, but only after, "the value of liberty as an essential condition of excellence in human things." [2] But as the great idea took possession of him he became increasingly the champion of liberty for all mankind. If Bomba was imprisoning and torturing his subjects in Naples, Gladstone made Europe to ring with indignation. If Italy was struggling for unity and independence, if Greece or any other of the dependencies of Turkey were writhing to escape the fetters, if Ireland were groaning under the economic and political disabilities which centuries of ignorance and indifference had inflicted upon her — it mattered not who were the sufferers, the call never came to him in vain. The great measures, proposed or carried, which filled the years of his three administrations are not his chief title to remembrance and gratitude. His unrivalled popular eloquence, which swayed vast multitudes as easily

[1] "Studies in Contemporary Biography," by Right Hon. J. Bryce, p. 480.
[2] "Life of W. E. Gladstone," by John Morley, i. 180.

as it dominated the House of Commons, will be a tradition, but not a lasting claim to a nation's devotion. His splendid mental and physical powers pale before the moral and spiritual greatness which enthralled contemporaries and will be the growing wonder of posterity. It was this which shed lustre on the political arena, and made corruption and low ambition ashamed to show their faces. By a personal elevation of character he saved Parliament and public life from the degeneration into which democracies are prone to fall.

At the age of thirty he wrote, "The longer I live the more I feel my own intrinsically utter powerlessness in the House of Commons." He lived to be the most commanding force in that House that there has ever been. In the midst of an admiration — and be it added, a hostility — which made him the cynosure of every eye, the best-known name in the civilized world, he was utterly unconscious that he was even distinguished. Mr. Bryce records a charming incident:

"Once in the lobby of the House of Commons, seeing his countenance saddened by the troubles of Ireland, I told him, in order to divert his thoughts, how some one had recently discovered that Dante had in his last years been appointed at Ravenna to a lectureship which raised him above the pinch of want. Mr. Gladstone's face lit up at once, and he said: 'How strange it is to think that these great souls whose words are a beacon-light to all the generations that have come after them, should have had cares and anxieties to vex them in their daily life, just like the rest of us common mortals.' The phrase reminded me that a few days before I had heard Mr. Darwin, in dwelling upon the pleasure a visit paid by Mr. Gladstone had given him, say, 'And he talked just as if he had been an ordinary person like one of ourselves.' The two great men were alike unconscious of their greatness."

The secret of this almost incredible humility is, perhaps, revealed in a passage of the Rectorial Address at Edinburgh: "The thirst for an enduring fame is near akin to the love of true excellence; but the fame of the moment is a dangerous possession and a bastard motive; and he who does his acts in order that the echo of them may come back as a soft music in his ears plays false to his noble destiny as a Christian man, places himself in continual danger of dallying with wrong, and taints even his virtuous actions at their source." [1]

In England at least no man has an excuse for abstaining from public life on the ground that it is sordid; every one has a reason for interest in it in order to maintain its great traditions. Here, for many centuries, politics has meant the application of religion — of the Christian religion — to the life of the State. There are many defaulters, men who abstain from politics on the plea of religion, others who enter politics without religion, but there have

[1] "Life of W. E. Gladstone," by John Morley, i. 634.

ever been the "sifted few" from the days of Alfred the Great until now, they who sacrifice everything for the welfare of their country and mankind, and work

"As ever in the great Taskmaster's eye."

CHAPTER V

SOCIALISM

THERE is something almost droll in the glibness with which Sir William Harcourt's *obiter dictum*, "We are all Socialists now" is quoted. The grim irony which came naturally to that witty statesman is not intelligible to the man in the street. The man in the street took the saying of the statesman as a piece of news from a higher sphere, and has been repeating the statement ever since, until he almost believes it. The irony of the dictum is exquisite. The Tories are not Socialists, nor are the Liberals; the Labour Party is not Socialist; but, what is really astonishing, the Socialists themselves are not socialist. So far from being all Socialists, none of us are. The suspicion of a socialistic tendency in the Liberal Party leads at once to a Tory reaction. If a great municipality acts on one or two of the admitted axioms of Socialism, the Progressive Party is swiftly annihilated. Every one is allowed to call himself a Socialist; the name is considered harmless; but if any one attempts in the faintest degree to be a Socialist, our English world gives him short shrift. What Sir William Harcourt referred to in his witticism was, no doubt, the Pharisaic profession of Socialism made by men of all parties. Just as Disraeli announced himself on the side of the Angels, and every one saw the humour of the situation, so every one now professes to be among the Socialists, and Sir William Harcourt saw how funny it is. Probably others are gradually seeing the joke, and will presently laugh.

It may seem an extreme statement to say that the Socialists are not socialist. But they are not, and never have been. It is true that they advocate Socialism, while it is impossible. But every one can see that, if it were possible, they would be its most pitiless opponents. The first rebellion in a Socialistic State would be moved by men like Mr. Hyndman. Who can seriously picture to himself Mr. Hyndman taking his allotted place in a socialistic community and keeping it? Indeed, the strongest argument against Socialism is that no one can even think of a plan by which men like our *ci-devant* Socialists could be made to live and work in a Socialist community.

The Fabians have very wisely adopted a policy of delay. Fabius Cunctator wore out Hannibal by refusing to fight, and so saved Rome. The Fabians hope to bring in the Socialist millennium by refusing to be Socialists. They continue to talk about Socialism; that is felt to be always interesting. But they must not be supposed to mean anything practical or immediate. If talking about Socialism, or advocating it, entitled men to be called Socialists, the Fabians might claim the name. But if the name means doing anything socialistic, or taking any decisive step to realize the ideal, the Fabians are no more Socialists than the Primrose League. Indeed, strictly speaking, the Primrose League is the only socialistic organization in the country. It must have been, when one comes to think of it, with a view to that pretty institution that Sir William Harcourt uttered his epigram. In the Primrose League, Cavaliers and Dames mingle freely with the lower orders. Feasts and entertainments are equally shared. At a Primrose League beanfeast a Duchess has no more cups of tea than her gardener. Every one enjoys a real, if limited, equality, in the defence of the Constitution and the resistance to — Socialism! But the League is itself the nearest approach to Socialism that we have attained. Where else do the rich and the poor meet together on such friendly terms? Where else does every one cease to call what he has his own, and share it unsparingly with the rest?

But the Fabians and Socialists do not share anything. They do not bring classes together. They do not promote camaraderie. Many of them, like Mr. Ruskin or Mr. William Morris, have good incomes, derived from investments or from their own industry. But they do not divide their money among those who have not, or even among themselves. Mr. Ruskin denounced the practice of living on the interest of invested money — which he called usury—

and continued to live on it all his life. Mr. Morris lectured superbly upon the evils of competition, the "each for himself and devil take the hindmost" theory of life; but in his own Art business he was a most successful competitor. He drove other furnishing establishments out of the field. His Socialism was only talk. So it has been all along. Frederick Lassalle, whose portrait is drawn by George Meredith in the "Tragic Comedians," did not live as a Socialist, except in the negative sense of ignoring the conventional morality. I do not remember that Karl Marx was more socialistic than William Morris. There are, no doubt, Socialist orators in the parks and open spaces of London who are quite willing to establish the socialistic State to-morrow. With nothing to lose they stand to gain by a readjustment of society. But if they had anything to lose they would become "Socialists of the chair"; they would advocate an economical rearrangement, which is practically impossible, and meanwhile they would enjoy the benefits of the individualist *régime* under which they live. But the orators of the parks do not any more than the Socialists of the chair share their wages or their homes with the Have Nots. I have known a Socialist agitator fall ill; not one of his Socialist "comrades" has come to see him or to help him; the help has come from some humble Christian worker, prompted by that faith which the Socialists had been furiously denouncing.

Aristotle made a shrewd if somewhat cruel criticism on Plato's "Republic," the first and by far the most brilliant dream of a socialistic State in Europe. "If it had been good," said the cool analytical thinker, "it would have been tried before!" If there had been anything in Socialism, the Socialists would have become socialist by now. They would have formed socialistic communities here, or in some new country they would have shown us how it could be done. I shall be told that Owen did establish a socialistic community in America. Yes, and there was the phalanstery attempted or proposed by Fourier in Europe. Indeed, the article on Socialism in the Encyclopædia contains an interesting, but not encouraging, account of many such attempts. But they all broke down; they were destroyed, not by external force, but simply by the facts of human nature.

Now if select communities of convinced enthusiasts cannot maintain a socialistic State, however small, into a second generation, what prospect is there that any State, great or small, can become socialistic? Or if it were socialistic for a moment, how could the equilibrium, human nature being what it is, be maintained? If the Socialists could, in any favourable part of the globe, establish a socialistic State and show how it works, the world would take heart, and would not despair of becoming Socialist. But in the reluctance to make the experiment, and in the failure of such experiments as have been made, ordinary men recognize this plain truth: Socialism is only a dream; it is attractive as an ideal, it may be useful as a guide to action which is practicable; but there are not, there never can be real Socialists, there can only be talkers of Socialism, the discontented denouncing their fellow-men in the name of brotherhood, the poor abusing the rich for the sin of possessing — damning the sin, that is, which they have no opportunity of committing. Probably the solid sense of mankind, at any rate here in England, sees through the matter pretty clearly.

Plato's ideal State was communistic rather than socialistic. It could not be taken seriously. The "Republic" is full of grave irony, a satire as keen, though not as cruel, as Swift's. It is a kind of prose poem, abounding in exquisite pieces, ending in a great vision of the future world, where the wicked, like Ardiæus, are eternally tormented, and where souls choose blindly the lives they will live in the next stage of the metempsychosis, and some, not saved by wisdom, drink more than they need of Lethe's waters!

Indeed, we are astonished at so serious a person as Aristotle taking this great feat of the imagination as a proposal in practical politics at all. One may criticise Henry George's "Progress and Poverty," but who would criticise Edward Bellamy's "Looking Backward," or William Morris's richly coloured pictures of the better order that is coming?

If we were to treat Plato seriously, there are

features in his scheme which take the breath even of a Socialist to-day. To begin with, equality and liberty are excluded from the State. On the analogy of the human soul, which is made up of reason, will, and passion, the State is an organism with its semi-Divine element, corresponding to the reason, persons who are the natural and hereditary guardians, or rulers, of the State; with its active element, corresponding to the will, people who are the soldiers of the State; and with its *canaille* of artisans, or rather slaves, corresponding to the hydra-headed passions, who are simply to be controlled and kept in order. Handicrafts are a kind of pandering to the hydra; therefore the workmen must be slaves of the best, that thus they may be ruled by "that which has in itself the Divine governing faculty." As the passions are controlled by the reason, so the people must be governed by the elect. It is an aristocracy of the most daring kind. The communism is only among the aristocrats; for the lower elements, even the soldiery, are left out of account.

The ruling class has all wealth in common, even wives and children. A wife is allotted to each, as a revocable gift, with a view to secure the best offspring. The children will be educated by the State for the task of governing. But home disappears. As Aristotle justly objects, parents would not know their own children; any murder might be parricide.

These are things imagination boggles at. And

if we are to have a socialistic State, we may be thankful that it will not be on the model of Plato's "Republic." The philosopher's dream was intrinsically a suggestion for the education of philosophers and a device for making the philosophers rule.

Plato set the world dreaming about an ideal State, but he can hardly be said to have contributed to its realization One is even tempted to wonder whether such idealizing does any good at all, whether the humblest effort to do good under existing conditions is not better than the bravest dream of improved conditions, under which at last one would endeavour to do good.

But the dreamers have their use, even those most unpractical of dreamers, the Socialists. It is incumbent on us to study, and to correct, those dreams which unconsciously shape the actions of men. Rousseau's dream produced, it is said, the French Revolution. His imaginary picture of men in a state of nature, entering into a social contract for the security of life and property, shaped the action of the revolutionists. And the fancy sketches of economic relations in which Socialists indulge shape our thought and even our practical legislation.

Perhaps it would not be extravagant to say that Socialism is a religion rather than a polity. Like Plato's Republic, or More's Utopia, it springs from an idea of God. It is the more curious to trace out the religious basis of Socialism because a large proportion of Socialists are under the illusion that they have renounced religion altogether But the great major premiss on which the validity of all their reasoning, and the power of all their proposals, depends is a religious dogma — a dogma, too, which is as hard to prove as the dogma of the Pope's infallibility, because, like that, it seems to be contradicted by the most obvious and frequent of facts.

What reason is there for thinking that men ought to have equal opportunities, equal advantages, equal enjoyments in life? Socialism is the heroic attempt to secure this equality, to pluck the fruit from the greedy hands of the fortunate, the fruit grown on the common earth, and to share it with all. But where is the sanction for demanding that equality? What evidence is there, in a world of inequalities like this, that such an equality is possible or intended? There is only one dogma which can justify the expectation or the demand. It is the dogma expressed with ineffable simplicity by Jesus: "One is your Father, even God, and all ye are brethren." If that be true, the ideal of Socialism has some justification; if not, it is "the baseless fabric of a dream."

It is as curious that Socialists cannot see how their theory depends on that dogma as it is that Christians, accepting that dogma, do not see whither it leads. The dogma may be held to be too daring; it may be considered unproven; but Socialism requires it, and Christianity, accepting it, is called to a distinct line of action. It certainly was inconceivably daring of Jesus to say, "One is your Father, and all ye are brethren," if He was speaking to all mankind, and not merely to His little group of followers. Yet no one to-day will deny that He meant humanity as such. The basis of the Christian view of life is that all men are brethren. The individual is merged in the family, the family in the clan, the clan in the nation, the nation in the world. The distinctions are not lost, but the distinct members are made one.

It is this dogma, which Socialists commonly repress, or even deny, that is, as a matter of fact, the most valuable, perhaps the only valuable, thing in Socialism. Keep this dogma steadily before your eyes, and you see an ideal of human society unfolding, an ideal of which Socialists gain brief and fragmentary glimpses. In the scientific view of man the individual is sacrificed to the race. There is a struggle for existence; the fittest survive; the unfit are eliminated. If the race advances, it matters not that the advance is made over the slain. Nature, as Science paints her, is careless of the individual life. Indeed, the scene of unlimited competition, the principle of "every man for himself and devil take the hindmost," is an exact counterpart in human life of what, according to science, is going on in Nature. Science treats man as a part of Nature, and cannot complain that man acts as Nature does. Socialism can get no logical foothold in this scientific view of man and the world, which has prevailed in this generation. It can secure a foothold only in that view of man and the world which takes God into account, sees man as the child of God and the world as under the government of God.

We cannot sacrifice the individual to the race. The worth and the rights of the individual must be maintained; the progress of the race can only be recognized in the full assertion of the individual claims. Life must be organized. States must be governed, on the principle that each one, however apparently insignificant, has a right not only to live but to live well. But this fundamental position, fundamental to Socialism and fundamental to religion, can only be maintained by that theological dogma, "One is your Father, even God, and all we are brethren."

Possibly, then, we must seek a new definition of Socialism, a definition which travels beyond the economic relations by which at first sight the subject seems to be bounded, and penetrates into those moral and even spiritual depths on which it actually rests. Human society is like an island which floats on the sea of the Infinite. All attempts to explain or to order it without reference to the ocean in which it floats necessarily come to grief. As Aristotle profoundly says: "Nature does not seem to be episodic, made up of phenomena, like a sorry tragedy." It is part, the phenomenal part — that is, the part which meets our human senses — of a great spiritual whole. Our chance of understanding what we see turns on our capacity to take in what we do not see. Human society, so far as we see it, made up of transitory and even shifting phenomena, is but a sorry tragedy. We get no key to it, no artistic completeness in it, unless we can read the prologue in heaven, and may have a prophetic view of the *dénouement*.

Our new definition of Socialism may be brief — the application of our religion to industrial organization and to State life. If a man has not a religion, he cannot be a Socialist. He can offer no plausible reason for treating society as an organism which has any definite life to develop or object to achieve. Or if he gets a brief view of humanity, plunging heavily through the seas of change towards some imagined shore, he can offer no chart of the voyage or steering for the ship. The first thing a Socialist needs is a religion. He must have some idea of a purpose in human life, of an ideal, of a Power which is set on the achievement of the ideal. Apart from this serene insight into the truth of things he may be indignant, to the verge of madness, with society as it exists, he may denounce the selfishness which has profited by the weakness and confusion of society, he may rouse the passion of the Haves by threats and of the Have-nots by promises. But hope of effectual redemption is not in him; he has no light to shed on the welter of chaos, no dynamic to apply, to bring in the Cosmos.

The Christian religion has not hitherto been

applied with conspicuous success to the social problem. But it is capable of being applied; it possesses both light and dynamic for the object to be attained. A new era for Christianity and a new era for the world opens when the question is seriously raised, What has the Christian religion to say about industrial organization and the life of a State?

It may be useful to glance for a moment at the reasons for delay in making this obvious application of religion to life. The tone of Christianity was in the first instance set by the necessity of conflict with a very powerful State organization, the Græco-Roman power. That figured itself to the sorrowful fears and hopes of the first Christians as a monster that must be overcome and destroyed. Instinctively these early believers clutched at the fragmentary promises of a life beyond this world, and passed lightly over the promises for the regeneration of earthly life, which were really the main burden of Christ's message to men. The fateful blunder of the eremitic and ascetic life crept in from Judaism and heathenism. Men fled to solitary cells in the Thebaid to escape from a corrupt and incorrigible world. That error haunts us still.

But when the Roman Empire itself became Christian, as Dante saw, the gift of Constantine was the Church's material blessing and spiritual malison. Fr m the age of Constantine to the Reformation the Christian religion left the ideas of its Founder and the Apostles, and developed an idea of a totally different kind. The Church replaced the empire and the Pope the Emperor. In the powerful imperial organization of the Western Church social reconstruction was not ignored; but it rested upon a false principle. The Church as a hierarchy used its power to make itself incredibly wealthy, while it taught the masses of the people the blessings of poverty. So inherent was the error that the religious orders, which invariably started with vows of poverty, drew to themselves more and more of the wealth of the community, until they became a peril to the State. The Catholic Church had the social organization of Europe in her hands, with practically undisputed power, for more than a millennium. But the results were enough to justify the Socialistic suspicion of Christianity. The poverty and degradation of mediæval cities, not so much relieved as fostered by the charity of the religious Orders; the helpless dependence of the people on their lords, in Church and in State; the ravages of the plague, the slaughter in the endless wars, the repression of industry by artificial restrictions, made a society which seethed with discontent and festered in misery. The Church clung to the position that she held the keys of the future life, and opened the gates of heaven or purgatory to her children at will; but she used these visionary and terrific powers to aggrandize and enrich herself. Here in England our literature begins in Piers Plowman and Chaucer with scathing revelations of the Church's greed and rapacity. The Catholic religion is hampered with the past; not only so, her principles, wherever they have free scope, always produce the same results to-day. When modern France found herself compelled to deal with the religious Orders as the main obstacle to national stability, and demanded their registration in order to assert some power of control, the same kind of facts came to light as in the dissolution of the religious houses in England nearly four centuries before. Vast accumulations of wealth, cruelties and abuses of spiritual power, and the other corruptions of the conventual system, had rendered these Orders a disease and peril to the state. Nothing, therefore, can be considered more demonstrated by experience than this, that there is no hope of social reconstruction in Christianity organized as Catholicism. The antagonism which is most plainly marked in the most Catholic country in Europe, Belgium, between Socialists and Catholics is radical and inevitable.

In this connection the achievement of Protestantism is rather in winning freedom than in the direct effect of its specific organizations on the social question. It is a melancholy task to follow the career of the Lutheran Church in Germany. Luther himself approved of the repression of the peasants, whose aspirations had been fired by the gospel of freedom which he preached and by the Bible which he had translated. Thus it became clear that the Reformation was not to be desired as another Catholicism, however reformed, but only as a liberation, once and for ever, from a discredited and outworn expression of the Christian religion. The Socialists of Germany regard the Lutheran Church just as the Socialists of Belgium regard the Catholic Church, with the same sick disappointment, the same deliberate hostility. Indeed, every Church which becomes strong enough to claim and exercise a magisterium over men falls to the same conclusion, incurs the same enmity, and becomes the same kind of obstacle in the way of social reconstruction.

We need not wonder, therefore, that Socialists have been, and are still, making their efforts apart from, and in hostility to, the Churches. And yet they are confronted by the radical impossibility of accomplishing anything without religion. If Christianity will not serve, they must wait until a serviceable religion emerges. But it may be submitted as at least an arguable position that Christianity would serve, and will serve, admirably, if only we mean by it the religion of Christ — that is to say, the religion that He taught, the religion which centres in His Person, His activity, His spiritual presence with men.

Let us go back for a moment to the religion of Christ, and see what bearing it has upon industrial organization and the life of a State.

Pure Christianity, before it was defiled by ecclesiastical ambition, or corrupted by sophistical casuistry, was, and still is, a Socialism of a very distinct, though unusual, type. Mr. W. L. Walker, in his book called "The Teaching of Christ in its Present Appeal,"[1] has succeeded in making this clear. Perhaps I may borrow a passage from this valuable source: "There were special reasons why Christ, if His teaching was not to be misapprehended amidst the conditions and expectations of His time, refrained from directly dealing with certain prominent forms of evil. But the same reasons do not exist for us. To His disciples He said, 'What I tell you in the darkness, speak ye in the light: and what ye hear in the ear proclaim upon the housetops.' The disciples could do what it was impossible for the Master Himself to effect. He looks to us to take up and carry on to its completion the work He began — the establishment of the kingdom of God on the earth. The means of social amelioration and, what is still more important, of the *prevention* of social evils were not at the command of Christ and His immediate disciples as they are at our command to-day. Opinions may differ amongst conscientious Christians who would fain be loyal to their Master in this great service as to what is just and right and best to be done for the sake of their poorer brethren. Here the *mind* as well as the heart must be exercised, so as to give the truest and most effective expression to our love of God and man. If we Christians will not make the needful investigations, and give the patient thought that these matters call for, we are

[1] James Clark & Co.

just as truly disloyal to our Master as if the love itself were absent from our hearts. We must love God with all our heart and soul and strength and *mind*. No doubt there are economic laws unalterable as are the laws of Nature. But Love can guide and modify and act through these laws just as it does with physical laws, which, left to themselves, would play havoc and cause devastation. There are no laws that will not serve a Love wisely directed; for that is God Himself in man. And while opinions may differ as to what is best to be done, we may, surely, say safely, in the light of Christ's teachings and purpose, and following the suggestions of the author of 'Ecce Homo,' whatever hinders the attainment of a true and full Humanity on the part of every man and woman ought to be removed, and whatever is essential to the very existence of human beings as our Father in heaven means them to exist ought to be supplied or made possible for all."[1]

It will be seen in these penetrating words that Christianity, understood as the religion of Christ, firmly establishes the presuppositions of Socialism, viz., the solidarity of humanity and the intrinsic right of the individual to a share in the advantages of the earth and the sea and the sky as the common habitation of men. It secures a principle by the highest sanction, which Socialists without Christianity cannot establish, or can establish only by that *force majeure* which it is the very object of

[1] *Op. cit.* pp. 140, 141.

social development to dispense with. The underlying foundation principles of Socialism, perhaps, rather than Socialism itself, are secured by the Christian religion. Socialism, as we know it, as it is commonly understood, may be an incorrect deduction from the premisses; and, indeed, too often, it is the fierce denial of the truth which alone is the major premiss of the argument, so that the red Socialist is often in the position of the man who sat on the sign-post to saw it down. But the deep, secure foundation of all social amelioration is laid by Christianity, not by the teaching of Christ alone, but by Christ being what He is. It would be well if we could succeed in stating this deep and abiding truth about man which is given to the world in Christ.

Mankind is conceived as one, an organism in which each individual is a member, and the Head of the whole is Christ. It is therefore at once established that while there are varieties of function, there are not varieties of importance. Each unit has its place in the body; the more prominent cannot depreciate the more obscure, the comely cannot slight the uncomely, the great cannot dispense with the small. In order to press the solidarity, the image of the Body is used. Each human being has his rights. It is all for each and each for all. They are members one of another. They are all their brother's keepers. If one member suffers, the whole suffers; if one is glad, all share the gladness. A system of motor and sensitive nerves connects all in one. The injury of one thrills through the whole system. The misconduct of one is the sin of the whole. No one can get out of the Body; no one can renounce his responsibility for the rest. The solidarity is not that of an inorganic mass; it is not even that of gravitation; it is that of an organism.

But in order to press the significance and value of the individual the image of the family is used. The true secret of humanity is that God is the Father, and all men are brethren. Mr. Egerton Young gives an exquisite episode in his mission to a tribe of red men, who had never heard the gospel before. He dwelt on the Fatherhood of God with great earnestness. Presently a chief, in his feathers and deerskin, rose and said, "White man, do you say that God is the Father of the white men?" "Yes." "And is He the Father of the red men?" "Yes." "Then the red men and the white are brothers?" "Yes." "Why did not our white brothers, if they knew it, come and tell us this before?"

There can be no perfectly right industrial or social relations between men unless they realize this fundamental fact of their common humanity. The Greeks had a glimmer of the truth that all Hellenes were related; but the rest of mankind were barbarians, and slaves were not included in humanity. The Jews recognized a kinship in Israel, and did not suffer an Israelite to be a slave. The Englishman has a kind of exclusive family feeling. Blacks and other foreigners are inferior. But he does not carry his admiration for his own race into any friendliness towards Englishmen as English; rather he brings his contempt for other races into his feeling for different classes among his own people. He repudiates the brotherhood of man; but he equally repudiates brotherhood with lower orders, or with Dissenters of every kind, or with persons of different political opinions.

But, in contrast with this racial or national or social exclusiveness, Christianity asserts the brotherhood of men, based on the Fatherhood of God. Of course, it is evident at a glance how thoroughly un-Christian, and even anti-Christian, much of the organized Christianity of our day is. But we are not now concerned with the petrifactions of obsolete systems which arrogate to themselves the Christian name. The fundamental principle of the Christian religion, as it stood over against Judaism and Hellenism at the beginning, and as it stands over against Churches and systems to-day, is a vast, searching, transcendental, and yet practical dogma, "One is your Father, even God, and all ye are brethren."

Now, here is the only secure principle of industrial organization. We trade as brothers; our object is to benefit one another; if we have our personal ends to serve, they are strictly subordinated to the general good. A gain of mine which wrongs others is illegitimate. The only legitimate gain benefits the whole body. The system of greedy competition, the unprincipled exploitation of labour to pile up fabulous wealth, the steady use of an economic "law" of wages to press the wage down to a starvation limit, the brutal use of accumulated wealth to curtail or destroy the rights of the workers — this whole system stands revealed in the light of the Christian religion as not only immoral but criminal. The speculator or financier may come within the grasp of the law on technical grounds as dishonest, the millionaire may be mulcted by a progressive income tax, an outraged community may take vengeance on notorious delinquents. But behind all these outward signs lies the deeper reality of right and wrong. Every action between man and man which is unsuitable between brothers stands condemned in the eyes of their common Father.

If men are fallen into poverty, they are still brothers. The Union does not erect a barrier between the brothers, or snap the family tie. The poverty is a clear claim on the community for help and relief. A relief which feeds instead of removing the poverty is no relief. The interest of the rich is to remove the poverty of their poorer brothers. To enjoy vast wealth in face of hopeless poverty is inhuman; but it is un-Christian and godless too. From this point of view it is evidently the object of all political or municipal organization to equalize opportunities for all, to train all to take their part efficiently in the body-politic, and to succour those who, through infirmity or misfortune, are disqualified. It is a recognized duty to minister to the sick. The hospital, the nurse, the doctor are at hand for all diseases. It is no less a duty to minister to the unfortunate, to those who by a turn of the industrial machine, or by the fluctuations of commerce, or by the very nature of their employment, are put at a disadvantage and unable to earn their living. A useless individual in a community is a disease: the healthy organism brings its curative forces to bear on the diseased spot. The idle rich who waste their manhood in dissipation are a disease. The idle poor who cannot get work to do, or are untrained to do it, are a disease. The two diseases appear to be mutually related. A healthy community strives to cure them both. And yet prevention is more important than cure. Legislation and administration should study to prevent the diseases in the body-politic. We make too much of military defences against foreign aggression. We waste our substance in preparing for war, and in nourishing a hostile spirit to other nations, forgetting that they too are our brothers. But we do not give anything like sufficient attention to internal defence, to securing ourselves against the diseases which sap our strength. The ideal which is dictated by our brotherhood is, as a minimum, this: That every human being born in our country should be trained for a definite work, and prepared for a suitable and honourable place in the social organism; that each should count as one, and each one should be esteemed important and essential. Education, opportunity, discipline, correction, should be given to all, as in a family, with encouragement for dutifulness and efficiency and chastisement for idleness and uselessness, chastisement tempered with mercy and with the strong desire to redeem.

This may be called the fundamental Socialism of Christianity; and in this sense we would recast our new definition of Socialism, as Christianity applied to our industrial organization and to our State life.

But whether this fundamental principle can be best worked out by what is called State Socialism is a question which remains *sub judice*. Communism is abandoned. Fourier's phalansteries and Owen's communistic settlements are clearly impracticable. A Socialist, in spite of the lingering ignorance of the subject which still survives, is not one who asks for a crude redistribution of property. In the story of an earlier date the Rothschild of the time, confronted by the Socialist demanding the redistribution of his wealth, replied: "I have worked it out, and find that my property if divided would give fourpence a head to our population. There" — giving him a fourpenny-piece — "take your share and be gone." No, the Socialist is not a communist. But he thinks he sees a way of reclaiming for the community the land which has passed into private ownership; or he thinks that the capital of the country can be claimed by the country. Or possibly he confines his attention to municipal Socialism; the municipality can possess the commodities and conveniences — lighting, locomotion, etc. — on which the comfort and life of the community depend. Or it can assert its right to the land on which the town stands, and purchase it at its prairie value. It would be a great convenience if Socialism had a mouthpiece which could speak for all. As it is, using a common name for very dissimilar proposals, Socialists appear to be much stronger than they actually are. In the vast and wandering programme of Socialism there are things which are desirable and possible; there are other things which are desirable but impossible; it is to be feared that there are some which are possible and not desirable.

Nothing could be more desirable than the State ownership of all the land so that rents would go into the common purse instead of into the pockets of individuals. Henry George's noble eloquence and passion for humanity in "Progress and Poverty" made many think that what was so plainly desirable must be possible. But is it possible? In a State where private property in land has been admitted for centuries, can the land be advantageously bought back from the owners? To expropriate them would obviously be a fatal start for social regeneration; it would establish the principle of securing justice by injustice, of wronging a large number of individuals in order to right the rest. There can therefore be no serious thought of reclaiming the land from private ownership without compensation. But if it is to be bought, would it be worth the price? The principle of State ownership of land would seem to be admirable for a new country like New Zealand. But unfortunately, in a new country the first concern is to get the land occupied and cultivated, and a young community is only too thankful to make grants of land, and to offer as an inducement the "magic of property," that its citizens may do that indispensable tilling of the soil on which the prosperity of all States rests.

The proposal, therefore, which is most characteristically socialistic, to destroy private property in land, is as a measure of practical politics chimerical. It might be effected by a revolution, but only by such a revolution as would make a wise and stable reconstruction of society impossible for generations. It would always seem as if the new State had been founded on robbery, and that would vitiate its growth. It is difficult to grasp the truth that, if the sense of property and respect for the right of ownership were destroyed, the dissolution of all social ties would rapidly follow. "What's mine is mine" has an unpleasant and selfish sound to sensitive altruistic ears. But the negative proposition, if one can imagine it taken seriously, "What is mine is *not* mine," with the correlative truth, "What is thine is *not* thine nor is anything anybody's," would mean a kind of delirium, a welter of chaos, in which human life, at least as it is organized and civilized, might be submerged. The chimera, then, if I may venture to call it so, of land nationalization is injurious to Socialism — it is too Fabian; it hinders possible advance by distracting the imagination with the impossible. It serves a useful purpose only so far as it keeps before the community a truism, which owners of property too easily forget, viz., that the whole community has a *latent* right in the land of the country, and private property is allowed only on the implicit understanding that this latent right is secured. We are all bound to live on God's earth, and we depend upon it for our meat and raiment. Private ownership therefore is limited by the obligation of the land of a country to provide food and clothing, standing-room and housing for all its inhabitants. If a few thousands *own* the land of England, they must accept the responsibility of securing the necessaries of life for the other inhabitants of this island. Ownership of land can never mean the right to forbid the people of a country to live on the land, or to live by the land. The chimera of land nationalization may force upon the attention of the country this forgotten truism.

The socialization of capital and the means of production might conceivably be possible. As Edward Bellamy pointed out, the vast growth of the Trusts, and the complete organization of certain departments of the State service, armies, posts, railways, &c., seem to point in the direction of a final logical step, by which one Trust will own and manage all the industries, manufactures, and enterprises of the State, and that Trust will be the State itself. It may be that this is the evolutionary development which underlies the present chaos of industrial life. If it be so, the Fabians are probably right in thinking that it will realize itself by an inner necessity. It is needless for any one to expedite a Cosmic incontrollable force of this kind. But meanwhile the preliminary expressions of this coming State socialism, so far from being welcome, are the things which Socialism most dislikes. The Standard Oil Trust in America shows the most hopeful line for achieving a socialistic result. Competition in that industry is eliminated. In place of the fierce war of competition is the tranquil security of the Trust. The individuals have become the docile members of this larger organism, controlled by one authority. Substitute for Mr. Rockefeller the State, and extend the principle of the Oil Trust to all trades, and you have State Socialism as a *fait accompli*. But Socialists do not value or promote the process which is to achieve the end.

Just as little do Socialists like that military organization of a whole country, whether in Germany or in Russia, which furnishes the best ground plan on which an industrial organization of the State might be achieved. Even Germans resent the interference with their liberty which such an organization involves. Would Englishmen, who decline a conscription, consent to an industrial system on the same plan? Would they buy security of daily bread and clothing by the surrender of that freedom, and that joy of enterprise, which are to them as the breath of life? One cannot resist the feeling that, if the socialization of industries is the fate which looms in the future for Western civilization, if some day all trades will be like the Post Office in England, or like the railways in Germany, the emigration from these Western lands will be rapid. All who love freedom and enterprise, all who rejoice in the keen conflict of wits and faculties, all who realize that life is expansion, effort, and failure, and hope of success, will seek to escape from the new Socialist *régime*, and find their felicity in far Cathay, or any part of the earth's surface where Socialism is not yet established.

On the other hand, a more limited application of the Socialist principle to municipalities and urban areas, or even to agricultural districts, may be at once desirable and possible. And it is in this direction that practical Socialists for the most part, renouncing chimerical dreams, are pressing.

We are timid enough even here. The mere suggestion of a socialistic Council produces a wild reaction, engineered by affrighted Property. To municipalize the water, or the electricity, or the traction of a town, raises not only the opposition of the interests which have grown up by the exploitation of the community, but also the suspicions of those individualists and lovers of liberty who feel that the value of life and the efficiency of work are formed only in the untrammelled exercise of personal ambition. But most men can see the impolicy of allowing the water supply of a city to be in private hands, to yield vast profits, such as raised the £1 share of the New River Company to the value of £30,000, and to be purchased eventually by the community at a ruinous and well-nigh impossible price.

Most people are now prepared for the direction of the planning and building of cities by the municipality itself, to secure the health, convenience, and beauty of the whole. Most people see that in a city at any rate the unearned increment of the land values should be claimed for the public, and not left to private ownership. No theory of private ownership can show my title to the enhanced value of my acres which chance to be in a town area, a value which is not due to anything I give or do, but arises entirely from the industry of others.

And even in agricultural areas, the difficulty and the decay of the agricultural industry are opening our eyes to see that co-operation and the action of local authorities are needed to make this industry successful in the peculiar conditions of our insular civilization.

It will be seen, then, that the proposals which are held to be distinctively socialistic must be considered in a dispassionate way, and with an open mind. They must not be confused with the socialistic principle itself. That principle may be right — and, indeed, must be and obviously is right — and yet these proposals may be misguided or chimerical attempts to realize it.

The principle is firmly established in the Empyrean, and must by the favour of Heaven with more or less celerity invade and occupy the earth. It is one with the reality of God and with the truth of the Incarnation. Difficult or impossible of proof on empirical grounds, incredible to pagan thinkers like Aristotle, illogical to materialistic thinkers like Haeckel, it is proved and self-evident directly God is apprehended as the Father of men, and human life is seen as the probation and opportunity given to men on this planet to become in effect, as they potentially are, the sons of God.

Sacred and wonderful is this sonship and implied brotherhood. What joy or prosperity is possible for me while my brothers suffer or are disqualified, unless it be the joy of seeking to help them, and the prosperity which consists in succeeding? Of what intrinsic value is wealth unless it be in widest commonalty spread? What comfort in my mansion, what pleasure in my pleasance, which simply shuts out my brothers? What satisfaction is there in making money unless it makes men? If my money-making does not bless others, but even curses them, how can I sleep on downy pillows, haunted by visions of the waste and ruin and degradation of my brothers and sisters? What other thought can I form of my personal good than that which comes —

> ". . . when all men's good
> Is each man's rule, and universal Peace
> Lies like a shaft of light across the land,
> And like a lane of beams athwart the sea,
> Thro' all the circle of the Golden Year!"

CHAPTER VI

PHILOSOPHY

A WITTY and paradoxical philosopher of our time has maintained that every man must have, and has, a philosophy. He may not be a disciple of the Porch, or wear the Stoic fur, he may be ignorant of the distinction between realism and idealism, and may think that the sensational philosophy has something to do with detective stories or with the Yellow Press; but, for all his ignorance of technicalities, he is a philosopher. He has a mode of looking at things, his own explanation of the mystery of life, his vision of man and of God, of the world as phenomenal, and of the noumenal world which phenomena presuppose. And this purely personal interpretation of totality is his, or in the case of a woman — for I do not understand Mr. Chesterton to deny woman this kind of suffrage — her, philosophy.

There is something decidedly attractive in this universality of handling a subject, in this all-inclusive hospitality of the Philosopher's House. Surely the prejudice against philosophy — which we must own is widespread — will immediately give way, surely the suspicion of philosophers which practical men, for example, entertain will pass into genial appreciation, if it is established that we are all philosophers, if the practical man himself, and even the man in the street, is convicted of belonging to the suspicious gang. But the paradox is too sweeping, too disconcerting. It is even dangerous: for there is some fear that if all are to be counted philosophers, many of the philosophers proper will give up their profession in dudgeon. They paced their Porch, or occupied their Chair, on the understanding that they were persons apart; they will hardly continue in their occupation if the privilege of distinction, which is commonly their sole earthly reward, is taken away from them. I have heard it said that Mr. Herbert Spencer's great Synthetic Philosophy, and the publication of that immense series of solid books, brought him in little or nothing in the way of hard cash. His one compensation for his toil was that men recognized him as an original philosopher, such as the crowd could not hope to be. Plato, we are told, lived in great comfort, and even luxury; Diogenes, entering his house and treading his carpets, exclaimed, "Thus I trample on the pride of Plato!" "With no less pride of thine own," was Plato's swift retort. For philosophers have always been mettlesome, and have seldom minced words in speaking of one another. But Plato's wealth was hereditary, and not earned by his philosophy. The philosopher's, therefore, must be considered an unremunerative profession; and there seems little hope of keeping these benefactors of the race at their task, unless we allow that they, and they alone, are philosophers, and the rest of us are looking to them to do our philosophizing for us.

While, however, it will hardly do to say that all men have a philosophy, it may be wholesome for some men, and even for the philosophers themselves, to say that all men ought to have a philosophy, and that the true philosophy must be that which all men can have.

This consideration gives an interest to that movement among thinkers which Professor William James calls pragmatism. This is a reaction to what we might call common-sense, like the philosophy which bore that name in the last century. When Hume by his scepticism had made knowledge appear to be impossible, and Kant by his transcendental method had puzzled the ordinary mind, Reid propounded a philosophy of common-sense, which, in Scotland at any rate, had a considerable influence. In the same way pragmatism has come into the philosophical world, which was bewildered by the conflict between Hegel and Herbert Spencer, by the absolutism of Bradley and the monism of Haeckel. Hegel attempted to resolve the world into a dialectical movement, which could be made plausible by a judicious selection of facts. Spencer attempted to explain the world and life in terms of evolution, couched in a cumbersome formula, and justified by the manipulation of a vast array of heterogeneous and unsifted instances. Bradley elaborated a doctrine of the absolute, which, while distinguishing between appearance and reality, and denying reality to appearance, seemed to leave the absolute without appearance or reality. Haeckel, on the other hand, attempted a monistic explanation of the universe by firmly denying all that could not be explained. This philosophy, if it may claim that name, explains God and the soul by getting rid of them, accounts for the astounding process by which life evolves out of the inorganic, and species are developed, by which the universe is a universe and not a multiverse, and the million wonders of the great framework harmonize and evolve, by simply pointing to the fact that this is what happens. Monism of this kind leaves no logical room for man, for freedom, for personality. Man, as a moment in the series of phenomena, has a place in the evolution which is studied; but man, as the mind which is studying the evolution, as the cognitive consciousness which, if produced by the evolution, as certainly transcends it, has no place and receives no explanation. Haeckel explains everything, but is himself unexplained. His explanation depends on ignoring the mind, conscious of its own activity and freedom, which is the organ of the knowledge. But what trifling this seems! Knowledge is everything, but the knower and the knowing are nothing. The intelligible world is said to be explained by blotting out the intelligence to which it is intelligible. Herbert Spencer, moving on similar lines to Haeckel's, always saved the situation by an illogical admission of the unknown which explained the known. But Haeckel would have nothing to do with an Unknown. He asserted that the known was enough and explained itself. This innocent and childlike philosophy, too palpably absurd for any one who has begun to *think*, produced a reaction. Nietzsche, Schopenhauer, Theosophy, Mahatmas, anything was eagerly snatched at to save the mind from that annihilation to which it was condemned by being identified with that which, whatever it was, was certainly not mind. Schemes of idealistic monism have sprung into existence with that rapidity and crudeness which results from hurry and desperation. Any rope was seized to save the human mind engulfed in the whirlpool of the Haeckelian monism.

It may be that pragmatism is only one of the ropes snatched at in a moment of philosophical despair. It may be temporary and transitional, like the Scotch philosophy of common-sense. But, meanwhile, it has some very serviceable qualities, and certainly enables some of us, who have been bewildered in the clash of irreconcilable systems, to find a philosophical foothold. Now, pragmatism is a new term, not yet found in the dictionaries. It is a philosophy in being; and it may be as yet perilous to define it, for any of its advocates, or inventors, may start up and say, That is not what I mean by it. But the essence of the pragmatic situation is this, *that truth is that which works.* About truth, as an absolute, we are not able to speak, for it must be always relative to our minds as knowing. If any one is bent on distinguishing between what *is* and what appears to our faculties of perception and cognition, bent on asserting that what appears to us is only phenomenal, but that the real, or the noumenal, does not and cannot appear to us, the path of scepticism is immediately open before us. Reality *is*, but we cannot perceive it. Truth *is*, but we cannot know it. What we perceive is merely a phenomenal world; what we know is not absolute, but relative. Reality and truth recede into a world of unreality and fiction. The humble attempt to obliterate ourselves, who cognize, and to admit "a thing in itself" apart from our cognition, results in our losing all reality and all actuality. The absolute is there, but it is nothing for us; we neither perceive nor know it. Our perception and knowledge are only ours, and therefore not a reality apart from us. Kant, in his immortal "Critique," faced this situation, and saw clearly that his argument was leading to scepticism; the world of knowledge was a world made up of the forms and categories of our own mind, and must be distinguished from the world of reality, the *ding an sich*. The "Critique" would have led, and, taken alone, does lead, to scepticism. But Kant retrieved the situation and saved his own philosophy, perhaps at the expense of consistency, by his work on the Practical Reason. Here he recognized in the moral nature, and in the Categorical Imperative of the moral sense, an inner and immediate reality. The cognitive being, man, is also a moral being, committed to a life of action, of choice, of conscious freedom. If his metaphysics failed to establish a world of reality outside himself, his ethics established a world of reality in which he is an operative factor. Here is the fruitful suggestion to which pragmatism recurs. It is Kantian, in the sense that it blends the Critique of Pure Reason with the Critique of the Practical Reason, and emphasizes the latter as the key to the former.

Hence Mr. F. C. S. Schiller, the liveliest exponent of pragmatism on this side of the Atlantic, opens his book called "Humanism" with an essay on "The Ethical Basis of Metaphysics." The very title is caviare to the philosophers of the older school. Metaphysics and ethics were kept rigidly apart. In a world of the pure intellect knowledge was to reach its conclusions without thought of the living, palpitating personality that was conducting the inquiry. Mr. Bradley, for example, is momentarily disturbed by a doubt as to what might result in practice from a position he is maintaining; but he brushes the doubt aside: "But if so, I may be asked, what is the result in practice. That, I reply at once, is not my business." Now the pragmatist admits that it is his business, that not only is it his business to ask how a theory in metaphysics works, but that the only way of determining its truth is by the way it works. It is for the way it works that truth itself is desirable. A truth which has no bearing, no valuable bearing at any rate, on the life and practice of man, who is making the investigation, is not yet a truth at all. It passes into the realm of truth by that very workableness which the metaphysician of the old school loftily ignored. Thus Mr. Schiller's definition of pragmatism is: "The thorough recognition that the purposive action of mental life generally must influence and pervade also our most remotely cognitive faculties."

We do not distinguish between truth and practice; truth is that which works in practice. We cannot set truth as such over against our knowledge and use of it; of such a truth in the void we have and can have no knowledge whatever; but truth is that which enters into our experience and practice in such a way as to be verified by them. For example, the reason for believing in the reality of a world external to ourselves is that it works beneficially to hold this belief. In such a world men have always believed. That the earth is solid under our feet, and the canopy of heaven overarches us, that the trees stand waving their foliage in the summer breeze or bearing their fruit in autumn, and that the fields yield the grass for the cattle and the grain for ourselves, that the solid hills of our childhood are standing there practically unchanged up to the day when we finally close our eyes and are buried in the churchyard at their feet, that the metals are constant, that the chemical elements are true to their nature of permanence or change, that the order of Nature is calculable and trustworthy, neither the freak of an ingenious mind nor liable to be seriously altered by the greatest exertion of human power — all this is true, not because any evidence can be offered for it outside our own cognition, but because, within our own cognition, to take it as true practically works. On the other hand, to take it all as false or as doubtful just as surely does not work. When the Hindoo philosopher declares that the veil of Maya is over things and the world of phenomena has no existence, when he scorns the explanations which are offered on the basis of experience, and prefers any fanciful myth to a *vera causa*, he seeks for reality in ceasing to be. The truth of an external world, in the last resort, merely means the immensely superior result in practice of granting its existence, and the disastrous result, mentally and morally, of not granting it.

We have touched the fundamental question first. But what applies to the reality of the totality of things applies equally to the details. "True ideas," says Professor James, "are those that we can assimilate, validate, corroborate, and verify. False ideas are those that we cannot."[1] Even mathematical truths, which are supposed to be the most certain of objective realities, are truths of precisely the same character as the truth of the external world. That is to say, they are verified entirely by the fact that they work. Most mathematical processes are deductions from certain axioms and postulates which are given, and the conclusions are only the demonstrable results from these presuppositions. We are familiar with the amusing arguments which can be advanced if we start from the assumption of a space with four dimensions, or from the assumption of a spherical space, in which parallel lines would ultimately meet. But the sole distinction between mathematics proper and these fanciful worlds is that the axioms and postulates of mathematics *work;* experience confirms the suppositions that are made. If, on the other hand, we endeavoured to live in a space of four dimensions or in a spherical space, the practical results would be so confusing that our fellow-men would, however reprehensibly, maintain us in asylums at the public cost. In the last resort mathematical truth, notwithstanding all its show of *à priori* certainty, is only that which works. If in concrete experience we found a triangle in which one side was longer than the other two, we might fancy that we were in a nightmare; but assured of the fact, we should surrender the venerable definition. If we found that whenever we put two

[1] "Pragmatism," by Prof. William James, p. 201.

and two together another invariably crept in, so that the result was five, we should cease to hold the antique doctrine that two and two make four; for it would not work.

Turning now from truth in the cognitive sense to truth in morals, we are surprised to find how well the pragmatic principle helps us to an understanding of things. What is morally right is that which works best. The sole interest of men in knowing moral truth is practical. A morality which does not bear upon life, however ideal it might seem, would not be true. For example, a strained and exaggerated religiosity finds in celibacy the supreme virtue. On this theory a virtuous world would be one which would in a generation cease to be. No abstract doctrine, therefore, could establish the moral value of universal virginity. The cloistral purity which is held up to the imagination in convents is immoral. Kant's precept, "So act that the law of your conduct might become law universal," shows immediately that there is something wrong. If all the world retreated to convents, it would commit euthanasia. However pleasing that might be to the pessimist, it would not be morally good. Nothing can better illustrate the absurdity of an *absolute* morality. It is not possible to say that anything is good or bad in itself. Everything is good or bad relatively to the agent, the time, the circumstances.

The old Utilitarianism of Bentham, turning on the principle that good conduct is that which produces the greatest happiness of the greatest number, was subjected to a merciless criticism. John Stuart Mill attempted to close the breaches in the armour. Clearly there was some defect, for there is no "calculus of pleasures," and therefore it is impossible to know what is the "greatest happiness" of any one. Nothing is more uncertain or fluctuating than the idea of happiness. Aristotle gave the best definition which could be given, "the activity of the soul according to virtue in a perfect life," but every one must feel the vagueness and indeterminateness of the definition. We have to settle what is virtue, and what is a perfect life, and we must bring the two together and plant the individual soul in the environment so conceived. As a guide to conduct the idea of happiness is too indefinite to be effectual, too impalpable to be grasped, too shifting to be calculated. Furthermore, the Benthamite formula makes one uncomfortable about the minority. It is conceivable that the greatest happiness of the greatest number might be purchased by the greatest misery of the rest. We are by no means sure that this is not what has happened in our community, living unconsciously according to the utilitarian dogma. A country which is the paradise of the rich and the purgatory of the poor exactly fulfils this ideal, when the rich or the comfortable are the majority, and those living on the border-line of starvation are only a third of the whole. Our present system in England may plausibly be claimed as the apotheosis of Benthamism, and yet we are not happy!

But while our British utilitarianism has been riddled by criticism and seems to be disappointing in practice, it has far too much truth and value in it to let it go. It requires amendment. If instead of happiness we read "good," and if for "the greatest number" we read "the whole," and interpret utility in the light of these changes, we approach the pragmatic interpretation of morality. Whatever is and proves to be good for the whole of humanity is morally right. And there is no other possible meaning of right and wrong.

Clearly we must distinguish between the moral sense which discerns the difference between good and evil, and makes the good obligatory — Kant's categorical imperative — on the one hand, and the determination of what is good and evil on the other. For the moral sense, the categorical imperative, an absoluteness may and must be claimed. Kant's awe in contemplating the moral law within, parallel to his awe in contemplating the starry heavens above, is the eternally right emotion for the human soul. As the galaxy strikes the childish imagination with delight and grows in wonder and beauty with every fresh exploration into the depths of space, and with every new analysis of the composition and movement of the heavenly bodies, so this mysterious and authoritative "ought" in the human breast startles our childhood with the sense of the unseen eye, and amazes our maturity with the conviction of the moral government of the universe. When the stellar systems are mapped, and analyzed, and weighed, they do not lose their majesty. Neither does the voice of conscience lose its authority by any attempt to explain it; if it is the product of our social life, the gathering sovereignty of the social consciousness, the instinctive recognition that what makes for the good of the whole must be binding on each, this suggested origin does not weaken the mysterious power of its inner voice. Explain it as we may, or leave it unexplained as we commonly do, it is a constant factor of human life, a distinguishing characteristic of man, of which only the most rudimentary forms are traceable in the other animals. Men know the meaning of "ought," nor do they need a further explanation. When they disobey they know it is disobedience, and cannot justify it. Remorse fails not, if repentance lags. The hidden scourge is wielded, though justice sleeps. No change of opinion alters the fact of conscience. In Juvenal, in Shakespeare, in Plato, in Butler, in the moralist who seeks to explain it, or in the materialist who seeks to explain it away, it asserts its mild, insistent, terrifying reality. "Had it strength as it has right, had it power as it has manifest authority, it would absolutely govern the world."

But while the judge is always the same, the nature of the decision, and the estimate of the facts which are brought before the tribunal, must change, and advance. Moral ideas grow, and the standard rises. Actions which passed once unquestioned by conscience become questionable, and are finally condemned. Actions which to-day are passed as justifiable will in a better age be condemned. Possibly there are secret and suppressed protests of conscience in many acts excused and even admired, which a fuller knowledge of ourselves and others would discover. For instance, George Grenfell found among the Bengola of the Congo the most revolting cannibalism. Not only were slaughtered enemies eaten, but human butchers kidnapped, bought, or otherwise obtained human flesh, which they fattened for the human market. A morbid passion for this food was common; a chief would kill and eat his wives, and ask the relatives of each slaughtered woman to the banquet; many would dig up corpses in an advanced stage of decomposition for food — the origin, it is thought, of the early Arab stories of ghouls![1] These customs existed unquestioned and uncondemned. But Grenfell found, on closer acquaintance with the tribe, that all were perfectly conscious of the evil. They knew the taste was depraved, as the drunkard condemns drunkenness. At the touch of the Gospel the Bengole become the most devoted and loyal of Christians. They break with their old life; it passes as a horrible dream.

It may well be therefore that in much which custom allows and the world practises a secret and silent protest goes on in the human mind. It is

[1] See Sir Harry Johnston's "Life of George Grenfell," for the revolting details.

with hesitation that we admit that what seems evil now ever seemed good to men, or that what is evil now can really seem good to us, so instinctively does the moral sense strain towards the idea of an absolute morality. But a development has been, and is, always going on. The old order changes. The old customs are condemned. Things which were endured as inevitable become intolerable. Moral ideas come into being, they grow and become distinct. The judgment of Conscience applies to new situations, passes verdicts on things which it had seemed formerly to ignore. This change or advance in the material of moral judgments is pragmatically explained. What once passed as right comes to be regarded as wrong, because in the long run it does not work, it does not promote the good of the whole. What was beneficial to the few, to the fortunate, to the strong, becomes suspect, because it is injurious to the rest, and the few are found to be more injured by the injury of the rest than they are benefited by the coveted advantages.

Slavery was to the Greek mind a law of nature. Aristotle had persuaded himself that some men were "naturally" slaves. His conscience did not prick him when he defined tools as "lifeless slaves" and slaves as "living tools." The Jewish Law allowed slavery, though it forbade the permanent enslavement of a native Israelite. Christianity did not abolish slavery; it only claimed the equality of slave and master before God. The time was not ripe. Our great seamen, like Hawkins, carried slaves to America in ships which were named after Jesus. Nay even in 1712, by the Assiento Contract in the Treaty of Utrecht, England secured the slave trade of the world. The Treaty was celebrated by *Te Deums* for which Handel wrote the music.

Our cousins in America up to the time of the Civil War practised slavery with an easy conscience. Preachers like Henry Ward Beecher or Phillips Brooks were denounced by Christian Churches for advocating abolition. What has happened, that all at once within the last fifty years slavery has become "wrong," and the conscience of humanity protests against it? It is not the work of religion, of Christianity, it is not the result of a fresh revelation. It is only that with the growth of knowledge, with the advance of economics and the fuller study of anthropology, it has become overwhelmingly clear that the system of slavery does not work. The apparent economic gain to a few is balanced by the most appalling results to the rest, and ultimately to the few themselves. That fact the genius of Harriet Beecher Stowe flashed upon the intelligence of America, as it had been proved to England a generation, earlier by Wilberforce and Clarkson and Granville Sharp. Slave labour is wasteful. A slave population is demoralizing even to the masters. A genuine democracy cannot be maintained on slave labour, because the rights of man become invalid in sight of men who have no rights, and to treat the labourer as a chattel is to make labour degrading. Conscience has at last condemned slavery, on the same principle that it originally condemned murder; it is against the good of the whole.

It is difficult to realize that in the youth of men still living the duel was the recognized and legitimate way of settling affairs of honour. When a man killed his fellow in a duel he did not think that he had violated the commandment, "Thou shalt not kill." Wounds and scars received in duels were distinctions and the guarantees of honour. A woman loved her lover the better because he had killed his man. All this is, as it were, but yesterday. Presumably in the weakness of law and in the excitability of unrestrained temper, it was held to be beneficial to society to leave the honour of each man in his own hands, and to vindicate it by mortal combat. The practice died out in England, and is dying out in civilized society, not because a gentle woman as Queen of England discountenanced it, but because, as the scenes in a hundred novels remind us, it served no real utility. What advantage was it for a man whose honour was wounded that a rapier should be thrust through his body as well? The peppery sensitiveness which the custom encouraged was injurious to social intercourse. The country and the services were deprived of valuable men, killed not by an enemy or by disease, but by the bullet of an acquaintance or even of a friend, who in a moment of irritation had dropped an insulting word. To-day probably the ordinary conscience would condemn a murder of this sort as severely as one of the common sort. Where the law is open, and civilization is established, the duel is an anachronism and an immorality.

But we may surmise that the *duellum* between nations, which is called war, is in the way of passing under the same stricture of conscience which has condemned the duel. The enormous cost of war establishments, the drain on national resources to train vast armies for improbable contingencies, the possibility of building huge navies in problematic competition with other countries, though a scientific invention may render the fleets nugatory, and give the victory to the weaker power, the waste of brain and manhood on the art of destruction, when what the world wants is a richer and fuller constructive life, begin to strike the moral sense of mankind in a new way. What benefit does a successful war secure, which compensates the general and disastrous loss of keeping prepared for war? And further, the same doubt begins to invade the conscience of humanity about killing in war as rendered the killing in a duel impermissible. More than once in the Boer War the enemies found themselves unexpectedly face to face on a kopje, and, looking into each other's eyes, they could not fire, but parted as friends.

We may be approaching the time when, from two sides, the conscience of man will be compelled to pronounce war immoral. Pragmatically viewed, it ceases to serve its purpose, or any purpose. It is an incubus on nations, which have not yet conquered Nature sufficiently to have spare strength to bear it. The prodigious drain it makes on the masses is not compensated by the rewards and distinctions which it brings to the military and naval classes. It is a monstrous ill-adaptation of means to ends. It is as if the Dean of St. Paul's dragged out the garden roller to crush a snail. For example, the King of Abyssinia imprisoned some English subjects. To liberate them and to avenge the outraged honour of England, Napier was despatched with an expedition to Magdala. The Abyssinian King killed himself, the prisoners were liberated, everything was satisfactory, and the two countries, the great British Empire and the half-civilized, half-Christianized African kingdom went on precisely as before. This was surely a success, a clear argument and justification for war. But when the bill came in, it was found that to accomplish this trifling readjustment this country had spent nine millions of money! The thing was too ridiculous.

A war of that kind tends to become an immorality, because the misery and degradation of the poor at home, not to mention the poverty of India, cannot afford such an expenditure for such a trivial result. The thing, so to speak, does not work.

On the other side, conscience awakes over the death of that Abyssinian King. What right have we, fellow-mortals for so brief a season on this travailing earth, to take each other's lives or push each other to death so lightly?

> "Our life is like a narrow raft
> Afloat upon the hungry sea,
> Heaven is but a little space,
> And each man, eager for a place,
> Doth thrust his brother in the sea,
> And so our life is salt with tears."

So runs an old MS., but humanity awakens and disapproves. Life appears more sacred; love appears more natural. National honour wanes in comparison with the solidarity of the human family, as personal honour became subordinate to the honour of the country. The nation's rights begin to seem valid only in so far as they are consistent with the world's rights. "My country, right or wrong" already begins to sound as immoral as Catherine of Siena's counsel to obey the Pope, however bad and wrong he might be.

Thus Conscience, ever the same, advances in its judgments on conduct. Morality progresses according to the intelligible principle that only that which serves the good of all is morally right, and in the progress and shifting of things that becomes immoral which no longer serves the general good.

The need of a philosophy of religion is felt when men begin to think. A book on the Philosophy of Religion like Professor Caird's, or one on the Philosophy of the Christian Religion, like Dr. Fairbairn's, is the most powerful confirmation of faith where it exists and the most urgent inducement to seek it where it does not. Religion without philosophy easily slides into mere emotionalism or lifeless dogma. Unfortunately, however, philosophical systems are apt to take the place of religion, or to crush religion into conformity with the *à priori* demands of the philosophy. Hegelianism with its insistence on the reality and the sole reality of thought, seems at first to offer a favourable defence of religion. But the more one studies its effects, the more one questions whether religion gains much from it. The dialectic movement from thesis and antithesis to a fuller synthesis is too abstract. It does not so much explain phenomena as take their place. Religious phenomena, like the rest, melt away in the void of the great and universal abstraction. Instead of living souls entering into and experiencing a religious life, we have thought, abstracted from the individual, performing its endless and apparently purposeless gymnastic feat. Insensibly we are carried away from the region of religious life into a kind of easy mental formula, which derives its certainty from its disconnection with all concrete facts.

It is doubtful whether Hegelianism is not a narcotic rather than a stimulus to religion. On the other hand, the competing system of Monism, as explained by Haeckel, rules religion out of court altogether. "Atheism affirms that there are no gods or goddesses, assuming that God means a personal, extra-mundane entity. This godless world system substantially agrees with the monism or pantheism of the modern scientist; it is only another expression for it, emphasizing its negative aspect, the non-existence of any supernatural deity. In this sense Schopenhauer justly remarks: Pantheism is only a polite form of atheism. The truth of pantheism lies in its destruction of the dualist antithesis of God and the world, in its recognition that the world exists in virtue of its own inherent forces. The maxim of the pantheist, 'God and the world are one,' is merely a polite way of giving the Lord God His congé." [1]

The dread of philosophy among the simply pious is not therefore without some reason. The sensational philosophy of Mill, the synthetic philosophy of Spencer, the neo-Hegelian philosophy which obtained a power in Oxford through the personality of Professor J. H. Green, and the monistic philosophy of Haeckel — that is to say, all the philosophical systems which have made a distinct bid for universal recognition during the last half-century — have either been directly opposed to religion or have offered a support which proves on closer investigation to be fallacious. They are pantheistic or atheistic, and the two are, as Schopenhauer says, in practice the same.

But what is the religious effect of pragmatism? Or rather, what religious philosophy emerges from the acceptance of the pragmatic principle? First of all, it offers a defence for religion as such; its

[1] "The Riddle of the Universe," p. 298.

examination of the human mind results in the recognition of the religious instincts, the tendency to religious belief and practice, as a constant element in man. The proposal to ignore or to dispense with religion is recognized as impracticable. Religion emerges in man *quâ* man. If it could be eliminated, and finally disposed of, that result would have been achieved long ago. The evils of religion have been admitted before Haeckel. The bitter cry of Lucretius has rung down the history of Europe:

"Tantum religio potuit suadere malorum."

But, recognizing religion there as a stubborn fact, the pragmatist is able to recognize also the practical good that it does. It is by its good, not by its evil, that it lives. The genius of this philosophy is to go straight to things as they are and to view them in their relation with the lives of men. In this spirit Professor James, the mouthpiece of pragmatism, says: "The sovereign cure for worry is religious faith. The turbulent billows of the fretful surface leave the deep parts of the ocean undisturbed, and to him who has a hold of vaster and more permanent realities the hourly vicissitudes of his personal destiny seem relatively insignificant things."[1] Faith is a physiological advantage. Faith in a living and loving God is an advantage for the body and the mind alike.

[1] "Religion and Medicine," by Samuel McComb and others, p. 280.

The pragmatist has a perfectly open mind to religion. "If theological ideas," says the same authority, ' prove to have a value for concrete life, they will be true, for pragmatism, in the sense of being good for so much. For how much more they are true will depend entirely on their relations to the other truths that also have to be acknowledged."[1] That is to say, religious truth, like metaphysical truth, like moral truth, is tested only by the question how it works. Apart from that, truth has no meaning which is of any value to us. Our sole interest in knowing it is that it bears upon our lives. If religion, therefore, bears favourably on our lives, it is true. If it does not, it is false. The difference between a true and a false religion is not that the one has an *à priori* demonstration, an abstract and detached authority which the other has not; it is purely practical. The one makes men better, builds up and develops nations, produces nobler life, presents more effective ideals, is the final cause of progress; the other, the false religion, degrades and hinders the life of men, leads to the stagnation and decay of nations, produces lazy, useless, parasitical lives, and presents ideals which lead to corruption, to superstition, to fear and weakness, and paralysis.

On the pragmatic principle the proofs of religion are within the reach of every one. "By their fruits ye shall know them" is the master key to the situation. Evidently there are degrees of truth in most

[1] "Pragmatism," p. 73.

religions. The religion that is wholly corrupt and debasing is not proved to exist among men. It would be impossible. Hinduism, for example, though the caste and the family system has its fatal faults, and the actual worship is defiled with licentiousness, though woman is degraded, and millions of guiltless widows are condemned to suffer for the supposed crime of the death of their husbands, whom in some cases they have never seen, is by no means without its salutary effects. It brings religion into every detail of the household life; it holds the system of Indian society together in a framework of surprising strength, it opens up vistas of thought and contemplation, in which the mystic can escape from the earth and enter the world of ideas. Mohammedanism has, or has at least had, virtues of a very practical kind. The simple Theism, the pure worship, and the constant engagement to prayer, have produced men irresistible in battle, men from whom that great solvent of courage, the fear of death, has disappeared.

The religion which has made Japan, and suggested the ideal of the Samurai, Buddhism or Shintoism or Confucianism, or the unconscious blending of the three, justifies itself in the virility, the tenacity, the artistic sensitiveness of that remarkable people. These religions hold their own in the world by virtue of their practical value. Their ideas are true, not absolutely, but because they work, or in so far as they work, for human betterment and for national progress.

The strongest argument against Christianity is not theoretical, or historical, but practical. The degradation of life in Russia, the moral, and even political, decay of the Catholic countries — the apparent hopelessness, for example, of Ireland, the most loyal and absolute daughter of the Papacy — offer an argument against Christianity which it is impossible to overcome. We may surmise that Christianity in this form of papal absolutism must surely decay, because it no longer bears the fruit of religion; countries which renounce it swiftly surpass those that retain it. On the other hand, Christianity understood as the religion of Christ, the religion which was taught in His precept and example, the religion which grew out of His death and resurrection, justified itself at the beginning, and justifies itself now by its practical results. While the political system, the ecclesiastical machine, has become of doubtful utility to mankind, the religion itself bears its constant and obvious fruits. Bad lives are made good, men become unselfish and devoted to the interests of others, towns are purged, nations are built up, their commerce extends, their political institutions grow, and grow better, liberty and order are increasingly reconciled; and all this is the result of taking the New Testament as the guide of personal and public life. The pragmatic value of the Bible and of the Christian teaching in its purity is distinctly marked in the lives of families and nations as well as in the experience of individuals. Indeed, the challenge may well be made, What produces a cleaner, wholesomer life, a life of greater beneficence, a life of higher ideals and more shining hopes, than the faith in Jesus Christ? What model has superseded Him? What power for imitating the Exemplar has equalled His?

This is clearly the safest and strongest line of evidence for the Christian religion. It is irrefragable. Christian truth is established, not by authority, which is itself in need of authentication, nor by wavering lines of critical or historical proofs, but by the fact, which may be at once verified, that it works, it produces fruit, and that the best fruit which is hitherto found in humanity.

This general position is illustrated by the astonishing appearance and development of a new movement within the bounds of Christendom itself, viz., Christian Science. The criticism that is directed against this system, which is said already to number a million members in all parts of the world, is searching, and often effective. It is much to be regretted that the text-book of the faith, "Science and Health," should seem to countenance a metaphysic which no pragmatist can allow. The writer of the book, who is not in any sense a philosopher or a systematic thinker, announces the paradox that matter is not real. The supremacy of mind, in her judgment, involves not only the subordination, but the annihilation, of matter. She cannot tolerate the foe for a moment, it must be repudiated and denied and denounced. There is but one real existence, that is God, the holy wisdom and love that must express itself in a perfect world. Evil, disease, whatever is other than good, is delusion, the creation of an ignorant and perverted mentality. When the thought is right, evil and disease are not there; God is all in all, and God is perfect. To make quite sure of the supremacy of spirit, matter along with evil, physical or spiritual, is treated, by a high *à priori* method, as unreal. But this denial of the reality of matter is, as we saw a few pages back, untenable. Reality is not a quality which we can say exists out of relation to our cognition, our perceptions and concepts; it is for us made by the process of our experience. That is real which for us works. As against the idealist, and equally as against Christian Science, we are bound to assert that the world of matter given in our experience is precisely as real as that experience which gives it to us. Nothing is gained by disintegrating the whole, which is made up of the subjective and the objective, to the discredit of either. Experience is a totality which at each point and in every detail necessarily contains the two elements. There is always the ego that experiences, and there is always the world, which relatively to it is external, that is experienced. The only unreal is the phenomenon which results from this unnatural dissolution. If the subject, by dreaming, or by disease, or by perversity and false philosophy, dissociates itself from the object, and constructs airy nothings out of itself, the product is unreal; the definition of unreality is, that in the subject which has no correspondent in the object. Reality is the consistent union of the two in the experience of a personality; reality is demonstrated by the concurrence of many personalities in the same experience.

Thus matter is as *real* as spirit. We cannot say that the one is more real than the other. Reality is only the result of their combination. The assumption of a reality which is thus given and maintained is justified. It works. The truth of experience, philosophically considered, is this demonstrated workableness. It is therefore a misfortune that Mrs. Eddy should have cumbered her religious principle with a metaphysic which is indemonstrable, unconvincing, and purely dogmatic.

But there is a truth in Christian Science which establishes itself pragmatically. Its evidence is in the way it works. As a doctrine, a dogma, an assertion of religious truth, it produces health of body, tranquillity, and cheerfulness of mind, love to men, and the anxiety to help them. The results reproduce the effect of Christianity in the earliest times. The Church, at the beginning, was a healer. It would seem that the first Christian ministers undertook the healing of disease as part of their Divine equipment. A peace which passed all understanding possessed those primitive assemblies, and a joy unspeakable gave meaning and hope to life. This verification of Christianity in its inception is not wanting to its latest and most astonishing development. The pragmatist, therefore, is profoundly interested to estimate its truth. His philosophy obliges him to recognize truth in it, and his philosophical duty is to guard against the error which easily invades a movement of the kind. Christian Science is a curious name to give to a movement which denies the reality of matter, and renders the researches of science, as commonly understood, nugatory. But the name Christian Philosophy would not be inappropriate. And, working along the lines which Professor James has laid down, the pragmatist might build and secure a very genuine philosophy which is essentially Christian — indeed, the very wisdom which the first Christians set over against the wisdom of the world and the reasonings of the schools. Entering into human life at every point, and influencing it in a thousand beneficent ways, this philosophy of God and man, of body and spirit, of life and death, might rapidly transform the human race. It would be Christianity universalized, denationalized, in order to be humanized, demonstrated in experience as the salvation of the world.

This whole wisdom was in Christ, and, indeed, was Christ. Nay, before the historic coming of Christ, this reason, or Logos, was the creative principle of the world. God is omnipresent, absolute love, holiness, power, supreme over matter and spirit alike. Fully realized and operative, as He was in Jesus, He showed Himself seeking and saving the world, removing its ignorance and folly and sin. Whoever enters into the mind of Jesus, and realizes His work in the world, becomes in his degree partaker of the Divine nature. In Him the Infinite Spirit operates and realizes Himself. Forthwith comes the same healing, cleansing, re-creation, which followed on the activities of Jesus among men. Conscious of the Divine indwelling, the weak is made strong, and is able to accomplish the things which appeared to be impossible. This Christian philosophy is verified by its practical working, and is thus, in the surest sense, true.

CHAPTER VII

SCIENCE

It is evident to every observer that the old enemies, science and religion, are coming to terms. At first they agreed to a delimitation of frontier, and entered into an engagement not to invade each other's domain. That delimitation has not lost its value, but the relations of the high contracting parties have become more friendly. The two confess a mutual need, and neither wishes to remain rigorously marked off from the other. On the one hand, religion is borrowing more and more daily the methods of science. On the other hand, science is interpreting the nature and necessity of religion.

It is slowly dawning on the intelligence of our time that the antagonism never was between science and religion, but only between science and dogma. When the Church took the place of the Empire, and constituted herself the mouthpiece of God on the earth, she took over the assumptions and claims of the Emperor. To question her authority, and not to bow down to her decisions, was *læsa majestas*, a kind of high treason. She not only claimed a universal knowledge, but reserved the right to torture and kill those who would not accept the knowledge she offered them. It was quite in the spirit of the Catholic Church when Cosmas Indicopleustes declared that it was heresy to maintain the possibility of sailing round the world; not a physical or geographical impossibility, observe, but a heresy, a sin which, according to the mediæval view, was punishable with death.

The most humiliating scene that ever occurred in Italy — humiliating, not for science, but for the Church — was when Galileo was compelled by ecclesiastical authority to declare that the earth does not move round the sun, and left the august presence murmuring, "E pur si muove." Science rightly resents this interference with the sacred pursuit of truth, this blatant and insolent infallibility of ignorance claiming to control the sunlit realm of knowledge. Just so far as mediæval ecclesiasticism survives, science is in antagonism with it, and must continue the war to the death. Science is the champion of the human spirit against the tyranny of superstition, of obscurantism, of degrading ecclesiastical ambition.

But, in enlightened countries to-day, it is well understood that ecclesiasticism and religion are not only not the same, but necessarily antagonistic. Ecclesiasticism is not more the enemy of science than of religion. Religion and science have drawn together in the recognition of a common foe.

Thus Professor Duncan, closing his review of the

New Knowledge, by which he means the new theory of matter, which results from our latest discoveries in physics and chemistry, uses language which would have smacked of superstition to Tyndall. It is the language, not of religion, but of science, and yet it is profoundly religious:

"Now that we know, or think we know, of this infinite treasure-house of inter-elemental energy, lying latent for the hand of future man to use, it is neither difficult nor fanatical to believe that beings who are now latent in our thoughts and hidden in our loins shall stand upon this earth as one stands upon a footstool and shall laugh and reach out their hands amidst the stars.

"Meanwhile we feel that we know this: In the beginning God created, and in the midst of His creation He set down man with a little spark of the Godhead in him to make him strive to know, and in the striving to grow, and to progress to some great worthy unknown end in this world. He gave him hands to do, a will to drive, and even senses to apprehend, just a working equipment; and so he has won his way so far out of the horrible conditions of pre-history." [1]

This is more like the first chapter of Genesis than Haeckel's "Riddle of the Universe." But it is the new spirit coming with new knowledge. Haeckel belongs to a past which has already fallen very far

[1] "The New Knowledge," by Robert Kennedy Duncan, p. 257. Hodder & Stoughton.

behind in the swift onrush of our knowledge. His facts are a lasting possession, his theories of the universe a childish incompetence which his admirers will strive to veil from view and to blot from remembrance.

Indeed, the opening chapter of Genesis is gaining recognition as so surprising an epitome of the Creation story, which modern geology has read in the rocks, that there seems no possibility of explaining it from any knowledge which existed at the time that it was written. It is the common Semitic version of Creation which is found in the clay tablets of Babylonia; but it is that account — making allowance for certain symbolical language, *e.g.*, the use of "day," or "evening and morning," to describe vast periods of time, which had to be reckoned before the sun marked the day of human experience — brought into an amazing conformity with the discoveries of science. How was that epitome written, centuries before Science had read the rocks, and, by laborious and patient studies, determined the process and order of creation? Science goes near to proving that the account of creation in Genesis i.-ii. 3 must have been a revelation, communicated supernaturally to an inspired prophet.[1]

Religion is not now inclined to vex science, nor science to envy religion. There is a mutual goodwill, a desire to understand each other, which can

[1] See a most remarkable little work "God's Week of Creation Work," by F. W. H. Nisbet & Co. Price 2s. 6d.

only be regarded as one of the fairest signs of progress in our times.

Perhaps the most striking feature of science in these times is its voluntary recognition of its own limitations. After a period of delirious intoxication, it is returning to the sobriety of its youth. In England Bacon is the father of science and the scientific method; he recognized the limitations from the first, and offered an admirable example of the mingled enthusiasm and modesty of the genuine explorer of Nature. In the Preface of the "Instauratio Magna," he says, using that splendour of imagery which suggests that he might have written Shakespeare's plays if he had given his mind to poetry instead of science: "Laying aside that poison of science, infused by the Serpent, with which the human mind is inflated and swells, let us not be loftily wise nor beyond sobriety, but let us cultivate truth in love. For, as Philo Judæus says, the senses, like the sun, reveal the face of the earthly sphere, but close and seal that of the heavenly. Let us reflect that Science has her limits. By the craving for power the angels fell, by the craving for knowledge men."

This exquisite modesty of the true man of science exactly conforms to the judgment of the true theologian. Thus Butler's fifteenth sermon is on the ignorance of man, and nothing better was ever, or could be, said on that subject. The bounds of our knowledge are designed and firmly set. It is not in knowledge that our happiness is found, but in obedience to the moral law. Our highest wisdom is "that we learn to *keep our heart;* to govern and regulate our passions, mind, affections: that so we may be free from the impotencies of fear, envy, malice, covetousness, ambition; that we may be clear of these considered as vices seated in the heart, considered as constituting a general wrong temper; from which general wrong frame of mind all the mistaken pursuits, and far the greatest part of the unhappiness of life, proceed. He who should find out one rule to assist us in this work would deserve infinitely better of mankind than all the improvers of other knowledge put together." [1]

This modest temper is the characteristic of the masters of those who know, and it is always refreshing for this reason to turn from the sciolists to the men of science, from the controversialists, whose interest in science is to find weapons against religion, to the genuine discoverers whose love of science will lead them to religion, if science but points, not obscurely, in that direction.

No book of science was ever treated so scurvily by the religious world as "The Origin of Species." The worst absurdities of the mediæval Church were repeated, at least by the temper and tongues of theologians, in the second half of the nineteenth century. When Wilberforce at the Oxford meeting of the British Association attempted to dispose of Darwin

[1] "Gladstone's edition of Butler (Sermons), p. 273.

with a sneer, and when Huxley attracted the attention of the world by the trouncing which he administered to the eloquent bishop, it was natural to conclude that religion and science were at daggers drawn. But what does Darwin himself say, in that very book which challenged the traditional theology of the time? He makes no presumptuous claim; he neither denies God nor disputes the validity of religion. He is the first to admit that the truth of science leaves the ultimate causes unexplained. "It is no valid objection," he says, "that the theory throws no light as yet on the far higher problem of the origin of life. Who can explain what is the essence of the attraction of gravity? No one objects to following out the results consequent on this unknown influence of attraction, though Leibnitz formerly accused Newton of introducing 'occult qualities and miracles into philosophy,' and it was subversive of natural and inferentially of revealed religion." [1]

How admirable is this scientific temper, the clear purpose to see and know what one can, in spite of the fulminations of entrenched authority, but at the same time the frank and ready recognition of the unseen and unknown, as the determining factor of our attitude to life. Precisely similar is the attitude of Lyell, as he draws near to the end of his great work on the Principles of Geology: "We aspire in vain to assign limits to the works of creation in space,

[1] "Origin of Species," *sub fine.*

whether we examine the starry heavens or that world of minute animalcules which is revealed to us by the microscope. We are prepared therefore to find that in time also the confines of the universe lie beyond the reach of mortal ken. But in whatever direction we pursue our researches, whether in time or space, we discover everywhere the clear proofs of a creative Intelligence, and of His foresight, wisdom, and power."

This is the temperate wisdom of science. There are of course blatant personalities that utter themselves in their scientific work, just as there are blatant personalities that utter themselves in their religious work. But science must not, any more than religion, be discredited by its unworthy representatives. There are religious men who are definitely antiscientific; there are scientific men who are antireligious. But truly religious men will always respect science, and truly scientific men will always respect religion. There was a delirious moment for science in the seventies of the last century, when certain scientific investigators imagined that they had got on the track of a materialistic explanation of the universe, including life and man. The fallacy was quickly exposed by thinkers. But it is that false confidence of a past generation which is finding its belated expression in the minds of the multitude to-day. The totally changed attitude of genuine science will presumably affect the multitude in the course of another generation. The masses live on

Tyndall and Huxley still, because their works are just popularized and within the reach of the half-educated. Lord Kelvin and Sir Oliver Lodge will reach the masses in another twenty years. The limitations which Science in her perfect modesty admits will be generally known and admitted. Haeckel's "Riddle of the Universe," which now excites the gaping wonder of the ignorant, will be recognized, not as the promise of a new dawn, but as the murky cloudrack of a day that has passed away. But to know the spirit of the science which is truly science to-day, let us examine the position of the Regius Professor of Natural History in the University of Aberdeen. Professor Thomson has written a book called "The Bible of Nature," which gives a more accurate view of modern science than the layman is likely to acquire by an attempt to examine all the sciences for himself. Here we find recognized the fundamental limitation of science. "The aim of science is not to explain but to redescribe in simpler terms, to find a common denominator, but its interpretations are always in terms of conceptual formulæ, such as matter, energy, ether, gravitation, chemical affinity, and so on — which are not themselves self-explanatory, which are, in fact, intellectual counters, symbols of the mysterious reality. . . . Scientific interpretations do not deal with causes in the sense in which we speak of a personal agency as a cause."[1]

[1] "The Bible of Nature," p. 85.

Science observes a world developing; it formulates the law of the development; but the cause remains beyond the observation and analysis of science. She is bound to recognize that cause as there at the same moment that she confesses her inability, by the methods at her disposal, to discover or to explain it. If she denies the cause she belies herself; she denies that which is absolutely necessary as the explanation of all that she is affirming; she ceases to be Science, just because she refuses to recognize what is beyond her. For, as Kant said: "The universe must sink into the abyss of nothingness, unless we admit that, besides this infinite chain of contingencies, there exists something that is primal and self-subsistent, something which as the cause of this phenomenal world secures its continuance and preservation."

There was a time when Philosophy and Religion pointed out this limitation of Science in an offensive way, as if they were only interested to deny her knowledge in order to advance their own pretensions. To twit Science with its agnosticism was a favourite recreation of Philosophy and Religion in an era which is, we hope, finally passing away. "A creature whose sphere of vision is a speck, whose experience is a second, sees the pencil of Raphael moving over the canvas of the Transfiguration. It sees the pencil moving over its own speck during its own second of existence in its own particular direction, and it concludes that the formula expressing that direction is the secret of the whole."[1] But now it is Science herself that proclaims her limitations. She only urges her claim to know what she does know, and ventures to say to her insolent critics of a former epoch, "My knowledge, however small, cannot be offset by your ignorance, however great."

"If we ask Science to tell us of the great clockmaker, she will be *quite silent*, for no man by searching can find out God; but if we ask how it precisely is that the mainsprings work, or why it exactly is that the weights go down, Science will answer that *she does not know*. If we ask Science to tell us why there is a world-clock or a succession of worldclocks at all, she will again be *quite silent*, for Science takes no stock in purposes; but if we ask how the first clock from which all the other clocks are descended came into being, Science will answer that she does not know."[2]

Science, then, frankly and eagerly avows that she cannot tell us the cause or the origin, the purpose or the end. If these are to be known they must be discovered by another method. She does not deny that we want to know them, she may even admit that, as men bound to live a human life, we must know them, or surmise them. She has no grudge against another method, another mode of knowing,

[1] Prof. Goldwin Smith's "Lectures on the Study of History," ii. p. 49.
[2] "The Bible of Nature," p. 45.

always provided that it does not conflict with her own or dispute the knowledge which is by her most certain ways established.

Let us make a note of this, for it is fundamental. The knowledge of cause and purpose is outside the field of Science altogether.

Within the limit thus defined Science with her ingrained modesty admits that though she knows much, there is more that she does not yet know. She is engaged in perpetual and fruitful discovery. In view of her rapid progress, she is justified in hope. She cannot explain the tides, or the weather, or the formation of the worlds, she cannot account for the eighty odd elements out of which apparently all things are formed, but she follows on to know. If the explanation eludes her she will not pretend that she knows; but if she discovers it she demands its acceptance. She is exploring a boundless country not hitherto explored. As she blazes the trees, and marks the track in the log-book or on the map, noting the natural features as she passes, she is well aware that she leaves the country on either hand untouched, but she is dogmatic about the path she has made, because on it she intends to return and from it to start out on fresh explorations.

The energy and certainty of Science within her limits are very easily mistaken for presumption beyond them. Her determination to know all that she can looks a little like a claim to know all things. But this is to misjudge. Granted that she cannot explain life itself, and cannot even give any completely satisfactory definition of the word "alive," she does not feel precluded from experiments to find whether life can be resolved into some other form of activity, chemical, physical, electrical. And in any case she knows it is her function to chronicle all the characteristics, changes, developments of organisms.

She does not know how man arose or whence he came or when he began, or where his first home was. We are in a deplorable state of ignorance on the whole subject. But she has no hesitation in tracing his connections with other animals by comparative anatomy. Anthropology collects and formulates all that can be known about man, his primitive state, his growth, his distribution over the earth, his customs, his institutions. If she cannot trace his origin or his destiny, she will spare nothing to know all she can about him between his unseen cradle and his unknown grave. She does not deceive herself, she does not boast; knowing how much she knows, she also knows how little. As Professor Ray Lankester, the typical man of science, says: "The whole order of nature, including living and lifeless matter — from man to gas — is a network of mechanism, the main features and many details of which have been made more or less obvious to the wondering intelligence of mankind by the labour and ingenuity of scientific investigators. But no sane man has ever pretended, since science became a definite body of doctrine, that we know or ever can hope to know or conceive of the possibility of knowing, whence this mechanism has come, why it is there, whither it is going, and what there may or may not be beyond and beside it which our senses are incapable of appreciating. These things are not explained by science, and never can be." [1]

Nothing can be more explicit than this. "Let us admit, as scientific men, that of real origin, even of the simplest thing, we know nothing, not even of a pebble." Sir Oliver Lodge is speaking for the whole body of scientific men.[2] Could anything be more debonair, more unpretentious. It is this temper of mind which has conciliated the goodwill of the modern world, even of the religious world, to science. After all, it is only vain pretensions to knowledge, and the arrogance which comes from claims of infallibility or omniscience, that we resent. Directly Science surrenders baseless claims, we all very gratefully admit the claims which are well based. Her frankness begets frankness. When she tells us that she does not and cannot know the origin or the purpose, we listen eagerly to all that she does know. We heartily accept her implied counsel, that if we desire to know origin and purpose we must necessarily apply elsewhere. We begin to see how we have misunderstood her intention, and have interpreted her agnosticism as a declaration that knowledge was impossible, and not merely a

[1] "The Bible of Nature," p. 234.
[2] "Ideals of Science and Faith," p. 27.

declaration that she, as Science, did not know. On calmer reflection we perceive that even Huxley, the father of Agnosticism, was by no means so negative as his truculence made him to appear: "It is very desirable to remember that evolution is not an explanation of the Cosmos, but merely a generalized statement of the method and results of that process. And further, that if there is any proof that the cosmic process was set going by an agent, then that agent will be the creator of it and of all its products, although supernatural intervention may remain strictly excluded from its further course."[1] This is very handsome! Huxley after all is not unwilling to admit God, if the theologians will not be so cocksure that they know all about Him.

But this noble confession of science evidently carries us a little farther than it at first seems to do. The science which makes the confession is physical science, or natural science — that is to say, it is the knowledge of Nature which the human mind can acquire. This knowledge of Nature is restricted within the limits which have been stated. But the human mind, the organ of investigation, is able also to investigate itself. Being itself a cause, it is ever impelled to inquire into causes; living of necessity a conscious and purposeful life, it cannot be indifferent to purposes. When therefore natural or physical science declares its inability to discover cause or purpose, the mind, by an intrinsic necessity, turns in

[1] *Op. cit.* p. 233.

upon itself, and by its discovery of cause and purpose within, it attempts to interpret the world without. And because of the certainty of itself, though *à posteriori* in experience is genetically *à priori*, it insists on regarding this field of inquiry also as scientific. In other words, there is a mental science as well as a physical. Psychology comes into existence as well as physiology, and with the same claim to be heard.

What Science, understood as physical science, confesses its inability to discover, Science understood as mental science may discover, and establish, at least pragmatically, as certain.

But without pursuing the discoveries which mental science is making and may make in the realities that lie behind and produce phenomena, we may turn back to press the value of science, and of the scientific method, understood in the narrower, the physical, sense.

Let it be granted for the moment that there are two fields of investigation, the field of natural law, the field of contingency, the field of physical facts, the field of what common-sense regards as the most real, the most certain; and the field of first cause and ultimate purpose, the field of spiritual experiences, the field which to the philosopher or to the mystic appears most sure, but to the man of science vague and uncertain.

Suppose these two spheres of thought and observation to be related to each other in the same way as the solid earth and the impalpable heavens. The sphere of science is the solid earth, the sphere of metaphysics and of religion alike is the circumambient heaven in which the earth is embosomed. Solid under our feet, real, practical, open to experiment and research, is this field of Nature. With its land and sea, its hill and plain, its rushing rivers and its central fires, its minerals, its vegetation, its animal life, its restless human inhabitants, it is a fact concrete enough. We may spend a lifetime in exploring it, and be with Newton like a child upon the sea-shore handling still only a few of the golden sand-grains. The circumambient sphere, on the other hand, is impalpable and apparently infinite. The waveless heaven itself,[1] to use the phrase of Plotinus, though it touches us, is remote, impalpable, untouched by the agitations and the cataclysms of the Nature we know. The starry sky is not stained by our smoke, nor affected by our cries, nor shaken by the earthquake which ruins cities. Its life glitters and proceeds in lofty disregard of the dim spot which we call earth.

Adopting for the moment the convenient symbolism suggested by the analogy of our terrestrial habitation, set in the midst of the celestial environment, and calling natural science earth and the other science heaven, it is worth while to realize how much better it is, in discovery and in teaching, to move from earth to heaven than from heaven to

[1] αὐτὸς οὐρανὸς ἀκύμων.

earth. The movement in the past has been from heaven to earth. The *à priori* road, derisively called the "*high priori road*," of metaphysics and of theology has been to bring abstract theories, authoritative dogmas, certainties which disdain and repudiate proof, to override the earthy knowledge, to browbeat the humble investigators into physical uniformities and causes. It is with a crimson sense of shame that we record how the Sorbonne, the Theological Faculty of Paris, treated Buffon in 1751. It declared that fourteen propositions in his Natural History were reprehensible as contrary to the creed of the Church. The first of these was the theory, more and more adopted by modern science, that the continents were produced out of the sea, and will by denudation relapse again, when new continents will be formed. Yes, we blush for our humanity to hear the great naturalist compelled by the theological tyrants to forswear himself: "I declare that I had no intention to contradict the text of Scripture, that I believe most firmly all therein related concerning the Creation. I abandon all in my book respecting the formation of the earth, and generally all which may be contrary to the narration of Moses."

No wonder that natural science learnt to dread and to hate theology. I remember with what amazement I, as a youth, heard Benjamin Jowett, in St. Mary's, Oxford, lay down as one of the indispensable conditions of true religion a ready and candid acceptance of the facts of science. In contrast with that *high priori road* of mediæval theology, it is now recognized, as the result of the teaching of such theologians as Jowett, that the better and safer course is to proceed from earth to heaven. The reasons are plain: here we are, obviously on earth, here are our verifiable facts, here the certainties which give us the sense of reality. If from the basis of this solid earth we can rear our heads into the heavens and assay the starry way, well and good, but to posit ourselves among the stars and descend on the earth with corrective formulæ and stage thunder is a method now out of date.

I read the other day an interesting book by Dr. Leighton, entitled "The Greatest Life." It promised more than it fulfilled, but the promise was excellent. He set out to show how religious teaching misses the mark because it will not start from the assured truths which are the common possession of the modern world. He presented in strong colours the feeling of the educated man for his religious teachers, the mingled contempt and irritation with which the man in the pew listens to the man in the pulpit, finally ceasing to listen and staying away. The argument was to show that religion should be presented along the lines of common knowledge, of science. All this was excellent. The proposed lines were suggestive enough to consider, and to supplement. Man, says our teacher, is made up of physical and non-physical elements, which, in both cases, are either innate or acquired. These consist of susceptibilities to what is favourable to life and immunities from that which is injurious to it. The greatest life, therefore, is produced by acquiring, if we do not already inherit, the susceptibilities, physical, mental, moral, and emotional, to the best, and immunities, physical, mental, moral, and emotional, against the evil, in our environment.

By a formula of this kind life and knowledge are unified, the religious is brought into line with the secular, the religious is explained in terms of the secular. The theorem is worked out in detail. A picture is drawn of the personality, physical and mental, acquiring the derived susceptibilities and immunities. The final sentence is: "There is a record in a book of a man who was entirely good, immune to evil and yet of human parents. His mother's name was Mary."

Now, I cannot pretend that the working out of the theorem exactly fulfils the promise of the vigorous criticism with which the book opens. But as an illustration of method it is admirable. Let us travel from the observed facts of the world and of life, treating them with reverence and fidelity; let us deny to any theory, however imposing, the right to dispute any fact, however humble. If all we can know of the earth is its gradual formation out of a fire-mist, through the solidification of rocks, the action of water, the emergence and development of life, the story which geology unfolds, let us hold fast to that knowledge and be by no means tempted to deny it because a Book or a Church, which gives us help in other directions, is on this point uninstructed. Scientific knowledge may, if you like to say so, be lower, less satisfying, less important, but it is knowledge, it is sure and indisputable. Our first duty is to accept that; the chance of our gaining a correct knowledge in the transcendental sphere depends on our honesty in receiving the knowledge which is given us in this so-called lower sphere.

Here there are things we can know. We can distinguish between food and poison, between health and disease. We can learn what makes the healthiest body at any rate, what improves the race, what constitutes physical progress for mankind. All this is sacred knowledge. If we get no farther, it is, as knowledge, divine. If religion can take no higher range, this, at any rate, is religious. To know the organism and its environment, to make and to keep the organism healthy, to modify the environment in order to secure this result, this is religion. Religion springs out of the earth. It does not wholesomely expand in the empyrean unless it is firmly rooted in the ground.

As we have seen, the extreme modesty of modern science enables us to concede this position without misgiving. While earth denied heaven, the human spirit could but spurn the earth, for its affinity is elsewhere. But when earth admits the heavens and does not affect to climb them or to explain them, we can with gratitude stand upon the earth to attempt the climb and the explanation. The reward for such fidelity to humble fact is rich and growing. Since this attitude has been adopted progress has gone on apace; a reformed religion is taking possession of the world; it is the religion which is securely rooted in science, in the knowledge and confession of things as they are.

The scientific spirit has been like the breath of life to biblical study, to dogmatic theology, to the claims of the Church. It is intrinsically more reverent than the credulity which gulps down the superstitions and the improved dogmas and the unsupported claims of tradition. That credulity is the mother of superstition, and superstition is by far the most deadly foe of religion. A big dogmatic claim, bearing down on the intelligence, and claiming instant and absolute submission, has the appearance of securing the authority of religion. But in reality it has precisely the opposite effect; it secures the power of superstition, which in its turn is the death of religion. That dogmatic claim, of an infallible Book whose fallibility may not be suggested, of a venerable Creed which must be accepted whole as the major premiss of every argument, of an infallible Church which enforces its authority by temporal power or by ghostly terror, is in the working the sure death of religion. The Bible, the dogma, the Church takes the place of the living God; the soul's submission to these authorities takes the place of that reasonable, voluntary, and lively surrender to

God Himself which is the essence of religion. It is the scientific spirit which has undermined these usurping authorities, and, though the result is not immediately seen, driven us to God Himself. These authorities may in a sense substantiate their claims in the face of the scientific spirit, and may become as real and powerful as ever. But if they do so, their influence is wholesome. For the difference between the pre-scientific claim of these authorities and the post-scientific claim is the difference between an absolute and a constitutional monarchy. A constitutional sovereign exercises his influence because he is appointed and acknowledged and supported by the nation; and for that reason he can do what for an absolute sovereign would be dangerous. In the same way a religious authority, established in the face of science, can go even farther than the absolutism of an *à priori* and indefeasible authority, which is not established by truth, but claims to override it, and even to determine what truth is.

The scientific spirit is cautious; it proceeds from fact to fact, and from the accumulation of tested facts to provisional inferences; but the inferences are always open to correction, if fresh facts emerge. This is the indispensable temper of science; it is also the indispensable temper of true religion. What is, is, and we do not want to imagine or to pretend that it is other than it is. Truth overrides all authorities. The authorities may be venerable and lofty as the perpetual hills, but truth is the overarching sky. This is the conviction established by science. It becomes ingrained in all the true workers in science. To get this conviction equally ingrained in religious men is the security against superstition, error, fanaticism.

It is worth while for a moment to mark this scientific spirit of our time at work upon the established authorities of religion, compelling them to justify themselves, and enduing them with a new influence only when they have passed its searching tests. Let us take the Bible. Invested with the adventitious power of a supposed inerrancy, regarded as the actual utterance of God from beginning to end, a Word which settled every point of truth as surely as the Word of God created the universe, the Bible was necessarily the enemy of science. If the Bible spoke of the sun going down and rising, it was heresy to say that the earth revolved and went round the sun. If the Bible said that the heavens were spread over the earth as a curtain, it was blasphemy to speak of the interstellar spaces which, with their sparkling and crowded solar systems, form the apparent arch of heaven for inhabitants of the earth. If the Bible said that the whole earth, sun, moon, and stars were made in 144 hours, it was impious to read the record of the rocks, and to recognize the slow work of countless millenniums in the organic forms and the physical transformation of the globe. The Bible, thus understood, was the enemy of science, opposed a bar to the progress of knowledge, condemned the seeker after truth as a heretic.

At the same time, the biblical authority was hardly less disastrous in the sphere of morals. Everything contained within its cover, a Word of God intact and complete, claimed a moral authority and finality. Cromwell cracked the skulls of the defenders of Drogheda on the strength of a military regulation, a word of God, in Deuteronomy. Pious men roused Protestantism to the carnage and cruelty of the Thirty Years' War by an appeal to the bloodthirsty Psalms. That most dismal of superstitions, the belief in witchcraft, was supported for centuries by the authority of Scripture. Many feeble and deranged women have been drowned or burnt because in the Mosaic Law of two thousand years ago it was said, "Suffer not a witch to live." For was not this the word of God? Hideous superstitions and cruelties have been perpetrated on the authority of the New Testament. Because an epistle says that a believer is not to eat with a heretical teacher, Calvin spurred the Church-commonwealth of Geneva to burn Servetus. Because in a parable the Lord says, "Compel them to come in," Torquemada racked and burned ten thousand heretics in Spain, and the Duke of Alva was sent to exterminate a nation, with the papal benediction. On an ambiguous text in Matthew xvi. is reared the stupendous despotism of the papacy. On a blind literalism in taking the words of the institution of the Supper rests that monument of human perversity the dogma of transubstantiation. The Bible, therefore, misunderstood and misapplied, has been used to enforce error, cruelty, and spiritual tyranny.

But the scientific spirit, like a cleansing fire, is sweeping through the Bible, with the most salutary results. It has shown that the Bible is pre-scientific, and, therefore, whatever religious authority it may possess, it can never be set up against any scientific conclusion. Science, which is God's word in the facts of Nature, and the verifiable development and laws of things, must correct the Bible, which is God's word in the evolution of religion. The same spirit has completely altered the perspective in the moral teaching of the Bible. Here evolution has made it necessary to see a progress in moral ideas. No moral precept for a nomadic people two thousand, or three thousand, years ago can possibly, as such, be binding on us. Moral precepts are relative to the environment. They are shaped by the social institutions and standards of the time. The stream of moral ideas purifies itself as it runs. Its authority is in the conscience, in the Spirit, and in the precepts which are dictated by the growth of the Spirit in the body of humanity.

Polygamy cannot be justified because Abraham practised it. Witch-burning is not right because Moses enjoined it. Slavery is not Christian because Christ said nothing against it. It is no defence of war to say that it is assumed and foretold in the Bible even to the end. The scientific spirit has entirely liberated us from the bondage of the letter, and given us moral truth by which to interpret the Bible in place of the Bible to override moral truth. If the Bible retains an unrivalled place as the handbook of morality for Christendom, it is because, tested and interpreted by the scientific spirit, it leads up to the purest and strongest moral principles that man has hitherto discovered. To interpret the moral law in terms of love, and to find all that law fulfilled in love, because God is love, is the highest hitherto attained, or, we may add, likely to be attained.

The same scientific spirit has reformed, and must still more reform, religion. It is fatal to the method of persecution as a means of promoting religion. Its methods with heretics is to convince, not to burn, them. No biblical authority can ever again justify a Torquemada or a Calvin. The scientific spirit, cool and collected, blows out the fire at the stake. Tyranny, masquerading as religion, is reduced to shame before the clear grey eyes of science, inquiring how truth can gain by forcing men to profess what they do not believe, or by making an irrational acceptance of formulæ compulsory, with or without the conviction of the heart.

Huxley went one day to dine with William George Ward, the typical English Catholic of the modern Catholic reaction. He stepped to the window and peered out of it. Ward asked him what he was doing. "I was looking," he said, "in your garden for the *stake*, Dr. Ward, which I suppose you have got ready for us after dinner." It was not a joke.

Ward's relentless logic was prepared for persecution, if it should again become possible or expedient.[1] Huxley was more religious than Ward. From his bracing air of exact inquiry and fearless acceptance of truth the soul can easily pass into true religion. But from Ward's stifling atmosphere of authority and coercion the soul can only sink enervated into modern Mariolatry and worship of the Pope.

It is not necessary to go into details to show how the scientific spirit is regenerating dogma and the creeds, and breaking the power of a blind ecclesiasticism. We may shiver as we emerge from the drenching douches of modern criticism; we may, like children in their first sea bath, fight with the hands which insist on submerging us. Why cannot the modernist be silent? Why should he unsettle our faith? Why should rationalism be always denying? Surely the Pope is well advised in excommunicating the Abbé Loisy and Father Tyrrell? Would it not be well if we, too, could silence Mr. Foote and suppress the *Freethinker?* Tossed on the uneasy waves of modern thought, swept from one uncertain foothold to another more transitory still, never able to get an inference from an established principle before the principle itself is questioned and begins to give way, we are sorely tempted to fly to *any* authority which will make itself responsible for us, to recite the creeds with sonorous har-

[1] "William George Ward," by Wilfrid Ward, pp. 159, 168, 176, 316.

mony, as if voices would make up for conviction, or to fly into the bosom of the Catholic Church, which is prepared to settle all our religious questions, if we will only leave them to her, though, unhappily, she settles our religion for us, too, by turning it into superstition.

But this relentless bath is the tonic of the soul. Only by such douches do we get a grip of truth. The creeds are not for reciting, but for believing; the Church is not for obeying, but for upbuilding by our faith and service of love. The Articles of our faith are only religious if they can establish themselves in the face of criticism. A Church is only authoritative if it leads us to the authority of the Spirit and teaches us to recognize and bow to that authority.

The Creeds, like the Bible, only preserve a living power when they are fearlessly questioned and corrected, if necessary, by the later discoveries of truth. For instance, "I believe in the Holy Catholic Church" is a cramping and deadening tenet if we mean by that Church the Church of Rome, the system which has blighted all the countries where it is dominant, and is kept comparatively pure only where the majority of the population has found a purer faith. To believe in the Holy Catholic Church only becomes an Article of religion when the Church in which belief is expressed is both holy and Catholic — that is, a Church which rests upon moral goodness, and embraces all who are truly Christian.

The tyranny of the Church, the golden age of Innocent III., to which men like Ward look back with longing and admiring eyes, has been the most difficult of all yokes which the human spirit has had to break. For that tyranny has claimed to be the authority of God, in His fullest and perfectest manifestation, Jesus Christ. A spiritual reformation raised the banner of revolt; the unspeakable degradation and demoralization of the Church called the virile nations to that standard; but it is the scientific spirit, the indubitable breath of the Spirit of God, truth, wisdom, beneficence, which is accomplishing the liberation. Thus religion owes much to science, directly, for its fearless criticism, its love of truth, and for its method and spirit; but in our day the debt is increased by the recognition, growing firmer and more decisive every year, that science has its limits. The genuine man of science to-day frankly recognizes that, as a man of science, he can say nothing about ultimate things. He can trace the succession of phenomena, but not the cause; he can tabulate what happens, but never can say why it happens. If therefore it is necessary to find out the cause, the why, there is need of another method, another discourse, as Plato would say. A generation ago, when he reached this modest confession, he was disposed to say, that because he could not know it could not be known. "What I don't know isn't knowledge" was the confident dogmatism of Agnosticism. But now he has recovered from the triumph in not knowing, and is increasingly ready to recognize, first of all, that we, as men, must continue to seek the cause and the why, that we are ourselves causes, and therefore can never rest in the ignorance of the cause, whether of the universe or of ourselves. And if in our own causality, the nearest and surest fact of our knowledge, we have an impulse to find the cause of all, it is growingly recognized that in this known causality there may be the clue to that cause that is unknown. By a method, which is not *scientific*, and yet must be allowed by science to be valid, that cause may be known. The scientific man of yesterday was so scientific as to forget that he was a man; but to-day he remembers that he is a man, though a scientific one. He allows the imperious necessity laid on the human spirit to find out its origin and its destiny, as he recognizes that the origin and destiny are not given in the study of the sequences and contingencies of the external world.

It is therefore with the blessing of science, and not, we trust, without the continued guardianship of its watchful and critical spirit, that we set out, in our days, to answer the great question. Science no longer opposes, but approves; if she cannot help, she does not hinder. Practically, she admits that there is, beside the knowledge of which she is mistress, another knowledge, where she is helpless. She bids the human spirit to search out that knowledge, as Herod bade the Magi to find the Child, and promises that when the object is found she will come and worship.

This wise and temperate attitude of modern science gives a promise of a brighter future. Our knowledge will not be divided into opposing hemispheres, but unified in a revolving and advancing globe. The dreary spirit of yesterday was well described by Sidney Lanier:

> "O age, which half believest thou half believest,
>   Half doubt'st the substance of thy own half doubt,
> And half perceiving that thou half perceivest,
>   Stand'st at thy temple door, heart in, head out."

This halfness will yield to a wholeness. There is a promise abroad:

> "Nay (so, dear heart, thou whisperest in my soul),
>   'Tis a half time, but time will make it whole."

Science looks with a longing eye towards Divine philosophy. Her heart is hungry to know what, on her own lines, she cannot know.

Catching this changed tone of Science, I seem to hear her say, through the lips of her chief ministrants and most authoritative exponents: "Though it is not my function, or within my province, search out, O soul of man, what is in thyself. Thou art, as thou hast always surmised, in a sense greater than the whole universe of phenomena which science explores,

> "'For, though the giant ages heave the hill
>   And break the shore, and evermore
>   Make and break and work their will;

> Though world on world in myriad myriads roll
> Round us, each with different powers
> And other forms of life than ours,
> What know we greater than the soul?'

See what the soul involves. It may be that the causality there is the microcosm of the cause that initiated and sustains the macrocosm. Perhaps the life there, the personality, the thought, the moral nature, the heart, point to the qualities of the cause of the whole. It may be that the indomitable demands of consciousness for continued existence and for progressive unfolding point to a life outside phenomena, a life which I, as Science, am unable to investigate. Possibly in the story of man, and in the great souls that have been or are in the world, thou canst find a solution of thy problems which is not to be found in that infra-human life which alone I can investigate. Push thy inquiries along thy own lines, while I push mine along my lines. Possibly while I unfold the harmonious universe, thou wilt find its Orderer and Ruler. In the claims of thy own moral nature thou wilt light upon the great Teacher. In the hunger for love, for life, for immortality, thou wilt find God."

Such a magnanimous behest coming from Science, freely recognizing the function and the scope of religion, is the encouragement also for the prosecution of theology, the discipline which searches for that which Science cannot give.

A bright day is dawning for humanity, a day of

wider views, of completer and more reconciling theories. In that day science and religion will supplement one another. Each will regard the other as indispensable. Then,

> ". . . mind and heart according well,
> Shall make one music as before,
> But vaster."

CHAPTER VIII

THEOLOGY

IN the Middle Ages, and while the spirit of the Middle Ages survived, it was customary, at least among theologians, to describe theology as the Queen of the Sciences. Since God is above the world, theology, as the science or knowledge of God, must be above the science or knowledge of the world. But in the restricted sense which the word "science" has now assumed, theologians themselves will be ready to admit that theology is not a science at all. Science is the formulated knowledge of the contingent; theology is the quest of the absolute, which science despairs of knowing. Science is not concerned with causes or purposes, but simply seeks to trace uniformities and successions in phenomena. Theology is concerned chiefly with the cause and the purpose, which Science deliberately excludes from her survey. It is therefore a confusion of terms to speak of theology as the queen of the sciences, if by "queen" is meant the science which is chief among the sister sciences. The description is only correct if the queen is recognized as belonging to a different order altogether, not the science which rules the other sciences, but the discipline, not itself a science, which must account for and justify all the sciences.

Theology is a discipline rather than a science; it is the orderly and rational attempt to know that which science confesses her inability to know. There is an advantage in Herbert Spencer's nomenclature: the sphere of science is the known or the knowable. But the explanation of the known is the unknown — that is, the scientifically unknown. But the unknown is so far known as that it is the cause of the known. The effects to some extent define the cause. Granting that science has no method or instruments for exploring the unknown, yet the human mind cannot cease to inquire. Phenomena themselves suggest much concerning the unknown, as, for instance, that it is not only powerful, but intelligent, that it has within it the love of, and the search for, beauty, and morality, and goodness. But the mind itself, which is engaged in the scientific quest, is sure, on self-examination, that it could not be the product of the phenomena that it is investigating. It, at any rate, knows that the unknown cause of itself is so far like itself, and unlike phenomena, as to be mental, spiritual, a cause of the same kind as itself. The unknown, therefore, of science cannot remain unsearched. Not only is the human mind impelled by its own constitution to search out the Mind of the world, but, by virtue of it own consciousness, it is possessed with an inalienable conviction that the Mind of the world can reveal itself, has revealed itself, does reveal itself. That universal characteristic of human life, religion, is the witness to this fact. Apart from science, before science begins, where science has ended, the human mind recognizes, seeks, desires to know, God. The results of this search are embodied in theologies. Clearly a theology, to be true, must not only be a thought about God, but a self-communication of God to the human mind. For of what value would be a theory of God, however complete, an idea of the Intelligence which produced the human intelligence, of the Being which accounts for all being, including ours, if that intelligent Being were completely cut off from all communication with us? A God that does not or cannot reveal Himself is, therefore, a *caput mortuum.* Theology has no vital bearing upon us unless it is a theology of revelation, what can be known of, and from, a God that reveals.

The nature of the quest, then, is evident. It is not scientific. Scientific people may excuse themselves from engaging in it. But the human mind cannot be dissuaded from it. At one time the quest was pursued, not only without the sanction of science, but in defiance of it. Now the temper of the quest is changed. The theologian, knowing that Science cannot do his work, yet asks Science to aid him. He asks Science to teach him her spirit, which sets truth supreme over desire; he asks her to lend him her method, her patience, caution, and candour; he asks her to afford him a critique, a critique of reason, that may at all points chasten him and test his conclusions. Since science declines to launch out into the sea to understand the Infinite, confining her interest to *terra firma*, the theologian, launching out fearlessly on the sea, requests Science to hold the ropes, and to bring him back if he is losing himself.

In this sense we may have, and ought to have, a scientific theology, a theology which heartily accepts science, and seeks to know that which science presupposes but cannot know — God. Theology is not a science, but is in strict harmony with science, and offers itself as the solution of problems which science cannot solve.

This discipline has also a point in common with the sciences; it is always progressing. That is the common feature of the 'logies, whether they be of earth, or stars, or God. The knowledge of God, theology, must change, just as the knowledge of earth, geology, just as the knowledge of life, biology, just as the knowledge of man, anthropology, passes from stage to stage of advance. Here it comes into line, and takes its place with the sciences.

If theology claims an absoluteness and finality, she discredits herself. She is best advised when she reviews her past and traces the progress hitherto, as a reason for expecting further progress in the future. Perhaps it is the claim to remain stagnant which has most discredited theology among the 'logies. Astrology advanced into astronomy; the visionary and fanciful uses of the stars, to forecast human fates, passed into the discovery of the vast sidereal systems in which our solar system is but a point of light, and men learnt to smile at the simplicity which could fancy the constant planets hung in the heavens and moved and combined, in order to determine the destiny of an infant born on the earth. Alchemy passed into chemistry; the attempt to transform the less precious elements into gold opened the door into that wonderland of the chemical elements which offers a treasure compared with which gold itself is worthless. The study of shells found in the rocks has advanced with giant strides, until within a century men have learnt to read the history of the earth and the evolution of life on the earth in those silent records. If the knowledge of earth and sky has thus advanced, we are likely to suspect a knowledge of God which shows no similar progress. At any rate, if any authority claims that theology is fixed by the Power that made the sciences, clearly and finally complete from the beginning, the claim must, by the scientific spirit which rules the human mind, be fearlessly questioned. At least it must be admitted that theology has changed in the past. Christian theology is an advance on Jewish; Christian theology itself is a record of advance. It is impossible in the light of experience to deny that theology may develop further, without and within, the Christian interpretation.

Thus, without identifying Theology with the sciences, we must assert the quality which she shares with them, the quality of advance, of growth, of progress. Let us admit that we live in a breathing, progressive world, in which knowledge is ever growing from more to more, and the thoughts of men are widened with the process of the suns. Let us catch the spirit of the system to which we belong, and we shall see that God must be revealing Himself progressively. As the human mind expands, as knowledge increases, as wider and deeper views are taken, God, if He be God, must become larger, richer, more wonderful, to the human mind. To say that we hold the theology of a former day, and to be unconscious of the progress, is to strike ourselves out of the lists of life, and to write down our theology as dead, as a *hortus siccus* at the best.

I have heard men in later life boast that their theology was fixed at the outset, and has never changed; but that did not seem to me a proof of the theology or a credit to them. But how much more beside the mark is it to hold the theology of the eighteenth century, or that of the seventeenth! If we have not gone beyond Butler, we shall get small good from reading him. If we are to be bound by the theology of John Owen or Richard Baxter, we had better keep clear of them altogether.

Or what reason can there be in clinging to the theology of the Reformers, when the whole value of it was that it was presumably an advance on that of the Mediæval Church? How can we remain fixed to Augustine, when we honour him only for his resistance to the narrower or less vital theology of his time? They who stick in the theology of the Fathers are not only involved in the meshes of contradiction, but they shift their point of view from the truth of Christ and His Apostles to an authority which had not yet learned to understand *Him* and had already got out of touch with *them.*

The theology of the Early Church is of value historically; it does not bind; it only suggests. The theology of the New Testament is more like a garden of burgeoning and shooting plants, which seem ever to live and to bear, than a neatly constructed system of cut and polished timber.

This point of contact between theology and science is not so much in danger of being lost as once it was. But we should accustom ourselves to it, and exercise our minds in the idea that theology, like all human knowledge, grows.

For is not a stagnant theology a denial of the living God, and of that law, which must be His, the law of development, the key and interpretation of the world and of life? The most interesting change in the modern view of the Bible has been the discovery of this progressive movement in it, of which apparently our Reformers were unaware. There is not only a progressive manifestation of God in Scripture, but there is an enlarging and deepening understanding of Him. This fact is hidden by the non-chronological arrangement of the literature; but when the dates are approximately fixed — when, for example, it is understood that the opening chapter of Genesis belongs to the latest and not the earliest theologies of the Old Testament, and that the primitive conceptions of God are to be sought in the Book of Judges and the Book of Samuel — we are able to detect the orderly and impressive development. In the eighth century B.C., when Micah wrote, the idea still prevailed that Yahwé was Israel's God, and every nation had its own god (Micah iv. 5); but when the Old Testament closes, in the latest books, like Daniel or Jonah, Yahwé is the God of all the earth, God is one and His name one.

The New Testament is a new theology; it is an orderly development out of the Old; to it all the lines of Old Testament history and doctrine have led up, but it is like a new revelation. God, who has spoken by His prophets, now speaks by a Son. What formerly had been a Word about God, uttered by inspired men, is now the Word of God, manifested in the flesh. The theology of the New Testament, therefore, is a climax. To it everything led up, and nothing further could be achieved until it was mastered and understood. But this theology, even within the narrow spatial limits of the New Testament, is seen progressing. The theology of the Fourth Gospel is an advance on that of the Apocalypse. Nay, even in the epistles of St. Paul the curve of this progress can be distinctly traced.

We cannot, therefore, imagine that the new theology of Christianity was meant to be stagnant or stereotyped. A line was registered from which theology could not legitimately recede; but there was nothing to prevent, there was everything to promise, an advance beyond that line. Polytheism was for ever impossible; God was one; Judaism was transcended; God was the God of all men. Deism was out of court; God is a living, present, immanent Spirit in the world that He has made. Theosophy, with its endless vagaries and vague relapses into mysticism, was guarded against its besetting danger by the historic Person of Christ. God's goodwill to the world and determination to save it were put beyond question as the starting-point of all further developments.

But there is no authority for maintaining that in the New Testament theology came to a stop, that there all that could ever be known of God is finally put down. The stagnation which has arrested Christianity in the old Churches, like the Syrian, the Coptic, the Armenian, the Nestorian, not to mention others, is due to this radical heresy of believing in an ancient, final, and unprogressive revelation. The Bible becomes a fetich, and essentially irreligious, if it blinds us to truth outside itself, or if it is set up to hinder the incoming of light from other quarters. The Bible never intended, and never could have intended, to establish such obscurantism. It is from first to last an appeal to truth and an incentive to discovery. The error has rested on an oddly misapplied text. In Revelation

xxii. 18, 19, which happens in our Bible to come at the end, through chronologically it should come nearer the beginning, of the New Testament, there is a threat against any one who should add unto, or take from, the words of that mysterious book. The ignorance of past generations applied this threat to the whole Bible, which was not, and could not, have been in the writer's mind; for this Apocalypse only attained a place in the Bible after running the gantlet of criticism and objections for two or three centuries. To quote this text, then, as a proof that the Bible is final, and as a warning against adding to or taking from the canonical Scriptures, is an example of sheer ignorance, such as becomes more and more impossible every day.

The Bible, if we may put it in this way, is not in the least anxious about its own integrity. Nor has it any need to be. Like the globe itself, which is spun out of the fringe of a nebula, and coheres by its intrinsic quality, not altered essentially by the exhalations or fragments which it casts into space, nor by the meteorites or accretions which it gathers out of the path of its orbit, the Bible holds together its parts by an inward principle, and can bear composedly the freest criticism. No power on earth can tear out of it a document that is in it or put into it a document that is outside. Its integrity and solidarity are vouched by time, the slow work of the compressing centuries.

But never does the Bible claim that its theology

is final, or forbid its readers to receive new light or truth which may break out from it or break in to it. The better we have understood the Bible, and the more we have caught its spirit, the more we shall realize that widening knowledge must widen the theology which we have derived from its pages. It gives us a theology which has within it the potency of growth; it gives us this theology, not to press in a herbarium, but to plant in the world, that it may grow.

In times of swift expansion, when new fields of investigation open up to the human mind, and legions of new facts crowd in to enlarge the point of view, theology must widen too. Theology must always allow for all the facts that are discovered. The theology of every age must dwell, not only harmoniously, but cordially with all the knowledge of the time. Thus as Christianity was the new theology of the first century, it requires us to find the new theology of the twentieth. We shall not part with Christianity in this enterprise, for it is a permanent and verified truth with which the world must always reckon; we shall not be tempted to part with it, because of its own eager encouragement to press on to higher knowledge, and even to greater works than were possible at the beginning.

The search for a new theology is not only permissible, it is imperative. Unless theology is new it is not true; the theology of yesterday is not true for to-day. But experience shows, the Bible itself shows, that the new theology always grows out of the old, is the natural development of the old, conserves and carries on all the vital power of the old. There is no breach. There is no razing to the ground, to build a new structure on the ruins. The old house is enlarged and modernized, but it is the old house still. A new theology which breaks with the past never succeeds in establishing itself. God is too orderly, His method of self-revelation is too continuous, His leading of the mind by steady progression is too settled to admit of revolutions. Evolution is His way. When therefore any one proposes to offer us a brand-new theology, in glittering and derisive antagonism to the old, we miss the Divine note in the offer; we know the thing will not prosper.

We remember that ingenious person who approached Talleyrand with the complaint that he had a brand-new religion, much better than the old, but he could not induce people to accept it. What should he do? "Be crucified, and rise again the third day," was the sagacious answer. We may surmise that no new theology will successfully establish itself which breaks with Him who was crucified and rose again the third day. The new theology must include and develop the best and greatest elements in the old.

In the search for a new theology we have many advantages. We are firmly persuaded of the inductive method of inquiry as the best and the only valid way. A theologian of the past generation would start out with the cheerful assurance that theology was a subject confined within definite limits. If he was a Catholic he had only to interpret the creeds, the encyclicals, the infallible utterances of the Church, to exhibit what the Church teaches, and there was the theology complete and authoritative. If, on the other hand, he was a Protestant, since "the Bible, and the Bible alone, is the religion of Protestants," his only task was to arrange the Scripture texts in an orderly system, and there was *his* theology, definite and decisive, more compact and more authoritative than the theology of the Catholic Church itself.

It has been complained that the theologies produced in this way are dull. They must necessarily be so. They are mechanical, formal, completely out of touch with life, with fact, with knowledge. Thomas Aquinas or John Calvin can be read with pleasure, because they were men of genius and masters of literary style. But their theologies, the one a deductive system from the Papal Church, the other a deductive system from an infallible Bible, cannot possibly grip the modern mind. Their logical cogency, as deductions from the premisses, is admirable and fascinating, but the premisses, unless granted, cannot be established. And all our knowledge, our conscience, our moral development, our intelligence dispute, and will always dispute, the validity of those premisses.

The theologian of to-day will not think of walking this "high priori" road. He will not dream of admitting papal infallibility as the bar to the discovery of God; nor will he start with the Bible as the *hortus inclusus*, from which his discoveries are to be derived. The modernist spirit has discredited those fatal fountain-heads of dulness, unproved and unquestioned authorities, endowed beforehand with infallibility, so that that quality may flow into the remotest deductions drawn from them.

The interest is returning to theology, the charm of the pursuit begins to captivate ardent minds again, because we no longer start from the Creeds, from the Bible, from the Church, but from premises which are verified or verifiable. The Creeds, the Bible, and the Church must find their place and their justification in the advancing inquiry: we may arrive at them, and may find them justified, but they do not impose their authority on our theology. On the contrary, the theology revives the authority in them which had decayed and was passing away.

Now, what are the assured premises from which the theologian starts to-day? What is it that affords hope of a new theology which can grip and hold the modern mind? We start now, as St. Paul suggests in Rom. i., from the known. "The invisible things of Him since the creation of the world are clearly seen, being perceived through the things that are made, even His everlasting power and divinity." Our first conception of God is that of the Maker of this mystic frame. That wild spirit of revolt the late Professor Clifford was, though he was not recognized at the time, the herald of a new theology. He believed that Cosmic emotion would take the place of religion; the thrill and awe of the universe, as its wonders and powers are unveiled to the inquirer, will be the worship of God.

Here is the first guarantee of a theology which will be real and vital, and therefore interesting. There is a second guarantee in the modern interest in psychology. The human mind is explored: its aspirations, and faiths, and experiences furnish a rich and verifiable material. In the human mind is the idea of God, the search for Him, the discovery of Him. Here is a fruitful field of inquiry. What is the Being that is discovered there in the soul's depths? What is the experience which the soul has of the Being with which it is in contact?

Now, the modern theologian moves along these two assured lines of inquiry. There are two worlds, but they are correlated and indivisible. There is the world of phenomena, the world which science explores and reveals; and there is the world of the investigating and discovering mind. We are bent on finding the Being who is the Author of these two worlds; we cannot doubt that the Being is One; for to suppose that the two worlds are out of relation, and that they spring from different causes, is to make all inquiry futile and all discovery meaningless.

Our theology will be the best and most demonstrable account we can obtain of that Being which is at once the cause of the universe as we know it and of us who know it, the cause of the intelligible and of the intelligence. We start with the known, with the world we know, and with ourselves who know, not divided, for, to us, they have no existence apart. Here is an intelligible, a rational universe, and here am I exploring it, living in it, and yet over against it, related to it as subject to object. This whole, given in experience, which by abstraction may be conceived of as apart from me, self-existence, but in introspection appears only as the sum total of my perceptions and conceptions, and therefore in a sense existent only in my knowledge of it — this whole, of subject and object combined, exists. What is the cause of it, what the purpose of it? Granted that the name we give to the cause and the purpose is God, what is God? what is known of Him? what relation have we with Him?

We start straight away from the facts which are before us, the most indisputable facts within our reach, facts which are certain, or certainty can be predicated of nothing. We start with ourselves and the universe, and we endeavour to answer the question, If God is the Purpose and Cause of all, what or who is God?

The best thought of our time recognizes that the only explanation of a universe is intelligence. There would be no order or cohesion, no uniformity on which scientific conclusions could be built, no intelligible system, unless the whole were the outcome of intelligence. The informing mind of things is not our mind, nor the sum of human minds. It preceded them and produced them. The discovery of a law of evolution running through things does not dispense with, but only serves to exhibit, the mind. Those minute adaptations of means to ends in Nature, interesting and important as they are, were far too narrow a basis for the teleological argument. It is not that in Nature innumerable instances may be discovered in which a purpose is betrayed, but it is that the whole of Nature, in sum and in detail, betrays a purpose. Millions of years ago the coal measures were stored, the continents formed, the seas shut within their limits, the atmosphere thrown round the globe. An abode for life, for human life, was prepared. In every part of this abode, which is open to our examination, there is an Intelligence at work, which makes the life that is produced possible, which sustains with food the living creature, and maintains, not only the comfort, but the beauty of the dwelling. This intelligence is in the mosses which clothe the hoary rocks with filigree of porphyry, and in the obscure worms that by their ploughing give to the soil its fruitfulness. We find no point, whether in the galaxy or in the electrons which form the atoms, where the Intelligence is not at work. In the standing miracle of our own bodies, with their complicated arrangements and adjustments, we carry about with us an exhibition, directly we come to reflect, of an Intelligence, far other than our own, which gives us life and being. Behind all particular wonders which open as we investigate and reflect there is the supreme wonder of the Being which produces and orders all, the Mind, which is to our mind as the universe is to our body. The *Anima Mundi* is not outside, but within the world. It is in the world as the life is in our body. The Being we are ever in search of is immanent.

"The direction is *from within*, the Cosmos was already in the nebula, there never was any chaos at all, there is nothing in the end which was not also in the beginning. And if you like to add, 'In the beginning was the Logos,' science has no word to say against it." [1]

God, then, to the modern mind is much nearer than He used to seem. He is in the heavens, but not exclusively there. He is in the earth just as much as He is in the heavens. He is in us as much as He is in the intelligences which piety placed about His distant throne. In Him we live and move, and have our being. Novalis felt that in touching a human body he touched God. By God we now all mean a Being —

> ". . . far more deeply interfused,
> Whose dwelling is the light of setting suns,
> And the round ocean and the living air,
> And the blue sky, and *in the mind of man*."

The starting-point of our theology is the immanent God.

[1] Prof. J. Arthur Thomson, "The Bible of Nature," p. 88.

We are thus led to move out from our own minds which afford us our most certain knowledge to the knowledge of God, whom once men described as the Unknown. We are not now alarmed by the inane charge of anthropomorphism. We almost smile at the crudity of the judgments in the last generation, as, for example, that while the Bible declares man to be made in the image of God, as a matter of fact God is made in the image of man. How completely has the standpoint shifted! We do not *make* God in our own image, but our own image, or personality, is the mirror in which He is reflected. Nay more, our consciousness is God welling up within us. The mind of the world emerges in our finite minds, not affirming that our finite minds contain the Infinite, but showing that they are or should be in contact with the Infinite. We do not make God in our own image, but in our image we are on the sure tracks of finding and knowing Him.

When Hume and Mill dissolved causality into a mere unvarying sequence, and tried to make us believe that by a cause we meant only an antecedent which was followed by a consequent, they did an unconscious service to our theology, for they led us to see how definite the idea of cause is, and how totally distinct from what they would have it to be. They prepared us for the capital discovery of modern psychology, that the idea of causation comes from the fact that we are ourselves causes. Our will is the fundamental fact in our experience through which we interpret everything else. We are, therefore, depending as we must on our own personality, obliged to conclude that what is not caused by ourselves, by the sum total of human wills, including ourselves, is caused by will not ourselves. The intelligence of the universe is will, and one will, otherwise there would be only a multiverse; and will is of course personal, not necessarily limited, as our own personality is, but, considering the vastness and complexity of the stupendous whole, more properly described as infinite.

We conclude, with a confidence which grows with every further effort of thought and every extension of knowledge, that the Cause of all things is an infinite Personality, a Will, an Intelligence — God.

At this point in our search we are Pantheists. God is the indwelling Reason, or Logos, that makes the whole. God is in the world what the soul is in the body. But here, in the investigation of our own personality, which is the one clue we have for the discovery of God, we light upon the fact of conscience. What is right and what is wrong is a matter for ethical research, and the idea of right and wrong must grow with the growth of the human organism, or society; we find, and are likely to find, in that no finality. But what is fundamental and invariable is the distinction between right and wrong as such. We are all far too definitely aware of seeing the better and approving it, and yet following the worse, to admit of any question on this point. And in this factor of the soul, the ethical, we gradually learn to recognize that the good is what agrees with God and the bad is what does not. We escape Pantheism through the door of the moral sense. The escape, as we saw in the chapter on Morality, is only gradual and imperfect, but it is sure. If we may say so, God, in spite of our reluctance, ultimately makes it plain. God is the author of everything except evil; God is in everything except the resistance to good. Slowly we make the capital discovery that evil is the resistance to God in our own or other wills, but that good is God.

If the fact of sin is neglected or slurred over, thought swiftly relapses into Pantheism. But that fact is so palpable, and emerges so definitely and necessarily from the moral nature which is ourselves, that Pantheism is sure of ultimate refutation. Thus the soul leads to God, the infinite Intelligence and Will that produced and sustains all things; but sin leads to the discovery of a Holy God, whose will is thwarted in our finite limitations and perverse resistance. To be rid of sin, to come back into perfect and conscious harmony with the will that is holy, must be the one aim and struggle of religion.

Here what is called natural theology comes to a stand. It does not appear how we can ever draw our foot out of the flux of things and arrive at any firm standing ground, how we can distinguish between the Holy God that is infinite and our finitude which resists Him, unless God, the Holy One, the Infinite Being, communicates with us, and defines, unless He shows us Himself over against us, as the Holy over against the unholy, and yet as the Holy bent on making us holy, by reconciling us to Himself.

Here, then, we come to a stay in theology, or we become Christian. As Christianity enters into our theology a new vista opens out; much may be discovered that seemed beyond our reach. Theology must turn aside to establish the proofs of Christianity, a whole discipline of apologetics develops itself, reasons are given for believing that Christianity is a revelation of God, not merely the human speculation about God, but God's own self-communication to man. The growth and preparation of the Christian truth are traced embryonically in the religion of Israel. The coming of Christ is established historically. His life and teaching are studied. His cross and resurrection and ascension are recognized as the starting-point of an evangel. The New Testament writings are examined as the foundation of a new theology which results from these facts. Into all this we cannot enter. But, assuming that theology has now become Christian, we go on to tread the opening vista, and to make the fresh and rational discoveries.

The most general and illuminating dogma of the Christian revelation is that the Logos — the reason in the whole Cosmos, the cause of the Cosmos, the sustaining principle of the universe — the reason which is in God, and, indeed, is God, which was in God and was God, from the beginning, was incarnate in Christ. This is the dogma which must either be believed or rejected. Only if it is believed on in the world does it become the light of the world.

We assume that it is believed, we take our stand with those who believe it and proceed to trace out the theology of the Incarnation.

The first and the last, the alpha and the omega, of Christianity, considered as a revelation, is that it establishes the simple proposition, God is love. It makes clearer than ever before that God is good. It identifies goodness with God in such a way that evil is shown to be in radical opposition to Him, and He is seen to be the declared foe of it. That emerges from the teaching of Christ, from His Person, and, above all, from the Cross, for there the evil in the world assails with malignant fury the incarnate Good, and overwhelms it with anguish, shame, and death.

But much more remarkable than the demonstration that God is good is the argument which shows that He is love. Christ asserts it on the ground of His own intuitive and eternal knowledge of God; He manifests it by His own character and conduct as the expression in human life of God's Spirit and nature; making no compromise with evil, He yet loves human beings that are stained with sin and sunk in guilt; but, above all, in the cross He dies to deliver men from evil; He bears the sin of the world in His body on the tree; God in Christ is seen as self-sacrificing love, which suffers even the death of the cross in the love that would save the world.

The argument by which Christianity establishes its capital conclusion, that God is love, is cumulative, and grows in strength with every fresh understanding of the sources and every deepening experience of life. Into our theology has come the most illuminating and the most pregnant idea.

Let us pause to get this into line with the truth of God which we reached, or might have reached, apart from Christianity, and then let us mark the lines of thought which radiate from the central truth.

The immanent reason in things, the soul of the world, that Intelligence which contrives and that Will which executes the whole, God, is holy love. In the forum of the conscience, where the eternal pleading proceeds between right and wrong, He is on the tribunal uniformly deciding for the right. But in the chambers of the heart, where love and selfishness are at eternal feud, He is the love. He has produced a universe which admits of something alien from Himself, but only in order that the alien may return to Him in deliberate and convinced devotion. He will ever devise means that His banished may return. While, therefore, the concrete world of our human existence appears to traverse the idea that God is love, or at any rate to suggest that, if He is love, His power is limited, the clue that we have obtained leads us to the correction of this impression. The impression is due to the eyes on which it is made, the eyes of human beings that, being out of harmony with God, see things in the distortion of their own lovelessness and resistance to Him.

All through the world, rightly understood, runs the principle of love, the principle which is God. The power is recognized by science, the love by theology. And yet when it is recognized, science itself confirms the conclusion. Drummond, as we saw, in his "Ascent of Man," brought evolution and the struggle for existence, with the survival of the fittest, to show that love ran through it all; for the struggle for the life of others, with its attendant sacrifices, is the concomitant of all the apparent struggle of egotism. Such unlikely writers as Prince Kropotkin and Karl Pearson are the witnesses of the truth which theology establishes. The former, in his "Mutual Aid," traces the principle of co-operation, of love, running all through the animal world and the earliest communal arrangements of mankind. The Divine element in our humanity is illustrated by a fact mentioned in a note.[1] A prisoner escaped from a French prison. He managed to conceal himself, though the hue and cry were up against him. Lying in a ditch, he saw a fire break out in a village, and heard a woman cry to some one to save her child in the upper story. But no one responded. The prisoner's humanity made him forget his personal

[1] "Mutual Aid," by Prince Kropotkin, p. 278.

danger. He dashed out, made his way through the fire, and with scalded face and burning clothes presented the rescued child to the agonized mother. The prisoner was thus arrested and restored to prison. Humanity is drenched with love, the love that sacrifices, the love that saves. The fierce competition of the modern world, thinks the Prince, is due to a mistaken doctrine; it fancies itself a law of nature. Darwinism, a great half-truth, has dominated the world; it was thought that the struggle for existence and the survival of the fittest were the secret of the universe. The hungry generations tread each other down with the heroic thought that they are co-operating with Nature, that great power which, for the modern mind, replaces God.

But the other half of the truth must be brought out — nay, more than half, the whole truth which dominates the fragment called "struggle for existence." As Karl Pearson, the other writer referred to, says, the struggle as we see it is rather the struggle of nations than of individuals, and for that, co-operation and mutual aid within the nation are absolutely necessary. For the moment, the aspect of the world is a solidarity of mutual life under the name of nationalism, supported by patriotism, involving antagonism and suspicion between nations; but presently nation will learn to help nation, as man helps man, the area of patriotism will be humanity, and the united struggle of mankind will be to dominate the forces of Nature and to provide for the welfare of each human unit. That is the kingdom of God, as conceived by Jesus Christ.

Even men who do not recognize God are thus discovering the neglected factor in the being of God, the truth which it was the object of Christianity to supply.

> "From the first Power was, I knew,
> Life has made clear to me,
> That, strive but for closer view,
> Love were as plain to see.
> When see? When there dawns a day,
> If not on the homely earth,
> Then yonder worlds away,
> When the strange and new have birth,
> And power comes full in play."

But if a Christian theology has enabled us to apprehend the love that runs through things, and to find in love the ultimate principle of the world and of life, it will push on to further conquests, until it transforms all other theologies and realizes that triumph of love which is involved in the conception that God is love, for God must be all in all.

When we have learnt to detach certain principles from the whole and to identify them with God, so that we are no longer under the paralyzing spell of Pantheism, we have a clue which leads us to a totally new conception of the world and to a fruitful pratique. When once the clue is grasped it is wonderful, as the modern mind begins to see, how good and gracious the universe is; the warring influence is found to be in ourselves, in our jaundiced minds and warped views, and the practical life resulting therefrom. "Strive but for closer view," get the survey of the universe which we may reverently call Christ's, and what do we see? There is the beneficent Father of men, God, making and maintaining His human family in a world which is an abode for them, marvellously constructed and adapted. His impartial benevolence gives life, and food, and opportunity to all. His sun rises on the good and on the bad. The sufferings and limitations of the creature are vastly overbalanced by the joys and delights. The balance of pleasure over pain is incalculably great. The pain is a spur to higher good. It makes character, it elicits help, human benevolence. The greatest and best in human life is the Cross by which it is redeemed.

It is no lazy optimism which reaches a conclusion of this kind, but rather a frank and full survey of the facts of human existence, released from the warping view of the mind in a morbid or perverted state. The theory that God is love brings out a world of love, where much seemed forbidding and perplexing, as a burst of April sunshine suddenly shows an earth beautiful with promise and a blue sky bending over it in tenderness. This transformed earth is the real earth, and lasts just so long as we maintain the illuminating sun, the love of God.

There is a tendency to-day to regard God as the author of good and evil, and even to imagine that God suffers the evil with us, and is battling against it as we do.[1] This kind of Pantheism secures unity at too great a price. It is better to rest in an unexplained dualism than to compress the contradictory facts into a forced monism. Whatever may be the explanation or the origin of evil, for practical purposes — and it is only for such purposes that theology is of any use — we get the best point of view by maintaining absolutely that God is good, and nothing but good, love and nothing but love. Whatever is counter to good or to love is not God, but the obstacle which God is overcoming, and will some day completely overcome. We take our part, however small, in His victory in proportion as we succeed in realizing and in bringing to bear on the facts of experience the unflecked purity, the unmodified goodness, the mastering love that is God. *Omnia vincit amor*.

The Christianity of to-day is as yet only half-developed. It is far too precious a truth to surrender. Its theology is far too original and valuable to admit of being superseded. We cannot give up our theology in order to become philanthropists, for it is not shown that we can love men consistently and redemptively except by faith in God who loves. But the Christian truth must push on to its conclusion, and the theology must be recast to express the rounded whole. The half-development, broadly speaking, insisted that we should personalize God, and Satan, and should dwell on the two as opposing

[1] "The Living Word," by Ellwood Worcester.

forces. Whether it was an echo of Zoroastrianism, or simply a reflection of the stubborn facts of the world, a dualism resulted, and we had our Ormuzd and Ahriman, two contending world-powers, and the victory hanging in the balance. No one can deny that this dualism is reflected in the Bible, and that Christianity in its early stages accepted it. But Christianity, fully developed, cannot admit this kind of dualism. It turns wholly from the darkness towards the light; it does not spend its strength in personalizing God and Satan, but it devotes all its strength, its mind, its heart, to personalizing God and loving Him. It conceives the task of religion to be the realization of the living God, who is truth and love and goodness, as omnipresent, mastering evil of all kinds. The Christian is one who sides only with God, with truth and love and goodness, and so resists the devil that the devil flees and fades into thin air. Christ's way of putting it, a picturesque and forcible way, was that the prince of this world came and found nothing in Him. So He would have it be with His followers. The prince of this world, the Satan of the Dark Ages, should find nothing in us, not even the image, or the terror, of him. Love should have driven out fear, and light darkness.

But is it not a *tour de force*, a will to believe carried to the excess of blindness? Is it not making God what we desire, and insisting that He is, because we have formed this idea of Him? Does it not involve shutting our eyes to many of the most obvious and certain facts of life, and wrapping ourselves in an optimistic illusion? The answer is, No! We are driven along a line of rational argument to the discovery of what God is. Surely, then, we are bound to side with God against what He opposes. We cannot stand disputing how these His enemies became His enemies, or how these facts of concrete experience fell out of harmony with His will? That course of conduct is intelligible if we are not convinced what God is, what He must be. But the Christian is convinced. God in Christ is truth and goodness and love, nothing else, in spite of all appearances, that and that alone. Into that scale, therefore, as essentially the winning side, the Christian throws his whole weight. He, too, will be truth, and arise to smite the lies which vex the labouring earth. He, too, will be goodness, and flame with a steady fire against all that is not good. He, too, will be love, vanquishing hate in all its forms, not by hating, but by loving. When the objection is made: But look at the sin and suffering of the earth, the irrational calamities which overwhelm the good, the cruelty of man to man, the moral evil which persists and frequently triumphs; how can there be a good, an all-powerful God? his answer is unhesitating: There is a good and all-powerful God, and therefore I trust Him where I cannot see, and I go out with Him to soothe, to comfort, and to save the world.

But if the objector urges: How do you know there

is such a God? the answer comes, and it is surely irresistible: If I groan over the sin and the sorrow of the world, and if I suffer in the catastrophes which crush my fellow-men, what right have I to think that this sympathy, this saving sympathy, is *my* creation? How dare I suppose that there is in me a virtue which I deny to the Soul of the World, the Creative Intelligence, God?

Is it said: That is reasoning in a circle; you agree that God is good because you are, and then that you are good because God is? Well, in matters of this kind the argument, to be complete, must be a circle. The circle is its own evidence. For who can deny that it is good? What better conclusion can faith or practice reach than this: I must be true and good and loving, because God is truth, goodness, and love? This is the vision of our desire, the self-evidencing reality which carries conviction.

> "I saw Eternity the other night
>   Like a great ring of pure and endless light,
>   All calm as it was bright:
>   And round beneath it Time, in hours, days, years,
>   Driven by the spheres,
>   Like a vast shadow moved, in which the world
>   And all her train were hurled."

That vision is the true theology.

We may, then, vindicate the name of theology as queen of the sciences, understanding by it, not that theology is one of the sciences, but that it is a knowledge or a discipline which must explain and justify the sciences, and in its turn be justified and recognized by them.

This knowledge of the Cause and the Purpose, to which science as such cannot attain, is as necessary as anything to which science can attain. For if God is not, or if we cannot know Him, a doubt and a fear will inevitably steal over the human spirit, What use or joy or satisfaction can there be in any other knowledge?

CHAPTER IX

LITERATURE

Vita sine litteris est mors was a saying of Robertson, the Scottish historian — "Life without literature is death." But a sick doubt sometimes steals over the world, in the incredible multiplication of written and printed matter, whether life even with literature is much better. When books were few and rare, and (despite Bacon's pessimistic view that the weighty things sink in the stream of time and only the driftwood and the bubbles and the froth are carried down on its bosom) only those that were of weight survived, when a newspaper was an event, and even letters were written with care as if for posterity, the student in his library might easily feel that he breathed the air of the immortals and conversed with the good and great of all time. Such a commerce with what is noble in literature was a finer life; to be deprived of it would naturally seem to be death. But when the flood of written and printed matter assumes vast proportions, when the ephemeral writing of the day, in papers or books, leaves no time for reference to the solemn and silent monitors upon the shelves, when writing is a trade for wresting from the restless and curious mind of man a living, and journalism becomes the record of facts which do not happen for the benefit of minds that do not think, then literature, if all that is written and printed is to assume the venerable name, appears as a muddy and defiling deluge, in which, though the precious products of time are still tossed and whirled, the mind is more likely to be debauched and defiled by the flood than to be saved by the treasures.

Life *with* letters is a death for the unhappy minds that feed upon vanity, for children who use the art of reading to debauch their spirits with sensational stories, for men who use it to exasperate the fever of gambling, and the like. None but a pessimist would say that a cheap press means more evil than good to the world, but he must be a blind optimist who does not recognize that the evil goes near to balancing the good.

Life without letters is death! But in contrast with the city population feeding on the garbage of the daily press, with no palate for any writing which is not spiced with lubricity, or malice, or sensationalism, consider the illiterate, still to be found in remote and quiet places, old men who live in dumb contact with the vital earth, or the still more vital heavens, tossed on the crisp waves of the sea, bronzed with the weather, hardy with the handling of the rope or of the spade. These illiterates are at least in presence of the living forces of Nature, and know the solemnity and uplift of the eternal things. They read in the legends of the stones and the hedgerows more salutary messages than the paragraphs of the daily press; they hear in the twitter of the birds, and the timid rustle of earth's humbler progeny beneath the grass, the word of God which has been spoken since the Creation. The doings of the cottage, the birth, the marriage, and the burial, the uneloquent loves, and the unrecorded heroisms of endurance, are a better script than the fripperies of popular fiction, and the scraps which take the place of knowledge. It has become, therefore, more necessary than ever to discriminate between literature and literature, and, if possible, to retain the name "literature" only for writing which has a certain quality. If we could give to literature a specific and legitimate meaning, if we might stamp as "illiterate" all who have no taste for real literature, all who wallow by choice in the writing which is the negation of real literature, we should be in the way of amendment.

There is a kind of human swine, unclean feeders, that eat with equal relish food and garbage. Before them the pearls are cast in vain.[1] Surely, and often quickly, the taste becomes morbid, and, like those Africans who acquire a craving to eat earth, which is

[1] What the literature is that at present starves the souls of London children is told in the answer made by one of the boys to the question, what *books* they read in their country visit: *Chips*, *Comic Cuts*, the *World's Comic*, *Funny Cuts*, the *Funny Wonder*, *Comic Home Journal*. ("Towards Social Reform," by Canon Barnett.) They ought to grow up humourists, but they do not. The comic view of life ends in tragedy.

ultimately fatal, they eat themselves to death in the noisome realities or lewd fancies of the written page. If such swine might be rightly stigmatized, if the line of distinction might be drawn, not between those who read and those who do not, but between those who read cleanly and those who read foully, if the illiterate might be defined as persons who are poisoned with bad writing, and cannot therefore understand literature, a certain guidance might be given, at any rate to the young. He shall not be illiterate who only has to confess that he must put his mark to a name written for him, but he who, to everything written, by himself or others, attaches inevitably the mark of the beast. For him, above all, life without literature is death.

It is curious that the original meaning of "literature" in our language, though the dictionary now marks it as *rare* and *obsolescent*, is not the vast unsifted mass of printed or written matter, but polite or humane learning. Thus Swift argues that the young nobility may be educated "that they may set out into the world with some foundation of literature," and Johnson speaks of one whose "literature was unquestionably great. He read all the languages which are considered as either learned or polite." This meaning just survives; for example, Mr. Howells speaks of a man as grotesquely ignorant — "He was a man of very small literature."

Thus the word started well. It implied discrimination, and meant culture. It was by a profane perversion that it came to mean anything that is written, until the vulgar and misleading posters which a political party issues on the verge of an election are designated "literature."

But the coin is not defaced beyond recognition, and is, perhaps, even now in process of re-minting. Thus Buckle, in his matter-of-fact way, was on the right track when he said: "Literature, when it is in a healthy and unforced state, is simply the form in which the knowledge of a country is registered." But evidently he had not captured the right definition. The bills of mortality, or the statistics of the excise, are a form in which the knowledge of a country is registered, but we hesitate to call them literature.

The realism which gives the minute details of vice and corruption justifies itself by claiming to "register the knowledge of a country," which is, it is argued, necessarily a knowledge of good and evil; but is it to rank as literature? We are reaching an agreement that literature is only writing of a certain kind or quality. We are feeling our way to an assured judgment that this or that book is literature or is not. But what is the *punctum discriminis?* In the absence of an Academy of Letters, who will define literature for us? Who will enable us to sort the printed matter into two great heaps — literature and the reverse? Who will cultivate the taste for the one, and the distaste for the other? Perhaps it may be said that no hard-and-fast line may be drawn, that there are approximations to the imaginary standard, some close, some more distant, and it is impossible to say where the remoter examples shade off into the indubitably unliterary. Perhaps there are writers who sometimes produce literature and sometimes do not, so that our task may be ruined by a bad work proceeding from a good writer. Or it may be argued that in one work there are parts, passages, sentences, which deserve the name of literature, while the rest does not. A paragraph in a newspaper, an effusion in a poet's corner, may deserve the *cachet* of the Academy better than a whole volume of dull and honest prose, or of mediocre verse.

The difficulties in reaching a definition are obvious. And yet a standard must be found. If we are to save our souls in the vast welter of publications in which we float or are submerged, we must have a criterium, we must have at hand some ready monitor to decide whether this book or paper is worth the eyesight and the brain expended on it — whether honest silence, observation, thought, or even reverie, is not preferable to this particular reading.

I have sometimes in a railway carriage watched half a dozen people with eyes glued to a printed page, while the train has been moving through country of rare beauty or of deep historic interest. There is a man feverishly reading the betting news in the *Sporting Times*, while the green meadows stretch away on either side of the line, golden with buttercups, defined by the silver with hawthorn-hedges; the white lambs frisking in the shadow, and the sky-blue kingfisher flashing down a stream. Or there is a boy poring over the semi-nudities and the nasty innuendos of the comic paper which delights his heart, while we are passing scenes of his country's history, which, by a momentary memory, might stir him to nobility of life and character. Up those smooth slopes of the downs, now gleaming in the sunshine, which is melting the mists, Alfred made his heroic onset on the Danes. In that old house, whose twisted chimneys just emerge above the sheltering trees, one of our great poets lived and wrote. In a word, the train is gliding through a pictured book, richer and nobler than is to be found on a library shelf; but the travellers are blind to its beauty and deaf to its lore, because they are *reading*, engaged in an occupation which has been commended as virtuous, but which, in this case, is quite the reverse. The good is the enemy of the best. We have given to reading a good name, and it is now one of the main hindrances to strenuous thought, to growth of character, to observation of life.

Before any reflecting mind, opens the world, let us even say the universe, the home of the spirit of man; and, under its lofty dome, on the countryside, or in the thronging town, the life of man is transacting itself — history and biography and poetry are being lived. Here, everywhere, is the still sad music of humanity; here, everywhere, is the forward march, the pressing to a goal. The whole scene is draped in solemn beauty; the whole movement thrills with unutterable meaning. Every pebble and flower is a library. Every human soul is an unsearchable mystery of being. God is certainly not to be evaded by any one who thinks and observes. He is too obvious, diffused in the glory and wonder of the whole, flashing out in the ingenuity, the wisdom, and the love, of every part. Here, indeed, is a Book to read, a veritable endless Bible, or revelation of the Divine to the heart of man. Here is a newspaper, issued morning and evening, with many editions during the day, recording the true events of the world, not liable to contradiction. The outgoings of the morning and of the evening rejoice. The sun publishes, and the stars take up the tale. But all this reading of earth, of man, and of God is precluded for these travellers along the way by their absorption in the base excitements of the racecourse, or the lucubrations of a scribe who has lost the power of thought and feeling, and can only issue from the noisome office and the midnight flare of an overwrought city — words, scenes, ideas, which have no relation with the facts of the universe or the truth of God.

But what is the criterium? What is the standard by which approximately we may distinguish literature from spurious literature? In the absence of any decisive verdict of an Academy, I venture to suggest that literature is only *that writing which combines truth and beauty*.

It may be said that truth is beauty; and there is

much to be said for the view that beauty is truth. But we are not defining things, or ultimate realities; we are trying to define literature. Writing which is at once true and beautiful, and such writing alone, deserves the name. A book may be true and useful, the facts it contains may be worth knowing, and they may be stated with accuracy and sincerity, such as a book of trade statistics or a medical or law book, and yet it may have no literary value, because it lacks beauty of form or diction. On the other hand, a book may be beautiful and yet putrescent. It may set itself to describe the alluring forms of vice, and to shatter the moral sense of the reader, by draping evil in the shimmering gold and the voluptuous folds which make it irresistible. But its want of truth excludes it from the rank of literature. It is true, perhaps, in the sense that it accurately describes the ways and the attractions of evil, but it is false in that it represents those attractions as real, whereas they are delusive. The apples of Sodom are beautiful to look at, but dust and ashes in the mouth. The book we are speaking of represents them only as beautiful, and does not reveal their inner meaning. It is not, therefore, true.

Our definition, it will be seen, cannot be applied by rule of thumb. Thought, reflection, conscience are needed to apply it. This should be no objection. But will any writing which combines truth and beauty deserve to rank as literature? Is there not something more? Must not the truth be of sufficient weight and value, and must not the beauty be original, something freshly formed in a mind which sees as others have not seen? Emerson said that the way to write what should not be forgotten was to think and write sincerely. But is that enough? May we not write platitudes sincerely, not knowing that they are not discoveries? And can a sincere reproduction of platitudes be welcomed as literature? Can Martin Tupper maintain a place among the immortals?

But, it may be answered, our definition will stand without an appendix if only we take account of the deep meaning both of truth and of beauty. Emerson is right. Truth in literature means sincerity in the writer. Every writer is a personality, distinct from all others. Let him be completely sincere, frank, gifted with power to utter himself and his thought, without subterfuge or pretence, and that self-utterance, if only it has the quality of beauty, will be literature. The writer may clothe his thought in poetry or prose, in history or in fiction, in science or speculation, but his sincerity will be the truth of whichever form he adopts. Literature, after all, is the reflection of writers. The writers must be good, sane, wise, clean, truth-loving, or their products cannot be literature. Benvenuto Cellini or Pepys can produce a book which has the stamp of literature, because, though the lives they present to the reader are by no means faultless, they have the crowning virtue of sincerity. Evil is in them as evil, not as good. There is no self-delusion. There is no pose. Here is a correct transcript of a soul, given in language which has charm and beauty. George Borrow may seem a singular example of truth, for no wit of man can discover where he is romancing and where he is describing what occurred. But his place in literature is due to "The Bible in Spain," and that book rests entirely on letters written from Spain. The book, therefore, is an actuality. With forthright literalness he presents the facts in language of singular correctness and strength. The book is literature. "Lavengro," much more brilliant, more interesting, more wonderful, owes its place, in our consideration, to the reputation of "The Bible in Spain." The element of sincerity is defective. There is a pose, an affectation; and though there are passages of great beauty, the book, as a whole, is not beautiful.

But it is time that we divided literature into its two most obvious branches — poetry and prose. Only, before we do so, let us notice the definition of literature in the discriminating sense offered by the dictionary, "writing which has claim to consideration on the ground of beauty of form or emotional effect." Here nothing is said of truth, except so far as it is implied in beauty; and here an opening is given for writing on the plea of emotional effect, which our own definition would exclude because the emotion is bad or false. We must firmly grasp our definition, then, that literature is only writing which combines truth and beauty, or we shall lose our foothold directly we enter the enchanted realm of poetry.

Plato firmly banished the poets from his Republic because they were liars. But his only chance of escaping from the charge of poetry himself is to restrict the definition of poetry to metrical form. The schoolboy's answer to the question, "What is poetry?" "Where every line begins with a capital," might show Plato not a poet. But essentially he is more a poet than Hesiod. Does literature begin in poetry because metrical language is easier to remember, a consideration of some importance before the use of writing? Is the rhythm or the rhyme simply a *memoria technica?* James Fitzjames Stephen said that Milton might have uttered "Paradise Lost" more effectively in a short prose pamphlet of half a dozen pages. Is that the truth? Certainly the irritating effect of doggerel — that is, rhymed lines without any beauty of thought or form — might give a distaste for metrical language as deep as Mr. Stephen's. But, on the other hand, the extravagance of Mr. Stephen's judgment reminds us that beauty of verse is an element in literature, though he may have been blind to it.

The reason why literature begins in poetry is that in the freshness of the world's youth and in the delight of song the rhythmical utterance is spontaneous. The measured language, the assonance or the rhyme, is an element of beauty. Where rhythm ceases to be beautiful it ceases to be poetry. Doggerel is admittedly more detestable than bad prose. But in poetry, if it is poetry at all, there is a beauty much deeper and more subtle than the charm of musical words and rhythmic movement. Of Mr. Swinburne, Tennyson said that he was a pipe through which every wind blew to music, but that does not give Mr. Swinburne a place in literature. In the famous chorus of the "Atalanta" —

"Before the beginning of years there came to the making of man,
Grief with a gift of tears, time with a glass that ran,"

there is a music of words, a swift, inevitable precision of rhyme and assonance, which make the reading of it an ever new delight. But there is something far deeper and more beautiful — the haunting paradox of the mingled elements in the composition of man, the glory and the shame of human life, the doubt and the certainty of human destiny, which gave to the Greek tragic drama its immortal charm. Half the beauty of human affairs is in the joy, the other half is in the sorrow. The charm is in the pathos. The mood of poetry is that in which pleasant thoughts bring sad thoughts to the mind, or *vice versâ*.

Thus Professor Gilbert Murray says, speaking of that old Greek tragedy: "It is a strange fact, this carrying power of a thing so frail as poetry, or of that creative effort in philosophic thought which is of the same stuff as poetry. Αὔρα ποντιὰς αὔρα ('Wind, wind of the deep sea') begins a chorus in the 'Hecuba,' and fifty others could be chosen like it. How slight the words are! Yet there is in them just that inexplicable beauty, that quick shiver of joy or longing, which, as it was fresh then in a world whose very bone and iron have long since passed into dust, is fresh still and alive still, only harder to reach, more easy to forget, to disregard, to smother with irrelevancy, far more in danger of death. For, like certain other of the things of the spirit, it will die if it is not loved."[1]

Matthew Arnold, in his curious analysis of poetry as "the criticism of life," struck into a most interesting and convincing vein when he took certain lines from Homer and Milton, and tried to show why they gave us this sense of inexplicable beauty, this quick shiver of joy or longing. That is the only way to open dull minds to the appreciation of poetry. That is the only, but sufficient, vindication of poetry.

Take those perfectly simple and apparently artless lines of William Allingham:

> "Three ducks on a pond,
> A green bank beyond,
> The blue sky of spring,
> Light clouds on the wing,
> Oh what a little thing
>   To remember for years,
>   To remember with tears!"

The beauty there is not in the words, for they are obvious and undistinguished. There is beauty, no

[1] "The Interpretation of Ancient Greek Literature," p. 18.

doubt, in the simple succession of brief lines, as in the little pantings and sobbings of reminiscence. But the beauty which captivates and then haunts us in the verse is deeper. The linked periods of human life, the pathos of childish memories in later years, the curious effect of Nature on the mind before its period of reflection begins, the stamped images of colour and form in the marvellous pageant of the world by which we are always surrounded — all this, and more, steals into the soul with the reading of the lines and floods it with beauty.

Or murmur these two magical lines of Mr. Swinburne's:

> "Where waves of grass break into foam of flowers,
>   Or where the wind's feet shine along the sea."

There is music of language unmistakable. But behind the language, beautified by the intricate though simple imagery, is the actual picture in Nature, and the mental delight of comparing the flowery mead of summer with the sea, and the swift movement of the wind on the waters with the passing of some goddess whose gleaming feet make tracks of light.

Or here are a few lines from a sonnet which paints the "pathos of the trees' decline" in autumn:

> "When all my last buds drooped in hopeless mood,
>   I took the valley road, of songs bereft,
>   Bordered with hanging woods, where Winter stood
>   Wrapt in the vivid garment Autumn left.

There, where he stood in bronzed gold of the brake,
Sprayed with the ruby of the bramble's leaf,
I made my suit for generous Autumn's sake,
That he would grant her children respite brief." [1]

Here a pensive beauty in language carries the thought into the pensiveness of a late autumn day, and links the mind with the processes of Nature, the succession of the seasons, the colour and change of the earth, which are themselves the poetry appealing to every child of man.

Perhaps in poetry, the earliest and the latest literary form, beauty predominates over truth, in the sense that we look for beauty before we are awake on the question of truth. But it must be observed that poetry establishes no permanent claim, and secures no recognized place in literature, except so far as it is *true*. We hope that Plato spoke satirically when he threatened to banish the poets from his ideal State. There are always enough poets who are false to justify an edict of expulsion. None the less, poetry is truth. Transparent sincerity and an almost slavish attachment to fact in its minutest detail are the distinguishing marks of all great poets. Thus, even in their less splendid passages they are worth reading; their truth emerges where their beauty fails. As Landor puts it: "Few consider that every page of a really great poet has something in it which distinguishes him from an inferior order, something which, if insubstantial as the aliment,

[1] "Poems by Two Friends." J. M. Dent & Co.

serves at least as a solvent of the aliment, of strong and active minds." [1]

Wordsworth, for example, has many pages, especially in the "Excursion," which would hardly be called poetry but for the (mechanical and artificial) cutting up into decasyllabic lines. But there is no page which is not beautiful with truth. His view of things is so just, his principles are so sane, and his sympathy with men is so deep that he cannot even in his letters be other than serviceable to his reader. His poetry, at times beautiful with a beauty which brings tears of joy to the eyes, touching the sensitive chords of the heart like a violinist's bow, and eliciting unearthly music, is at all times truth, solid reality of earth or of heaven, blending the two. Indeed, the impatience which reads only short lyrics, elegant extracts, and purple patches, does him a grave injustice, and never really knows him. No poet has so much prose in his poetry, but no poet's prose is so good.

A great poet is, without knowing it or intending it, a great teacher. Homer was the Bible of the Greeks, in spite of Plato's grave disapproval, not a Bible that could ever claim moral or spiritual infallibility, but a book of inexhaustible wisdom, from which texts can be found for all occasions.

Shakespeare is as much a teacher as Dante, though he makes no parade of it. Goethe is, next to Luther's Bible, the most powerful teacher of Germany. The

[1] "Pericles and Aspasia," Let. xxxii.

philosophers and men of science touch the public faintly and indirectly, but Goethe reaches every hearth, and does for Germany what Burns does for Scotland. The poets are not infallible. They see but in part, and often through a glass darkly. They have their pitiable lapses. Donne attempted by a life of piety to atone for poems that had gone forth from him in his youth which he never could recall. Marlowe might, if he had lived, have desired to burn whole pages of his translations and of his original work. Burns wrote things which are base and unclean, and, but for their lyrical ease, would have no claim to a place in literature. Byron wallowed in an affected vice, and tried to establish his claim to election, the election of the lost, by a daring violation of the principles of morality and even of decency. But for all their lapses, these, like the other great poets, are true teachers: their fundamental quality is veracity, even moral truth. In spite of themselves, unconsciously, they are, as poets, on the side of Heaven. Their truth reaches many who remain unaffected by Dante's austerity, by Spenser's golden mellowness of music, by Wordsworth's stainless mountain air.

"Don Juan" is unsavoury reading, but it would not tend to make, it would even tend to reclaim, a debauchee. The poet cannot be vicious, though he affects to be. A rush of elemental purity and rightness suddenly overwhelms vice with ridicule, which is more discouraging to it than reproof.

The poet does not set out to be a teacher. He only looks at things observantly and reflectively, and sees them in the light of their own ideal. He begins to celebrate them in thoughts which are to their own music chanted. He presents the world, the life, and time as they *are* to him, as, we may believe, they actually are. He enables others to see the reality, which to them at first appears to be only a dream. The poet seems to the unpoetical to be an idealist. But he is indeed a realist. His claim upon us is that he says, with a beauty which is his incommunicable gift, what is true. God Himself is the best poet,

"And the real is His song."

When from poetry we turn to prose, perhaps, like Carlyle, with a sense of relief, we have to observe that our definition of literature holds here, though the stress is laid on the truth rather than on the beauty. Here truth is everything. Bad prose is false, unreal, misleading. Any prose that is quite truthful, exact, and able to convey truth to the reader, is, like a block of unhewn marble, literature in the rough. But it must be carved and polished if it is to live as literature.

The main objection to the vast deluge of printed matter under which the modern world is submerged is that it has not truth as its motive or its substance. Journalism aims at effect rather than at truth. It is corrupted by party feeling. It records things which are not true and corrects them on the following day.

It deliberately excises, twists, suggests, in order to convey a convenient impression which is the reverse of the facts. The writers have no interest in truth as such; their interest is in a swift and enormous sale. It is this which prevents journalism from being literature. Here and there a journalist honestly aims at truth, and writes articles which rank as literature. When the articles are collected a book emerges. But, like Coleridge's "Friend," such writing will never sell a paper. Such writers are soon at a discount. Lord Morley began as a journalist, produced real books, and ended as a statesman. He is a great and shining example, but the Press has not laid the example to heart. And it must be admitted that John Morley's success as a journalist is not beyond dispute.

An immense proportion of current literature is fiction. Fiction may be true, and frequently is. No books are truer in the world than "Don Quixote" and "Tom Jones." But it is obviously more difficult to write true fiction than true history or true science. To write true history it is necessary to master the records of the past, and to have a capacious mind which can hold the causes and sequences of events; to write true science nothing is wanted but patience and close observation. But to write true fiction the writer must himself be wholly true and in vital contact with the realities of human life. A Balzac, a Fielding, a Dickens, is as rare as a Molière, a Shakespeare, or a Browning.

Unfortunately, to write bad fiction nothing is wanted but pen and ink and a lively fancy. To write popular fiction, prurience and a taste for sensual vice may be added as lure and seasoning. No knowledge of life is needed, except that knowledge which is only a euphemism for acquaintance with sin. No balance of judgment, no insight, no sympathy, no knowledge of science or literature, no acquaintance with goodness or with God is demanded. If a man, or, better still, a nimble-minded woman, lives in society, reflects its foibles, and catches its dialect, all that has to be done is to sit down and concoct a plot out of the incidents which are daily occurring; and the world will call the story true, because it corresponds to what it actually sees. But what it sees is not true; and the book that reflects its vision is false as the vision itself. Literature is truth, truth of fact, truth of feeling, truth of life. It is spoiled by false feeling, sentimentality, just as it is spoiled by false statements, lying, or by the suppression or distortion of facts. Fiction is only saved from being noxious by being true, more true than even a Blue Book or a table of statistics.

But if truth is the essence of literature, it might seem as if all solid essays on facts, all historical treatises, all sound philosophical speculations, would be literature. But this is notoriously not the case. What is it that is wanting, what is it that makes us hesitate to call the Annual Register or the Encyclopædia, however true they may be, literature?

It is the element of beauty. To this element the mind, debauched by bad writing of many kinds, may become almost insensible. Flamboyant descriptions, sounding rodomontade, invective, jokes, and tit-bits, may create a diseased palate, until beautiful writing seems tame as a marble statue, in comparison with the flaunting figures on the boulevard, or undistinguished as a rose garden after the glittering splendours of the stage.

But the beauty which is demanded in writing, if the writing is to be literature, is not all of one kind. The best literature presents a manifold beauty, elements of beauty which can be traced and analyzed, and a consummation which escapes analysis, like that element which we just examined in poetry, a perfection in which the varied beauties are harmonized.

There is a beauty of prose which is distinguished from that of poetry only by the substitution of a freer rhythm for the exact divisions of lines and stanzas. The description of the mosses in "Modern Painters," or the description of the ship in "The Harbours of England," Carlyle's description of Marie Antoinette as she first appeared at Court in "The Diamond Necklace," or De Quincey's description of the stage-coach rushing through the night, would quite justly be described as poetry. The music of the words, the rhythm of the sentences, the richness and colour of the diction, the depth of feeling, the imaginative insight into related facts, and suggestions of other trains of thought or associated emotions, are precisely the elements which make great poetry. We have no reason to regret that Ruskin, Carlyle, or De Quincey eschewed the vehicle of verse, and found themselves in this flexible and opulent prose. Or rather, the only reason for regret is that these great passages, buried in bulky volumes, and surrounded with prose of a pedestrian quality, may not survive so vitally in literature as single poems, like "The Elegy in a Country Churchyard," or "The Burial of Sir John Moore." Verse is curiously preservative. It furnishes wings which carry light pieces right down the course of time.

But there are some who question the legitimacy of this poetical prose, and in any case prose cannot live on these heights. If its beauty can only be of the poetical kind, it cannot establish its claim.

There is in prose the beauty of compact and neat expression, which makes a sentence stand out like a polished gem. Walter Savage Landor and Walter Pater have produced wonders in this kind. As we keep cabinets of gems, so we range over the pages of these writers, and find fresh delights for eye and mind each time we revolve the flashing and crystalline sentences.

"Ah! my Aspasia, philosophy does not bring her sons together; she portions them off early, gives them a scanty stock of worm-eaten furniture, a chair or two on which it is dangerous to sit down, and at least as many arms as utensils; then leaves them: they seldom meet afterward."

What a sense of satisfaction and wonder is produced by a sentence like this, which sums the history of philosophy in three or four lines!

Or, again, how we seem to pass into the clear, sun-bathed air of Attica in a remark like this: "Men may be negligent in their hand-writing, for men may be in a hurry about the business of life; but I never knew either a sensible woman or an estimable one whose writing was disorderly."

Or, once more, how unhesitatingly we know that we are touching real literature when we read: "Do not chide me, then, for coming to you after the blossoms and buds and herbage: do not keep to yourselves all the grass on the Meander. We used to share it; we will now. I love it wherever I can get a glimpse of it. It is the home of the eyes, ever ready to receive them, and spreading its cool couch for their repose."

For Pater, let these serve: "Certainly the mind of the old workman who struck that coin was, if we may trust the testimony of his work, unclouded by impure or gloomy shadows. The thought of Demeter is impressed here, with all the purity and proportion, the purged and dainty intelligence, of the human countenance."

Or this of Ladas, the famous runner, in the Capitol: "Of necessity, but fatally, he must pause for a few moments in his course; or the course is at length over, or the breathless journey with some all-important tidings; and now, not till now, he thinks of resting to draw from the sole of his foot the cruel thorn, driven into it as he ran. In any case, there he still sits for a moment, for ever, amid the smiling admiration of centuries, in the agility, in the perfect naïveté also as thus occupied, of his sixteenth year, to which the somewhat lengthy or attenuated structure of the limbs is conformable."

Here is a beauty of language which suggests a carved agate or a liquid amethyst. It is not the beauty of spontaneity or abounding life, but the beauty achieved by the craftsman, with deliberate purpose, who will not lay down his tool, or hesitate to cast aside a damaged stone, until he reaches what, at any rate for the moment, seems to him perfection. It is this kind of beauty which made Robert Louis Stevenson's work such hard writing and such easy reading.

There is a third kind of beauty in prose which may raise it to the rank of literature, viz., intensity of feeling. The human soul under strong emotion is very beautiful; the face flushes, and the eye gleams, and the body throws itself into striking postures; under this kind of inspiration a plain and uninteresting person is transfigured. When we meet the orator, the singer, the actor, in private, we can hardly believe that this ordinary, quiet person was the centre of that brilliant display. In his brain, and on his tongue, for the moment, the powers of the universe had rolled and thundered, the soft music of things had whispered, the fountain of tears had been unsealed, the vast mirth of the happy ages had rippled and laughed. So it is in books. Writing which succeeds in expressing genuine emotion, if that emotion is beautiful, becomes beautiful with that which it expresses; it is suffused with the light, the warmth, the sweetness, of its subject. Thus historical writing, like Macaulay's or Froude's, may attain the rank of literature, not by accuracy or impartiality, which are the tests of history, but by the conviction and feeling which burn through it.

The "Pilgrim's Progress" is literature, in spite of the judgment of the author of "Ionica" that it is "wretched stuff." The immeasurable seriousness of its theme is heightened by the wittiest characterization, and by gay pictures drawn from contemporary England. But through it all runs the deep feeling of eternity and human destiny. Its homespun stuff is shot through with threads of the cloth of gold.

There is a fourth beauty which will raise apparently pedestrian prose to the rank of literature — that is, lucidity, a quality hard of attainment and very rare. For few souls are lucid, and when they are they are surrounded with an opaque and obscuring integument which it is difficult to break through. Many people are capable of clearness to the length of a one-page letter, others can carry it to the length of a newspaper article, but only gifted minds can maintain clearness through a prolonged composition. A book which is lucid from beginning to end gains, and deserves, readers. If its theme is truth of permanent value, the book will become literature. This is how Hooker's "Ecclesiastical Polity" and Adam Smith's "Wealth of Nations" have attained their rank. Hume's philosophy is not of permanent value, but his writing is transparently clear, and he will be admitted to the slopes of Parnassus when the philosophical schools have banned him as barren. Defoe is a master of this fascinating lucidity; he will persuade you of the truth of everything he touches, because he makes it too clear to be classed with fiction. Cobbett, and John Bright, and Spurgeon have probably attained a permanent place in literature, and will outlast sounding names and weighty writers, for they are gifted with an admirable clearness. People have tried to explain it by saying that they use Saxon words in preference to the Latin and other foreign imports in our language. But that is not true. If you examine a paragraph of these writers, you are surprised to find that they use long words, like other men. Cobden has the same charm of clearness; that will be granted even by Tariff Reformers. According to these modern economists, he carried Free Trade by his lucidity. But consider the following passage, and note how free the language is from the affectations of simplicity, how unhesitating is the use of words of Latin extraction, and yet how clear and telling every phrase is:

"A famine fell upon nearly one-half of a great nation. The whole world hastened to contribute money and food. But a few courageous men left their homes in Middlesex and Surrey, and penetrated to the remotest glens and bogs of the west coast of the stricken island to administer relief with their own hands. To say that they found themselves in the valley of the shadow of death would be but an imperfect image. They were in the charnel-house of a nation. Never since the fourteenth century did pestilence, the gaunt handmaid of famine, glean such a harvest. In the midst of a scene which no field of battle ever equalled in danger, in the number of the slain or the sufferings of the surviving, those brave men moved as calm and undismayed as if they had been in their own homes. The population sank so fast that the living could not bury the dead; half-interred bodies protruded from the gaping graves; often the wife died in the midst of her starving children, while the husband lay a festering corpse by her side. Into the midst of these horrors did our heroes penetrate, dragging the dead from the living with their own hands, raising the head of famishing infancy, and pouring nourishment into parched lips, from which shot fever flames more deadly than a volley of musketry. Here was courage. No music strung the nerves; no smoke obscured the imminent danger; no thunder of artillery deadened the senses. It was cool self-possession and resolute will, calculating risk, and heroic resignation. And who were these brave men? To what gallant corps did they belong? Were they of the horse, foot, or artillery force? They were Quakers from Clapham and Kingston. If you would know what heroic acts they performed you must inquire from those who witnessed them. You will not find them recorded in the volume of reports published by themselves, for Quakers write no bulletins of their victories."

It may be thought that this passage exhibits some of the other beauties which have been enunciated, but its chief beauty is its transparent lucidity. The subject is one which might lend itself to dithyrambics, to turgidity, to hysterics. But it is clear as the revealing light of morning; it looks down on the sufferings and heroism of men with the tranquil radiance of the stars.

This leads us to a fifth beauty, which gives to some writing, of no literary pretension, an enduring place as literature — that is, the power of exact and exhaustive statement. For example, no writer ever eschewed ornament and fine writing more than Bishop Stubbs. His principal theme, constitutional history, precludes everything of the kind. But all he wrote may challenge a place in the literature of his country, because he can marshal an immense mass of facts, and place them in their proper connection. The fulness of truth that he conveys, with the parsimony of language, produces a sense of beauty, precisely like the beauty of an austere chalk down in Sussex, or that of a vast stream moving past treeless banks.

But no one illustrates this kind of beauty which

makes literature better than Darwin. He was under the impression that he could not write. When he attempted to record the results of his patient observation, and to reason out the truths which were demonstrated by the vast accumulation of facts, he felt that he was grasping an unaccustomed weapon. He expected no success; but he achieved a success which surpasses the achievement of the literary artists of his time. He struggled to put into the plainest language the truth which was in him. He aimed only at conveying to the reader what was proved to him. Of himself as the medium he did not think at all. The result is that his books are valuable, not only as works of science, but as literature. The *Origin of Species* is a masterpiece of English. Even the treatise on earth-worms is of hardly less literary beauty than Maeterlinck's exquisite book on the bee. This brings us back to the principle with which we start — that it is, after all, truth which makes good prose; the beauty of truth is the excellence which of itself will suffice to rank prose as literature. Beauty is not ornament or tinsel; it may be in form and texture.

To create the love of literature is a salutary object of education. Nor is anything else needed than to discriminate clearly between what is literature and what is not. Taste comes from discrimination. The mind trained to a love of literature will turn with fastidious distaste from writing which does not approach the standard.

The five beauties of prose-writing — viz., poetry which eschews metrical form, the construction of gems of thought or expression, the utterance of genuine and worthy emotion, clearness in style, exactitude and fulness of statement — are found in a remarkable combination and harmony in one English book. The Bible contains much poetry, though the metrical form is obscured in translation. Job, Psalms, and Lamentations, and even passages of the Prophets, are literally poems. But the Bible, taken as a body of prose, is unequalled in our literature. It has passages of concentrated poetical expression, in the Pauline letters or in the Apocalypse. It abounds with gems of thought and expression which have passed into common speech and have done more than anything else to enrich our language. No writing ever throbbed with deep and noble feeling more than Deuteronomy or the Gospels. Lucidity of expression has never been better attained than in the historical narratives, in the Book of Proverbs, or the writings of John. And though so much matter, and so great a tract of time, are compressed within the one volume, it contains passages of minute and exact statement, as in the Law, or in Ezekiel, or in the teaching of Jesus, which constitutes a supreme literary beauty.

Thus a man *unius libri*, as Wesley claimed to be, knowing only the English Bible, might know all that needs to be known for literary purposes, and should certainly have the unerring instinct for literary excellence.

CHAPTER X

ART

ART is like religion in this, that it suffers most from its devotees. But it is also like religion in this, that no extravagance or fanaticism of its schools or sects can ever destroy it; it is an inalienable accident of the human mind. From the time when Palæolithic man graved on his stone axe the outline of a reindeer, to the time when Pheidias moulded in marble the living forms of the frieze of the Parthenon; from the time when the Druids stained their bodies with woad, to the time when Gainsborough draped his ladies in folds of silk or satin and in exquisitely studied plumes, which blended with the landscape behind the sitter, until art and Nature appeared to be inseparable; from the gold ornaments found in the remains of the lake dwellings at Glastonbury to the coronals of diamonds which are sold in Regent Street, art springs up in the life of man as surely as season follows season in the year.

The schools and cults and affectations of art invest its devotees with an air which often provokes the contempt and wrath of the unregenerate, but the true artist is welcome to humanity as a child. Indeed, as George Sand said, great artists are great children.

It was my lot to be at Oxford in the days of the Æsthetes, and one of my contemporaries was that brilliant man, whose affectations were the prelude to brilliant achievements in verse and prose, but whose art was the cover for one of the most tragic moral disasters of modern times. It was he who filled his college-rooms with blue china, and said to his friends, "How hard it is to live up to one's blue china!" It was he who passed the severest censure on another man by saying that "he whistled while he took his bath — so un-Greek!" It was he who wrote the ballad of Reading Gaol, and that exquisitely poignant book, the consummation of literary art, in which humility and contrition and repentance were used as the material for a dramatic masterpiece.

The Preraphaelite Movement, which Mr. Holman Hunt has vindicated in his autobiography, that masterpiece of many-coloured prose, was, as it were, exploited and rendered ridiculous by the affectations of the Æsthetes. Mr. Justin MacCarthy's satire is almost literal truth. "The typical Preraphaelite," he says, "believed Mr. Dante Rossetti and Mr. Burne-Jones to be the greatest artists of the ancient or modern world. If any spoke to him of contemporary English poetry he assumed that there was only a question of Mr. Rossetti, Mr. Swinburne, or

Mr. Morris. In modern French literature he admired Victor Hugo, Baudelaire, and one or two others newer to song, and of whom the outer world had yet heard little. Among the writers of older France he was chiefly concerned about François Villon. He was an enthusiastic admirer of the paintings of the late Henri Regnault. Probably he spoke of France as 'our France.' He was angry with Germans for having vexed 'our France.' He professed faith in the philosophy of Schopenhauer and the music of Wagner, and he was greatly touched by Chopin. He gave himself out as familiar with the Greek poets, and was wild in his admiration of Sappho. He made for himself a sort of religion out of wall-papers, old teapots, and fans. He thought to order, and yet, above all things, piqued himself on his originality. He and his comrades received their opinions, as Charlemagne's converts their Christianity, in platoons. He became quite a distinct figure in the literary history of our time, and he positively called into existence a whole school of satirists in fiction, verse, and drawing, to make fun of his follies, whimsicalities, and affectations." [1]

The description, with slight alterations, will apply to the cliques and coteries of any day, the dupes of art, the parasites of great artists. I have heard it said of a much more recent specimen of the same type that "his back-bone had been removed, and in place of it had been inserted a ha'porth of Botticelli."

[1] "History of our Own Time," iv. 542.

These are the people who invent a formula like "art for art's sake," who are irritated when any one speaks of the morality, or even of the subject, of a picture. Art, according to these virtuosos, has nothing to do with morality; the subject is a matter of indifference. They are contemptuous of a painter who uses his skill with the brush to tell a story, or to make an appeal of any sort to the ordinary mind, which values a picture for its interest and not for its technical qualities. These are the people who would have killed art, if it had been mortal.

It is this affectation of the shallow minds, tricking themselves in the feathers of art, but totally unconscious of its depths or of its significance, that has made some of the greatest minds, themselves true artists, contemptuous, and even inimical to art. Plato would banish the poets from his ideal state as liars; Carlyle considered nothing worth saying which could not be put into prose. But both Plato and Carlyle were great artists. The "Republic" itself is a poem; so is the "French Revolution." The great artists are prone to sweep away impatiently the summer-flies of art which buzz about their ears. They take their art seriously; they are expressing through it the best that is in them, and the beauty, tragical or comical, that they see in things. The petty tribe of virtuosos and connoisseurs, therefore, with their shallow formula, "art for art's sake," and the like, and their ignorant theories, separating art from life and from humanity, are infinitely tedious and annoying to them. If *they* represent art, let art go. Let us have done with art, with tricks, and come back to Nature and reality.

But art is not the victim of its blind admirers. It survives because it is of the texture of life, and is incorporate in humanity. It is the instinctive effort of man to express his deepest ideas and his strongest emotions, to arrest in a form which may be permanent the beauty which he perceives everywhere, shooting through things, like the gleam on a silk robe, hovering over all things, like the changing sky. The artist is one who conceives it as his function to practise the forms of expression, that he may utter what is not only in him, but in his fellows. His work is no child's play. He must submit himself to the severest discipline, and train his faculties with assiduous care, if he is to attain success. The amateur and the dilettante have not the brain or muscle, the will and the resolution, to be artists. No one treading the primrose-path of dalliance acquires the superb self-mastery which makes expression sure, triumphant, and inevitable. As Ruskin put it in "Flors Clavigera," [1] the artist is "a person who has submitted, in his work, to a law which it was painful to obey, that he may bestow, by his work, a delight which it is gracious to bestow."

The artists, therefore, are the exact opposite of the dilettanti and the easy critics. They suffer the fools, sometimes too gladly, for few men are free

[1] Vol. v. 301.

from the love of admiration and even flattery. But the chatterers and poseurs of the cliques and of the schools know nothing of art. They have no conception of its strenuousness, its seriousness, nor of the vital and essential connection that exists between beauty and truth.

Thus art finds its place, as Professor Eucken shows, in the life of the Spirit. "The outer," he says, "far as it may fall short of being a factor with equal rights, yet seems indispensable in order to drive the inner to definite decision and complete organization; with its power of stimulation and reaction it is an important element in the process of life. All artistic creation proves the truth of this, and thereby furnishes, as Goethe said, the happiest assurance of the eternal harmony of existence. But the clearest proof of it is the indirect one from the experience of humanity. For wherever form has been despised and neglected, life has soon degenerated and finally sunk into barbarism. Form, with its close union of inner and outer, is indispensable in order to call forth spiritual life, bring it to full power, and make it penetrate the breadth of things. Hence it can be easily understood how it was possible that form should become the central conception of a cult of immanent idealism." [1]

Or again: "Without the creative activity of art there can be no successful construction of an independent spiritual world in the human sphere, for

[1] "The Life of the Spirit," p. 205.

this construction involves the severance of the subject from the confused initial situation and a creative effort in contradistinction to it. Would not a movement of this kind fall into the void unless imagination went on in advance, giving form to the invisible and keeping it constantly present with insistent, rousing, and stimulating force? The importance of this is most clearly shown by the historical religions, with their impressive pictures of new worlds, their pictures of the kingdom of God and the last judgment, of the future heaven and earth, or else of the endless succession of worlds — pictures which sometimes inspired men with deep longing and sometimes filled them with horror and dread. But in all the departments of life no essential progress is possible unless imagination thus opens up the way; and the life of the individual needs it as well, for it is only when an ideal picture of itself is constructed and kept in mind that this life can enter upon an inner movement of ascent, and thereby rise superior to the dull routine of every day. An activity of an artistic nature is also indispensable for the organization of what this inner ascent has enabled us to acquire. Such an activity alone can extend what has been seen on the heights to the whole breadth of life, and make what was at the beginning distant and strange in the end near and familiar. An artistic activity of this kind, which is grounded in the connections of spiritual reality, cannot be isolated, in spite of all its independence of other departments of life, and cannot lead men on the road towards a feeble and unnerving æstheticism." [1]

If the Professor, then, is right, art is not a matter of rouge and castanets, nor the work of mimes and dancing girls. It is rather a matter of life itself, and must be undertaken by the strongest souls endowed with peculiar gifts. That it gives such deep pleasure is apt to mislead us, for its object is not pleasure. That it adorns life makes us oblivious of the fact that it is life, a necessary part of life. It is, therefore, one of the gravest calamities which can befall a people, when art has degenerated and has become identified with emptiness and immorality. A fiery Puritanism feels itself compelled to banish it, and in its banishment human life degenerates.

Puritanism and the Restoration are swings of the pendulum. But Puritanism is nearer to truth and beauty than the Restoration, as even the most careless visitor to the National Portrait Gallery can see. For the sober-hued portraits of Walker's men of the Commonwealth are artistically more beautiful than the florid coarseness of Dobson's men of the Court of Charles II.

"Religious ideas and religious emotions under the Puritan habit of mind," says Professor Dowden, "seek to realize themselves not in art, but without any intervening medium in character, in conduct, in life. In an ordered life, an ordered household, an ordered Commonwealth according to the Puritan,

[1] *Op. cit.* p. 264.

the Spirit is to be incarnated." But Milton is a perpetual protest against the falsehood of the extreme. He stands at the heart of Puritanism, asserting, with the stoutest of his compeers, that the ordered life, the ordered household, and the ordered Commonwealth is the true incarnation of the Spirit, but also, with every nerve and fibre of his sensitive being, declaring how music, painting, verse are essential to the order of life, household, or Commonwealth. We cannot be indifferent to these things. The soul of a man, and the soul of a society, withers and perishes, unless some gifted minds "of imagination all compact" can body forth its ideal, and present it with the images towards which it is to grow. The intrinsic beauty is not always visible to the eye, nor is the harmony of the spheres always audible to the ear. The world looks drab and casual, a rapid succession of vanishing scenes rather than a paradise or a city of God. The sounds which assail the ear are often discordant, or unintelligible. The beauty we thought was there is gone, the music we thought we heard is silent. Discouraged and disillusioned humanity relaxes effort and stops its march. Now is the artist needed. He does not take the place of the prophet or the seer; he is the prophet and the seer. He does not usurp the work of evangelist and apostle, but he is needed to bathe the evangel in the iridescent colours of the heavens, and to carry the apostle forward to the sound of music. He begins the high chant of the things that always were and of the things that are to be. And the mighty process of evolution becomes an ordered march, a march to the melody of which the feet of men can move. "Mother," said a child, as the military band marched along the street, "how is it that the music makes me feel happier than I am?" The answer is one of the great secrets, and the justification of all great art.

The artist paints his picture or fetches his statue out of the marble, and immediately the world is seen to be a great landscape or seascape, blossoming, wind-swept, glinting with light; and human forms are seen to be beautiful, even divine.

The artist tunes his orchestra and sounds his prelude. Then the great piece proceeds. We are at a high music. All the thoughts of men seem to be transcended; all the experiences of men, the passion, the rapture, the sorrow, the pain, are blended and harmonized. The world seems noble and full of meaning; the heavens bend over it with conscious and palpitating stars. The claim of Abt Vogler does not seem to be extravagant. "God has a few of us He whispers in the ear. 'Tis we musicians know."

The function of the artist, therefore, is not mere pleasure. It is the highest or among the highest known to men. As Hegel puts it, the object of art in the State is to render visible the Divine, presenting it to the imaginative and intuitive faculty.[1]

[1] "Philosophy of History," p. 5.

Thus, there have been times when the religion of a community has lost its savour. The breath has passed out of it, so that it cumbers the ground with arid formulæ or lifeless ritual, a kind of dustheap to which none would resort except for the most terrestrial of reasons. And then men are kept in touch with God, and their true spiritual environment, for a time, by the work of the artist alone. The twin pair of Sirens, music and verse, or the imaginative work of the painter, the sculptor, and the architect, or, it may be, that attempt to combine all the arts in one, the drama, will carry home to an irreligious generation the reality of religion. The Divine will become more manifest in the hands of the artist than on the lips of the preacher.

Yes, great artists are great children; they are the children of the Father. In their round text-hand they copy His legends. Though they think they are playing, amusing themselves and others with their toys, their very games are doing what they have seen their Father do. Unknown to themselves they render visible the Divine.

It will be seen, then, that in relation to art we have a twofold problem which we do not very steadily realize, viz., to retain and yet to restrain it. If we cannot restrain, we shall not retain, it. But the retention is the main thing. If art vanishes, human life degenerates and decays. And yet if art is not restrained by the master principles of life and humanity, it becomes a corruption, instead of a salvation, of life, and, indeed, imperceptibly changes into another influence altogether.

For example, it is wholesome to remember that Nero was above everything an artist. Art for art's sake was the principle on which he lived. To be a musician and a poet was more to him than to be the Imperator. He desired the bay of Apollo more than the crown of the Cæsars. He scandalized Roman propriety by entering into the artistic competitions of his time. The German Emperor composes operas, and his subjects are pleased with the results of imperial relaxation. But the severity of the Roman spirit could not tolerate an artist as Emperor. The contempt of the artist in Italy lasted down to the Renaissance. Benvenuto Cellini defends Dante for referring to the miniature painter Oderisi, not on the ground that the craft of Giotto and Cimabue deserved recognition among the great achievements of mankind, but on the ground that the love of glory animates even the lowliest, "seizes on all men with so little distinction, that even lowly craftsmen are anxious to gain it, even as we see that painters put their names on their works, as Valerius writeth of a famous painting."

To Italian eyes, Nero degraded himself by being an artist in poetry and music, and his pathetic cry in death, "*Qualis artifex pereo!*" — "What an artist dies in me!" has been subject rather of contempt than of pity. But why was Nero's art not art? Why does the picture of his Court and of his reign leave upon the mind a blurred image of ugliness and horror? The most magnificent revival of classical splendour in architecture, painting, and music, and even the stage which presented the plays of Seneca, remain in the memory only as a confusion of blood and lust. The plain fact is that art without goodness changes into its opposite. It becomes "procuress to the lords of hell." It is blighted and blasted, and becomes first a devastating conflagration and then a calcined ruin.

This is very curious and interesting. For there is, of course, a sense in which art and morality are totally distinct. A dominant insistence on morality, as Puritanism showed, may repress art. Prudery may blunt the perceptions and draw a veil of decency over the eyes, through which beauty itself cannot be seen. A painter who sets about a picture to enforce a moral lesson, like a writer who composes poetry or writes a story with a didactic purpose, will very probably fail. Goodness may be very inartistic and may thereby lose half its charm. But while goodness may be divorced from art, art cannot be divorced from goodness. Licentiousness cannot long employ art in her service, any more than superstition can. In the hands of debauchery and idolatry, strange to say, art quickly dies. In Plato the good and the beautiful are covered by one word τὸ καλόν. Shall we gradually learn to hail the Platonic language as an omen? Beauty without goodness is a flower torn from its root; it is sure to wither.

This morning in the garden, lashed by the winds and rain of March, I picked up a crocus which lay prone. A sparrow had nipped the stalk and pecked the leaves. It was draggled in the soil. I opened its delicate-veined petals, which were limp and drooping. I laid bare its heart of fire, for the pistil and the stamens were still dusted with golden pollen, and unconscious of the ruin which had befallen them. And I saw before me the image of art dissevered from the mother earth of humanity and goodness.

The truth is concealed by the fact that the cut flower retains its apparent life for a time. The heart of fire burns when the corolla has decayed. A school of painting, for example, will survive though moral death has set in. A strange beauty, as of decay, will cling about it. Then it will be said, "See how art can live without goodness, how your artists can be licentious, non-moral, and yet preserve the cult of beauty." But this is a delusion which vanishes on investigation. The Italian schools of painting are instructive. Why did the mighty art of the Renaissance decay? Why should the perfection of Raphael, the subtle omniscience of Leonardo, the giant strength of Michael Angelo lead on to the pitiable decline of Julio Romano, the Carracci, Michael Angelo Caravaggio? The answer, that when once perfection is reached the successors of the masters must overstrain themselves and plunge into extravagance and decline, is too easy. Too easy, for surely there is nothing to hinder men of genius from taking their own line, and avoiding the fatal error of imitation.

The explanation lies much deeper. Very early in the Renaissance a profound moral corruption set in. With the models of Greek Art came an imitation of Greek morals. The schools of the painters were invaded by impurity and weakened by hypocrisy. Perugino was Raphael's master. His sense of beauty and technical skill were, in his time, unrivalled. The illusion he produces on the spectator is almost complete. It is hard to suspect evil in the painter of modest and delicate virgins. Surely the soul that could feel and represent those lucent Umbrian skies, with the blue mountain distances, and the dainty poplars pencilled against the living light, must be pure. How debonnair is the step of Tobias and of the angel? Could that be conceived by a corrupt heart? Our suspicion is aroused, perhaps, when Michael, the stern warrior that subdues the dragon, is represented as a carpet knight, whose armour is undinted, whose curls are unruffled, by the combat. But the transparent clearness and purity of colour deceive us. We fancy Pietro a devotee, kneeling before the Madonna, whom he worshipfully paints, and joining already in the canticle of his white-robed angels that wheel and sing on their filmy ground of summer clouds. But the secret is out in Vasari: "He was a person of scant religion, and never could get himself to believe in the immortality of the soul; wherefore with words suited to his own flinty brain he most obstinately rejected all good doctrine. He had all his hope in the gifts of fortune; and for money he would have undertaken to do any ill deed." Here was the seed of decay. Raphael's personal elevation, Michael Angelo's titanic religious faith and life of austere self-contempt, could not arrest the germs of evil that were latent in the schools of the Renaissance.

It is noticeable that a wave of spiritual life and moral reformation, like that which flowed from Savonarola, would arrest judgment and temporarily save art. Lorenzo da Credi and Sandro Botticelli submitted to the regenerating influence of the movement. In those pure Madonnas of the one, with the vases of flowers, and the glimpses into holy country scenes, and in those circling hosts around the throne, of the other, showing this common earth, even this actual Florence, with the open lilied tomb, overmastered by the ranks and companies of saints, martyrs, doctors, principalities, and powers, earth filled with heaven, we are aware how art revives and recovers its beauty when it is brought again into contact with the good, the true, and the spiritual.

But the moral corruption of the Renaissance was the ruin of its art. Beauty cannot live in an atmosphere of intrigue, assassination, and shameless greed. Italy is beautiful. Her cerulean seas and azure skies; her lofty peaks, often crowned with cities; her rivers, fed by the snows; her pines, her cypresses, her ilexes, her oleanders, oranges, and arbutus, endow her with a loveliness which never can decay. Virgil's passionate love is echoed in every observant heart that visits her still, as it sees with rapture

> "Tot congesta manu præruptis oppida saxis,
> Fluminaque antiquos subterlabentia muros." [1]

Moreover, every city of the enchanted land is filled with memorials of former greatness. Ruined viaducts and triumphal arches span the plains and roads. Vast amphitheatres still render faint echoes of the plaudits of an assembled city. Churches, sculptured, pictured with mosaic, white against the blue sky, rising serene above the crowded streets and lanes; palaces, ramparted, grilled, with fountained courtyards, glimpses of perpetual green and whispering shade; terraces, gardens, with statues and marble seats, and soft distances of hill and plain, speak of the toil, the passion, the faith of the past. Every city has its galleries of paintings and sculptures. Almost every church has its treasured masterpiece. It is the land sacred to beauty.

And yet modern Italian painting is muddy and trivial and coarse, without elevation of subject, without beauty of line or colour. The Italians are engaged in socialistic agitation, in struggles for clerical domination, and chiefly in comic opera and

---

[1] "The cities piled along precipitous peaks,
And rivers lapsing under ancient walls."

melodrama, apparently unconscious of their past, and untouched by the beauty which surrounds them. It is evident that art is the product of moral forces, and decays when goodness dies. Not even the splendid monuments of the past can revive it. Blurred eyes and palsied hands cannot profit by the examples of loveliness which were created by hearts that felt the impulse of the Divine, and learnt to paint by learning to pray.

Perhaps the moral foundations of art can be discovered also in the modern schools of France. The schools which produced Corot and Millet should be vital and inspiring. No eye ever saw more truly than Corot's the silvery beauty of a landscape under the delicate drooping of trees, crossed by gentle rivers. No heart ever felt more keenly than Millet's the pathos of labour and the humble piety which sheds light and romance on the bare furrows of the field. But Corot and Millet were religious men, and exceptions; the schools of France have taken a different course. The life of art-students is emancipated from moral restraints, and defies not only religion, but decency. The result was apparent in the instructive comparison of the French and English schools, when the pictures of the two were placed side by side in the Franco-British Exhibition of 1908.

Possibly the first impression made by the French pictures was the muddiness of their colours. The next was the ugliness of the portraits. Then, one realized the poverty of subjects. The Church furnished a few picturesque processions and ceremonies. For the rest, the Casino, the boulevard, and the bath-room of women seemed the chief stock-in-trade. If mankind should begin to weary of nakedness and shame, where would French art be? I can never forget the bewilderment with which I stood before a picture which in the catalogue was marked "Beauty." It represented, against a dun background, a semi-nude woman, with long, wiry hair, of the kind which one associates with savages. There was no beauty of feature. The flesh was not beautifully painted, in the way that makes Velasquez's Venus beautiful, in spite of itself. No beauty of form or colour or idea. A coarse, ugly, soulless woman, with brindled hair and inadequate garments — this was Beauty. Why? When goodness fades out of the brain, when purity, love, and the excellences of the soul cease to please, what is left for art is only lust and its sickening reaction. Beauty cannot long survive when goodness has been permitted to die.

Art is a necessary activity of the human spirit, an attempt to express the life of the universe, the soul of things, manifesting itself in many forms, the human form among the rest. It is as necessarily connected with God as man is. If man must be good, if morality is only the formulated doctrine of his goodness, art must be good too. If it loses touch with goodness, it loses touch with life and with reality. Directly it becomes indifferent to the good it becomes blind. Seeing only the evil and driven by the impulse to imitate or to reproduce, it eliminates the good, and reproduces plastically the evil, only the evil. It calls itself impressionist or realist. It eschews idealism. But under these morbid and debased conditions its only impressions are the passing, the evanescent, the unimportant. It gets no impression of the noble, the eternal, the exalting, which runs through life and the world. Its realism does not mean that it depicts what is real. The real is far indeed from seeing; this art has become radically incapable even of understanding it. What it mistakes for the real is that selection of coarseness and ugliness and corruption which its own diseased sight is alone capable of seeing.

Perhaps, then, we begin to see an answer to the question why, with all the examples of beauty before us, we do not necessarily produce or love the beautiful. We are puzzled why an Academy should be trivial, cheap, and thin, when all the artists had access to the National Gallery, and most of them have studied in France or Italy. We wonder why, with Westminster or Chartres before them, the architects of to-day cannot build beautiful houses, why the public buildings of our towns are for the most part ambitious imitations of the worst features of past styles. We ask why our furniture is not beautiful when our workmen have all the best models to imitate. How comes it that, with all that has been said and written on art in the last half-century, we build nothing like the Doge's Palace, and cannot even rival our own painters of a century ago, Reynolds, Gainsborough, Romney, or Constable?

The answer is that by the most misguided teaching on the subject art has been separated from life, from goodness, and from God. In that isolation it rapidly becomes idolatrous; it takes the place of God, of goodness, and of life. It is not religious, but becomes a religion. But when this occurs art declines; its peculiar possession of beauty slips out of its hands.

That is a strange passage in "The Stones of Venice,"[1] not sufficiently explained by Ruskin's admitted inconsistencies and contradictions, in which he wonders whether art is a real minister of religion: "I do not know, as I have repeatedly stated, how far the splendour of architecture or other art is compatible with the honesty and usefulness of religious service. The longer I live the more I incline to severe judgment in this matter, and the less I can trust the sentiments excited by painted glass and coloured tiles. But if there be, indeed, value in such things, our plain duty is to direct our strength against the superstition which has dishonoured them; since there are thousands to whom they are now merely an offence owing to their association with absurd or idolatrous ceremonies. I have but this exhortation for all who

[1] Appendix, xii. p. 371.

love them, not to regulate their creeds by their taste in colours, but to hold calmly to the right at whatever present cost to their imaginative enjoyment; sure that they will one day find in heavenly truth a brighter charm than in earthly imagery, and striving chiefly to gather stones for the eternal building, whose walls shall be salvation and whose gates shall be praise."

How wise is this from the greatest lover and exponent of art in the nineteenth century! A doubt invades the mind in some quiet cathedral city, where the trim decencies of the present enshrine the pieties and the art of six hundred years. For this exquisite and storied building does not produce or conserve a progressive religion. Round its venerable walls, close to its sculptured portals, human poverty and depravity and unbelief surge and beat defiantly. Even in the sleepy and corrupt community which has gathered about the beautiful monument of religion the vital religious work is probably being done in some building devoid of beauty, or in no building at all.

It all points to the same conclusion. "Art for art's sake" is an impossible formula. Nothing, not even art, liveth to itself. When art is for art's sake it ceases to be art. Art is for life's sake, for truth's sake, for goodness' sake, for God's sake, or it dies. It is the crested and iridescent foam upon the waters of life, beautiful, as it is thrown up by the deep, swiftly moving and proudly chafing stream, perpetual as the stream and as the sunshine into which its crystal beads are flung. But in vain shall you attempt to separate this delicate curtain of spray, or this gurgling joy of tumultuous foam, from the river which produces it. By the time it is separated it has lost its beauty, it has even ceased to be. As it is flung up by the infinite yearning and onward striving of the spirit of man, its vitality depends upon his life, its beauty comes from his beauty, its object is to keep him alive to the Divine atmosphere in which he moves.

George Meredith says of a brook that "it filled the lonely place with one onward voice." Art is "the onward voice" of the stream of life. Its music and its iridescence, its passion, its joy, lead him into his future, accomplish for him his destiny.

It is this which enables us to see the bearing of that other problem, how to *retain* the art, which admittedly we must restrain, how to save it from corruption, from the silence which has sometimes fallen on its music, from the pallid death which has sometimes dimmed its hues. It must be evident now that art is not an extra in the school of life, but a necessary part of the curriculum. It ranks with religion, and with morality; it is the blossom of life. Its loss implies deterioration and decay; its perversion is death.

First of all, for each person it is necessary to train and cherish the sense of beauty, and to develop whatever artistic faculties may be in him. It may seem dogmatic to assert that there is an absolute standard of beauty: for it has become an axiom among men that there is no disputing about tastes. But the margin of variations in taste no more disturbs the absoluteness of beauty, than the very similar margin of variations in moral ideas disturbs the absoluteness of morality. If we may use the language of transcendentalism, that which is beautiful to God is really beautiful; and the object of all culture is to bring the human mind into harmony with the Divine. It is a toilsome and even a tedious task. At first we count as beautiful garish colours, extravagant sounds, bombastic absurdities. Unaffected by the beauties of Nature we are captivated with a pantomime. The ingenuous girl who saw a moonlight effect in crossing the Atlantic, and exclaimed, "That's as good as a transformation scene in a theatre," represents the untrained childishness from which it is the object of education to deliver us.

But we are really educated just as we genuinely feel the beauty of what *is* beautiful, and are instinctively critical towards spurious or imperfect beauty.

I listened with interest the other day to a young man's remarks on the "atrocity" of Giovanni Bellini's "Garden of Gethsemane" in the National Gallery. He was perfectly candid and open, and of course the day will dawn when that faint flush of sunset in the West, the piled order of the town on the hill, the soldiers in the middle distance, the sleeping three in the foreground, and in the centre, on the bare rock of prayer, the Man of Sorrows, meekly accepting the "cup," which the ministering angel brings to him from heaven, will strike home to the mind of my young friend as a moment in the history of landscape, and as an eternal revelation of the mystery of love. But life must teach him.

In view of the necessity of art a country should not waste its artists. It is pathetic to know the struggles of the great painters; Richard Wilson dying unrecognized, Holman Hunt living down two generations of derision. The artists are generally children of artisans, born in humble circumstances, and condemned to a struggle from the beginning. Gainsborough and Morland are not born in the purple. Corot was the son of a barber. Wealth and ease discourage the strenuous discipline which is necessary to high achievement. But it is a calamity if an eye which sees, as Turner does, a colour sense which could produce the effects of Opie, a hand which can carve a frieze, or a heart which can conceive a new melody, should be lost to the world through the indifference of the public or the faults of an educational system. To see and to appreciate beautiful things is a gift which might be cultivated in many, but to produce them is a gift of more limited distribution. And we cannot afford to lose a single hand, or eye, or mind, which is capable of representing the divine to men, and of becoming the interpreter of life to those who only through art can learn.

The intense delight of painting, and the convenience of easel pictures, have partly obscured the function of art in beautifying the home, and in making even a small house the fit abode and school of human spirits. But beauty inwrought in the shape and furniture of rooms, in the outlook from windows, in the aspect of the house and garden, has more constant and beneficial effect than beauty shut up in an art gallery, or even artificially hung upon hooks. I stayed once in a house, which remains in my memory as a vista into worlds of visionary beauty. For over the mantelshelf of my chamber a daughter of the house had painted the "Water Babies." In a long sweep of gaily breaking waves, the tiny creatures danced: their auburn locks floated and mingled with the tresses of the breakers, their bodies seemed to sweep and swirl with the pliant waters, and to wreathe themselves in the eddies of the foam and the rapture of the spray. Their wide eyes of wonder, innocence, and delight looked down on the fortunate sleeper in that room. Here was Art doing her prescribed service to weary and world-worn men, bringing them back to the freshness of their dawn, and awaking in them their mysterious connection with the unknown forms of being which haunted our entrance, and await our exit, from this transitory scene.

Where the spirit of beauty works, a tiny house

may be made just as lovely as a palace. Nor is it a matter of expense. A flower, a fold of drapery, a patch of colour, an unexpected decoration on a door panel, a mere arrangement of lines and curves, may suffice to give distinction to a small suburban house. As the scarf of red on the shoulders of Ariadne in Titian's picture is said to be the most wonderful piece of red in the world — though in itself it is such a red as you may see anywhere, even in a shambles — so this fine sense of the beautiful can by a touch light up and redeem the commonest apartment. And it is beauty, not brought from without by unthinking wealth, but evolved from within by hearts that feel and love, which makes the charm and the spiritual value of a home.

And if it be important to invest the home with beauty, to make it at once the expression and the inspiration of the souls that inhabit it as their temporary tabernacle in their journey, it is even more pressing to make the towns and the cities in which more than three-quarters of our people live radiant and significant, rich in suggestion of a storied past or in hope of a noble future. It would seem that only religion can make a city beautiful. But art is the means which religion should employ. For a city made spiritually beautiful, and kept so, by an informing spirit, is the nurse of great men and gracious women; while a city which is foul and ugly stunts where it does not defile, degrades where it does not ruin, the character of its people.

The great cities were beautiful by reason of the service of God, and beauty will not again be possible in architecture and city-making until men can see again with Plato a city in the heavens, and with John the Divine that city in the heavens coming down to the earth. It was religion, sincere and passionate, which built the Parthenon, the Erechtheum, the Propylæa, and the Niké Apteros, to crown the Acropolis of Athens. No Athenian could work in his house, chaffer in the market, or assemble in the Pnyx, but he was confronted with the majesty and beauty of the divinities. High above the common life of men was the life of the gods. Gazing towards Helicon, with a sweep over the purple sea, Athene watched her worshippers and breathed into them the wisdom and the passion which have made Athens the intellectual mistress of the world. How could an Athenian be common or unclean, when through that translucent ether, against the living blue, struck with the glory of sunrise or sunset, he saw ever, in ivory and gold, the stainless symbol of purity and wisdom which the heart of Phidias conceived and the hand of Phidias executed?

High over Florence rose the Duomo, looking down on the little baptistery of San Giovanni, out of which had risen the city's growing glory, and flanked by Giotto's tower, like a flower in stone. Hard by in St. Mark's Savonarola lived and burned; there Fra Angelico saw his angels, and fastened his visions on the walls. Santa Croce on the one side, decorated by Giotto, contained the monuments of the great dead; Santa Maria Novella on the other held to the light the golden glory of Ghirlandajo, and in the dark vaults underneath the dream of Simone Memmi, the education of the youth of Florence conceived as the outpouring of the Spirit of Pentecost. Such a city produced great artists, and was made by them; Cimabue, Orcagna, Giotto, Donatello, Brunelleschi, Ghiberti, Fra Angelico, Fra Bartolommeo, Lippo Lippi, leading up to Buonarotti, Botticelli, and Luca della Robbia. Even now, when the spirit of Dante's city is flown, and the monuments of the great past look down on the sordid materialism and the trivial pleasures of modern Italy, a visitor can look through Casa Guidi's windows or through any other windows in Florence, and see the power of great men to build noble cities and the power of noble cities to make men great.

A city cannot be great whose chief building is a newspaper office or a music-hall. In vain will the hills curve its streets, and the suggestions of the sea bring health and expansion to body and soul, if individual greed is allowed to determine the buildings which shall be reared, and to poison its air with smoke or chemicals, and its moral atmosphere with heartlessness and lawless pleasure.

There must be a president beauty in the ordering and laying out of its squares and thoroughfares, of its central business houses and of its suburban dwellings, a spirit which readily controls the wilfulness and selfishness of its citizens, if it is to be great. Its river must be saved from pollution, and the banks must be adorned with terraces and the statues of noble men and women. The open spaces must be planted with trees and flowers. The streets must be clean, and intelligible. Old buildings which are beautiful must be preserved as treasure; buildings which do not contribute to the harmony of the whole must be disallowed or condemned. Especially the homes of the poor must be guarded against the disease and the dirt which are the cruel fate of poverty, and from the temptations which produce and seal the degradation of the weak and helpless.

Such a city, whether large or small, becomes the delight of those who visit it and the education of those who dwell in it. Thither the tribes go up; its blest inhabitants beautify the place of God's feet. For it must be evident to every reflecting mind that such a city can never be, unless it is a city of God. God must control the selfishness and inspire the dulness of men, before they can conceive or achieve such a city. God must be the glory in the midst and a wall of fire round about. For we cannot build a city of God on earth except in so far as it descends out of heaven.

Finally, art must come to the service of religion, not only in ordering the life of men, but in beautifying the worship of God. Notwithstanding the doubt which invaded the mind of Ruskin, and made him suspect the religious value of architecture, and

painting, and music, in worship, the irrepressible
instinct of mankind must be allowed. The mischief
appears when the art is summoned for pride and
vainglory, when the artist offers his service only
for money, when God fades out of the mind, and the
æsthetic effects are offered as a substitute for Him.
Then religion sinks into idolatry; art is defiled, and
indeed disappears.

But art has its place in worship, and worship is
incomplete without it. The mind which is truly
religious finds it intolerable to live in ceiled houses
while the house of the Lord lies desolate. It is
necessary to worship God; and the heart adds "in
the beauty of holiness"; yes, in beauty, such beauty
as we can command or express. That region of
delight which is made by music and painting, by
beautiful words in rhythm, chanted, recited, or sung,
by sweet odours and harmony of movement, is the
Gate Beautiful of the Temple. In that porch we
may not linger, but we may fitly pass through it
when we pray.

It need not be ostentatious or self-pleasing; but
the heart's love set on God, and eager to praise Him,
seeking some adequate expression of its mingled
reverence and delight, beats about for forms of expression. For it knows that its efforts will always
be inadequate, and its expressions will fall short of
the intention. Therefore it takes hold of all that
seems the most noble and exalted, in form, or colour,
or sound, and draws near to God in the house of

solemnities, where the light streams through storied panes; it uses the language of poetry and sets it to music for its praise, and offers the incense of flowers for its prayer. Knowing that all will come short, it yet does what it can to make the place of His feet glorious. It is not ritual; it is not lip-service. But religion has called her handmaid Art — busy as she is in the service of man — to see if she can do anything to help in the service of God.

I must close with a curious experience, one of those coincidences in life which incline one to believe that there is no chance or accident, but only the unfolding of a precedent design.

I was asked to preach in a school chapel on the annual prize day. I found that one of the features of the occasion was the unveiling of a window, the completion of a series which represented the life of Jesus. When the unveiling took place I found myself by accident close to the artist who designed the windows. He turned to me and said: "You did not know that you had any part in these windows, but you had. Some years ago I heard you preach on Giotto's frescoes in the Arena chapel at Padua. I thought to myself, 'Nothing would please me more than to have the opportunity of decorating a chapel in that way.' At last the opportunity came. I cannot tell you what it has been to me; for the study of our Lord's life, in order to make these designs, has given me a new and wonderful conception of Him. And now, when the whole series is completed, you come and preach in the chapel, and see the execution of the thought which your words inspired."

It would seem sometimes that God Himself is the great Artist; and we, ourselves and our lives, are His workmanship, His artistic creation, poem, or music, or painting, and that the artistic sense within us is derived from what we have the likest God within the soul.

CHAPTER XI

LIFE

> "Debilem facito manu,
> Debilem pede, coxa,
> Tuber adstrue gibborum,
> Lubricos quate dentes,
> Vita dum superest, bene est,
> Hanc mihi, vel acutâ
> Si sedeam cruce, sustine."
>
> — MÆCENAS.

THIS sentiment of the Epicurean Mæcenas is not at first blush very admirable: "Let me be feeble in hand, feeble in foot and thigh; pile a hunch on my back, shake my teeth crazy; while life lasts, all is well; that, though I should straddle a cross, however sharp, maintain for me." No, it sounds like a craven love of life. And we acknowledge that life is not to be desired too passionately nor purchased at too great a cost. In theory we are all agreed that a man should be ready to resign his life for a worthy object, and should not cling to it when it has ceased to be valuable.

But from another point of view the verses of Mæcenas are worthy of his fame as the leader of culture and the patron of literature at the Court of Augustus. They express with amazing energy, not to say fierceness, the truth that lies in Epicureanism, the *joie de vivre* which is or ought to be a fundamental fact of the world. Life is very good. To be alive is a sufficient reason for devout gratitude. Every living creature should each day offer a sacrifice of praise to the Source and Giver of life. Creatures that have no capacity to see beyond the sun may suitably render worship to that apparent origin of our existence. Creatures that are able to penetrate to the ultimate cause of that mediate agent must give thanks to God. Indeed, the instinct of praise in consciousness itself for being conscious compels a belief in a consciousness to which life is due. We find God in thanksgiving. The praise which life breathes for the gift of life is the intuitive evidence of the Giver.

But life is certainly very good. The diseased cling to it, in spite of their sufferings, the poor cling to it when they are deprived of all comforts. On the Thames Embankment — to the shame of our civilization — there are crouched every night the homeless waifs of the city. They are in rags, they are unfed, they are hopeless. They huddle on the seats, in the frost, in the rain, in the clammy fog of London. If the sun shines by day, these forlorn outcasts of the social system fling themselves on the turf of the parks, and they lie in all directions like slain soldiers after an engagement. They are indeed the victims of the fierce competitive battle of modern industrialism. Life is for them reduced to its lowest terms; they have life and nothing else, nothing to ameliorate or adorn it, nothing to give it value beyond what it possesses in itself. But life is to them sweet. They do not plunge themselves into the turbid river and permit the ebbing tide to carry them out into the blissful Nirvâna of the sea. They do not beg a copper to buy a dose of poison, and so end the weary struggle. Is it the interest of the struggle, the struggle to keep alive, which gives them energy to hold on? No, it is the positive sweetness of living itself. I fell into conversation with one of those wastrels the other day. A more pitiable object could not be seen. Hardly a rag held its place with security. Unkempt and cadaverous, he might have been a scarecrow set to guard the crops from the birds. But he was far from miserable. Strange to say, he was an American citizen, with the American firmness and deliberation of speech, and the American sense of dignity and equality. For ten years he had lived the wastrel life in this country, and had practically surrendered all hope or desire for the future. He had nothing but good to say of the country and the people, of the kindness and consideration which were shown to him, a penniless, helpless, and useless stranger. He had a firm faith in God, which could not be surpassed by Dives living in the mansion hard by. This Lazarus of modern civilization was in as fair a way to be carried to Abraham's bosom as the Lazarus of the parable.

My heart warmed to him. I encouraged him to try again, and harped a little on the energy and resource of the American character. For a moment an old light awoke in his eyes; but it quickly died away. He promised that he would make another effort. He accepted without effusiveness a small alms; but his eyes ranged over the open space and the distant horizon, and I saw that simply to live was enough for him. While there was air to breathe, and a crust to be found for asking, and now and again a night's shelter, he would be content.

Life is certainly very good. Paley, in that optimistic eighteenth-century manner, which in so many ways gets nearer to the truth of things than the extravagant faiths and unfaiths of the succeeding century, drew an inference to the goodness of God from a shoal of small fish, which he saw leaping in the line of the breakers on the shore and flashing in the sun. They were, he thought, obviously enjoying it, and their ecstasy argued a creative cause which was happy and happy-making. The closer observation of the natural world has greatly strengthened this argument since Paley's days. Once, on our western coast, — it was a bright December morning, — I was startled by what seemed a cloud rising out of the sea. But the cloud was vital, and moved and changed, not after the slow, impassive manner of clouds, but with a pulsating energy. Presently I perceived that it was a vast flight of dunlins. They rose, as if at the command of a choregus; they drew themselves out in long lines, like the wings of a vast bird of heaven; they wheeled round in ordered squadrons; they executed a maze of measured flights, all in perfect harmony, thousands of them moving as one. I picked up from the shore one of their number which had fallen out of the bright ranks, dead and stark, the glazed eyes seeing no longer the joy of his comrades. But there could be no doubt in my mind but that the swift, noiseless evolutions in the sky were the expression of a myriad-hearted delight. As I stood alone and watched, with no human companion to share or to disturb the doings above, I became aware of the vast, wide joy of the world. I thanked God that living creatures, from animals up to men, and beyond, are so infinite in number, because every life is a joy. Sensation, notwithstanding its possible or occasional pain, is rapturous.

Again, I shared with a friend a delicious sight. One morning in early spring we were at the Zoological Gardens, and came, we two alone, upon this scene. The gnus, those awkward and ferocious elf-like creatures, were out of their stalls in the paddock. They were, in sheer joy of the new spring, executing a dance. Their great heavy heads and horns were no impediment; they gyrated on their slender legs with the lightness of a Taglioni. Their movements were evidently prearranged during the winter, for they wheeled and returned, set to partners, locked and unlocked horns. It was a spectacle of such surprising gaiety that we stood entranced, and ever since that joy of the creation has returned in memory to confirm the belief that life, even for life's sake, is good.

It is a pity that we allow custom to stale, and the occasional sorrows and pains of life to dim, this obvious truth. Why do we not train ourselves to be surprised and to apprehend the joy of the world, the endless interest and charm of things? Some years ago a man named John Carruth, at the age of thirty, recovered his sight by an operation. In reading his first impressions, one felt heartily ashamed of not having made more of this wonderful world, of not having praised God more constantly for the gift of life and sight. Gazing for the first time on the landscape of simple beauty which surrounds his home at Crofthead, Bridge of Weir, he exclaimed: "There is bound to be a Creator for all this! I often dreamed that I could see the world, but I never imagined it so splendid as it is!" The rise and fall of the land struck him with admiration. He had not before understood why in walking it was sometimes harder, sometimes easier, to move; now the mystery was solved. He saw the shimmering water of Houston Head Loch, and another mystery was solved. He had been in the water, but could not understand how it gave way to him and why he could not hold it.

"Do you hear that bird singing?" he asked his companion. "Yes, it is a lark." "But do you see it rising in its song?" He watched it become a speck. He turned round, thinking of the birds he had heard, but never before seen, and asked, "Why don't people make more fuss about them?"

Yes, life is very good, to breathe, to enjoy the sun. All the senses give an exquisite delight. That beautiful spirit of Helen Keller, breaking out of the prison-house through the three senses of smell and touch and taste alone, has given to us all a new perception of the rapture in the senses of which she, dear soul! is deprived — the hearing and the sight. For it may be questioned whether there ever was a finer or a richer sensibility, more trained, more effective, more thrilling with joy, than this which never saw a sight or heard a sound. Her literary style is not only clear but coloured, not only strong but musical. She has told us how in a country walk all the landscape comes to her in the scents, and how she can feel by a vibration the running of a brook, or even, as she leans her head to the trunk of a tree, the whisper of the leaves.

No wonder all the resources of plastic art and of music fail to exhaust the delight that comes through the eye and the ear!

But Helen Keller's economic use of her frugal senses is the best possible comment on the resources of the soul. The soul is the life. In Greek one word is used for both. The soul communicates with the material world and with other souls, so far as they are embodied in a material tabernacle through the senses. But the life of man, at any rate (we can but faintly surmise the life of other creatures), is intrinsically the soul. It is not the sensations, nor the succession, nor the sum total, of sensations. It is the entity which receives sensations, and lives apart from them, the identity in the ceaseless flux of perceptions, the unity of concepts, the thread of personality. Life is the soul; it is the person. And because the soul is distinct from the material world, and from the lower life-forms, it reports differently of life. Personality admits of good and evil, a good exceeding good, an evil exceeding evil. While, therefore, speaking of life objectively, we can say and prove that it is very good, speaking of life subjectively, we are bound to admit that the soul is good or evil. When we wake to human life there is an appalling discovery — that it can be good or evil, unutterably good, unutterably evil.

The life of earth is good, only good. Its verdure of springing grass, its forests of leafy trees; its hidden treasures of minerals and gems, its rocks and stones and soil; its lucent air and gathering gloom, its pageantry of sunrise and noon and sunset, its arch of star-filled heavens above, and the star-filled heavens at the Antipodes, and around; its tiny amœba, the one undifferentiated cell alive, its range upon range of living things up to the mighty cachalot, which in the moonlight ocean struggles with and devours the lithe and clinging octopus; its swarming fishes in the river, the lake, and the sea; its birds migrating, or settling even in the frozen circle of the Antarctic pole; its animals of all kinds and sizes, burrowing in, or ranging over, its surface — this organic, bedded in the inorganic, springing out of it, passing into it, no one can tell how, is wholly good. It is true, life sustains life, species dies for species; the unit exists only for the whole, as a cell in a body, for the body. It is open, therefore, to a morbid and perverse human mind to complain that death pervades the life of earth, and that Nature is red in tooth and claw. But that is a manifest misreading, a jaundiced view which is corrected by the scientific purging of the eyes. It is the law of life that the grass feeds the graminivorous animals, and the graminivorous the carnivores. But the death of the animals is no more detraction from the goodness of life than the munching of the grass.

But the life which is soul may be good or bad. If it is good it continues the goodness of the lower forms, and leads to a transcendental goodness which connects itself with higher forms in the spiritual world; if it is bad it misreads the goodness of the lower forms, and connects itself with bad forms in the spiritual world, shaping for itself a mode of being which might conceivably be evil, whole and unredeemed. Edward Fitzgerald, commandeering, rather than translating, the "Rubaiyát" of Omar Khayyam, gives a faultless expression to the phenomenon:

"I sent my soul through the Invisible,
  Some letter of that after life to spell,
    And by and by my soul returned to me
    And answered: I myself am heaven and hell —

Heaven but the vision of fulfilled desire,
And hell the shadow of a soul on fire,
  Cast on the darkness into which ourselves
So late emerged from shall so soon expire."

The solemnity of the human soul is this, that it cannot by any possibility abide with the mere good life of the earth, rolled round with stocks and stones and trees, or sharing the life of the other animals. It is perfectly useless for Whitman to admire and to prefer that placid life:

"I think I could turn and live with animals, they are so placid and self-contained,
I stand and look at them long and long.
They do not sweat and whine about their condition,
They do not lie awake in the dark and weep for their sins,
They do not make me sick discussing their duty to God,
Not one is dissatisfied, not one is demented with the mania of owning things,
Not one kneels to another, nor to his kind that lived thousands of years ago,
Not one is respectable or unhappy over the whole earth." [1]

He might have added, Not one wrote a "Song of Myself," or could appreciate a line of "Leaves of Grass."

Life, when we are speaking of human life, cannot

---

[1] "Song of Myself."

be the life of the animals, any more than it can be the life of the mosses on the one hand or of angels on the other. It is a soul — that is to say, it shapes for itself a heaven or a hell, as Fitzgerald puts it, though it is by no means clear that it escapes by death the heaven or hell of its making. While proof is not available, human life cannot escape the doubt, the surmise, of the

> ". . . something after death,
> The undiscovered country, from whose bourn
> No traveller returns."

Indeed, whenever we come to work seriously at human life, we find its continued existence after death becoming first possible, then probable, then certain. We have no choice. We may covet life after death, or dread it. We may, with the Hindoo or the Buddhist, direct all our living energy to escaping it and to reaching the bliss of ceasing to be; or we may, with the Christian, strain every nerve to secure eternal life; we may have qualms of pain, as Huxley had, in thinking that at the end of the century he would exist no more than he did at the beginning;[1] or we may, with the despairing suicide, passionately desire to be "anywhere, anywhere out of the world." But a dispassionate inquiry leads to the irresistible conviction that we shall live and not die. We are destined for our eternity, whether we make that future the soul on fire from which we

[1] "Life and Letters of Thomas Henry Huxley," ii. p. 62.

recoil or learn to say with Obermann, "*Eternité, deviens mon asyle.*"

The dogmas, as Fitzgerald perceived, are in this case not the cause but the effect of the belief. Heaven and hell are not the creation of priests, who at the best have only garnished them, and at the worst have rendered them incredible. They emerge spontaneously in consciousness as the result of serious reflection on life, nay, as the result merely of living. I have heard of men vehemently declaring that they will die like the brutes, that they will cease to be, that there is no heaven or hell. But I have seen no evidence that any one seriously believes this. The belief in immortality is not a convention devised for the sake of influencing, or giving worth to, this present life (though it must be owned that it is difficult to give worth to life, or to maintain it as an upward progress, if personal life perishes in death), but it is an inevitable product of human life itself. Herbert Spencer quaintly explained it from dreams and shadows: primitive man saw his shadow and mistook it for his soul; he dreamed of a dead friend, and thought the vision a proof of his existence. This is far too naïve. When in his later life Spencer found out the defects of his own thought and deplored the loss of those spiritual experiences which he had failed to cultivate, he was awaking from the hypnotic trance into which his own system of thought had thrown him. With the utmost labour, and through a dozen weighty volumes, he had persuaded himself that his life was limited by the grave. But the delusion broke from him in the awaking. It is easier to persuade yourself that you are not existing now than that you will not exist after death. It is just as necessary, or as unnecessary, to offer proofs that we are now living as to offer proofs that we shall live. The one implies the other. Life, in the sense of soul, is persistent. It has come to be, not to perish. Explain it as you will, or strive to explain it away by any argument at your disposal, you cannot evade the conviction; it floats up to the surface of the mind in quiet hours, or in rare experiences: to say that "I am" is the same thing as to say "I shall be." To say "I die" is only to assert an experience of the Ego, a baffling experience, a plunge into the unknown; but of the words the "I" is dominant and persistent, the "die" is but transitory. "I," fully realized, is a term that precludes death.

The pressing problem is, not to show that life persists — for Nature sees to that argument — but how to use life, and to give value to it. Clearly a life that is already meaningless and purposeless cannot be improved by being made everlasting. A life that has become insipid, or a burden, here within the narrow limits of time, promises nothing but torture if it is continued into eternity. One may easily snatch at a Hindoo philosophy, and begin to covet Nirvâna, the cessation of personal consciousness, as the only desirable heaven, unless consciousness as we know it has acquired an intrinsic value, a flavour, a motive, an activity, which, prolonged to infinity, would be increasingly sweet and satisfying. Life must have an interpretation, a purpose, a positive quality, or the prospect of continuance may become no consolation, but a haunting fear.

How clearly in the sensuous life of the early Greeks this fact was realized is shown by the myth of Tithonus. The goddess had heedlessly endowed him with immortality. But old age and world-weariness came on. Her bright beauty and eternal youth ceased to charm him. The light of the sun oppressed him; the joy of the earth palled. It was death, not life, for which he panted; death, not life, of which his nerves were scant. The greatest terror that can fall upon the soul is not death, but a life which has become an intolerable *ennui*, which yet it is impossible to extinguish. Heaven may be as insufferable as hell for one who has not found the secret which makes life worth while, for one to whom the only delights of eternity are not attractive but tedious. There is no profanity, but a deep seriousness, in R. K. Stephen's apparently flippant epigram:

> "Though hell at the first
> Might seem to be worst,
> Yet time the annoyance might soften:
> But if you are bored
> With praising the Lord,
> You'll be more so by praising Him often."

While our thoughts are directed to external sources of joy or sorrow we can hardly apprehend the deep and tragical significance of eschatology. But when we examine the consciousness itself, and note how its joys and sorrows alike are the product of its own condition, the matter assumes an overwhelming significance. For facing eternity, that eternity which it does not seem within our power to evade, it is evidently necessary to have a consciousness which, at home with eternal things, has learned to live a life tolerant of an eternal continuance and growth. A life which has become entirely dependent on the things that are passing away might be hardly less desolate and forlorn in an eternal world than one which has heedlessly misused the things of the senses. A Dives in hell might suffer as much as a debauchee or a criminal. For to the thoroughly vicious character the indulgence has ceased to be pleasing, and hell only continues the habit of his life; but for Dives hell means the loss of the comforts and luxuries which were his only pleasures.

A man living the luxurious and self-indulgent life of the clubs had one night a dream, which altogether changed his course of life. He was in hell, and he knew it. But the strange thing was that he was in the smoking-room of his club, and everything appeared just as usual. He rang the bell, which brought in the waiter, alert and respectful. He asked for the evening papers. "Yes, sir," was the reply, and they were immediately brought. He glanced through them, but could find no interest in them. He rang again. The same deferential waiter was at the door. He ordered a brandy and soda. "Yes, sir," and it was brought at once. "Waiter," he asked, "where am I?" "In hell, sir," was the reply. "Is this hell?" he cried; "is it just like this? Will it continue so?" "Yes, it is just this, and will continue so!" "For ever?" "Yes, for ever!" Then the horror of it broke upon him. Life had consisted in killing time with the aimless indulgences of the club. He had always congratulated himself on getting through another day, or week, or winter. Though he had always dreaded death, each lapse of the years of life had been a relief. But now there was no time to kill. He might kill years, centuries, millennia, but he would be just where he was — the selfish meals, the cigars, the drinks, the sporting papers. He realized that he was in hell.

The supreme problem, then, is to obtain an interpretation, a plan, a mode of life which, having in itself intrinsic value, continued into eternity, would retain and increase its value. Not life is what we want, but life that is life indeed. "*Omnia fui, et nihil expedit*," said the Emperor Severus — "I have been everything and nothing is of any use." The same burden is in Ecclesiastes, though with a conclusion that offers a clue. It is a commonplace of thought — and it is this which makes Ecclesiastes the most delicately charming book in the Bible to a mind like Renan's — that all the experiences of honour, indulgence, wealth, and power, which are possible for a human being, may leave the soul as hungry and dissatisfied as ever. Though mistaken mortals start out on the old quest, defiant of the world's experience, it remains true that everything which the world offers is in the long run vanity and vexation of spirit.

There are two or three conclusions which may be considered settled, and it would save a world of disappointment and trouble if only youth could accept them as proved from the beginning. In the hope that one or another of my readers may be led to grapple with the subject in time, I will state three of these conclusions: In the first place, it is quite impossible that a human life should verify itself or become valid in isolation. Only as part of a social organism can the individual really live. In Aristotle's vigorous phrase, one who would separate himself and be apart is ἢ θεὸς ἢ θήριον, either a god or a wild beast. But Aristotle was not aware of the facts, whether of theology or of natural history, which make his comparison at either end unsuitable. For God, as we have learnt to know Him, is not isolated. In His intrinsic and Eternal Being He is Love. Within Himself is the movement which establishes relations, and goes out to make objects of love. So far from being isolated, God goes out like a Father to His children, and seeks to bring them into His family, reconciled and happy. The solitary human life, hoping to find a self-sufficiency in isolation from its fellows, is not Godlike, as we understand God. Nor is it fair to compare such a life with the wild animal, for all through the life of animals runs the principle of co-operation and mutual aid. The wild beast of the forest has its domestic life, its love for mate and offspring, its heroic struggle for the life of others. A man that separateth himself, and expects to make his life alone, can find no real justification in heaven or in earth. Every life consists and must consist of relations. A human life is necessarily a network of delicately woven and solicitously maintained relations. So far as it is selfish it is dead while it lives. It lives really in the extension of these finely spun relations with other lives, with other beings, with God. The first step in life is to find the true relations in the family, the reverence to parents, the consideration for brothers and sisters, the kindness to dependents, which make the home life. It must be owned that one who has missed these preliminary lessons of life is at a great disadvantage, and a wise state will do its best to provide homes for orphans, and those who, by the vices of parents, are robbed of that initial training. The second step in life is to realize the rights and claims of others in the world. This is the chief lesson that school has to teach, and is a reason for preferring a school training to a too lengthy course of education at home. The third step in life is to extend the relations with friends and acquaintances to the whole country. Patriotism is a necessary transition from the life of the family to the family of mankind. We cannot attain cosmopolitanism at a bound; our love of mankind is insipid and bloodless, if it does not pass through the love of the country to which we belong. But the fourth step in life is to gain the sense of humanity, to believe in its solidarity, and to hold oneself a debtor to the whole race. That life has become truly good and worthy of immortality, which throbs with the life of the whole. It could be wished that over every human grave might be written the epitaph which marks John Howard's resting-place in Russia: "Reader, whosoever thou art, know that thou standest by the grave of a friend."

Life is not achieved or realized until all human beings are recognized and potentially loved; until the life's work, however simple and humble, is done as a contribution to the life of the whole, a personal salutation from the individual to humanity. The fifth and final step in life, coming often, at least partially, nearer the beginning, is the recognition of the greater spiritual company to which we belong, the spiritual presences which occupy the world, and give meaning to the universe. Only then do we live in the fuller sense when we are come unto Mount Zion, and unto the city of the living God, the heavenly Jerusalem, and to innumerable hosts of angels, to the general assembly and church of the firstborn who are enrolled in heaven, and to God the judge of all and to the spirits of just men made perfect.

z

The family in which we were born is much larger than we knew.

In the second place, it is not possible to give a genuine value to life without God. No one hitherto has succeeded in doing it, though the pathos of human folly is that in each generation men renew the experiment. But it is only in relation with the supreme, ordering and unifying life — which is God — that the individual life acquires worth. There are times when the life of humanity seems enough, and socialism offers a substitute for religion. But again there are times when even humanity, conceived as a whole, and brought by supposition to its ultimate perfection of harmony, co-operation, and love, remains a *caput mortuum*, lacking explanation or adequate reason for existence. We can only keep humanity as an object of desire and love, when we succeed in regarding it as the life of God seeking self-expression. Human has its value as antithetical to divine. And if humanity as a whole is only of worth as the expression of the life of God, our individual lives acquire their meaning and value only by realizing the life of God in them. It may, and must, be evident that the life of God is at work in all things, and even the lowest forms of life betray the presence of that informing life which gives unity and harmony to all. But the life of God in humanity is God emerging to a kind of limited consciousness in the individual. It is a hint, a suggestion, a promise, a potency, not an immediate fulfilment. Consciousness is as it were a daring experiment. It is a particle of the Divine life, flung off, to try whether it will develop in harmony and love with the whole. It is breathed out from God in order to return voluntarily to God. But if this is the origin of the mystery of human life, it is evident that no human life can justify itself, or discover its own validity, until it realizes its origin and purpose, nor can final justification be reached until the purpose is accomplished, though life becomes of value directly the purpose is grasped sufficiently to make the result an object of desire and of quest.

Life without God must always be an abortion, an ache, an unfulfilled desire. The attempt to organize human life without God, resulting in the complicated atheisms of the world, the conventionalities and insincerities, the pitiless competition, the hungry generations treading each other down, the nations engaged in war or in ruinous preparation for war, in commercial rivalries instead of hearty and brotherly co-operation, is the clearest proof that only with God and in right relation to Him can human life be valid, successful, or happy.

Sit down in a calm moment and ask yourself: Why am I here? Why should I strive for goodness, for love, for life? What account can I give to myself for my existence, or what goal can I set before my eyes for my endeavour? Unless you may use the term God for explanation you will find that you can give no satisfying answer, no answer which does not leave your life a prey to sickening disillusion. The human soul, when it comes to reflect, has no choice. It is shut up to God. There is God or — nothing. Human life admits of no rational interpretation, except that its aim is "to glorify God and to enjoy Him for ever."

It is observed in every great picture that there is some object, some touch of colour, which gives unity to the whole. If that small spot is covered or removed, the picture, though it does not disappear, becomes flat and insipid. The genius of a painter might sometimes introduce into a failure from the brush of another that centralizing and vitalizing point which would redeem the whole.

In the picture of human life there must be such a point, round which or in reference to which the other lines, or colours, are introduced. If that point is omitted the whole composition is flat and tedious. No dashes of brilliance, no touches of loveliness here and there can save it as a whole.

That point in the picture of each man's life, central, indispensable, without which the life ceases to be a life and becomes a mere succession of vanishing sensations, "mere glimmerings and decays," is God.

But, in the third place, man is not able to give any but a poor, degrading, and threadbare meaning to life unless he has "Forever." The limits and the uncertainty of human life reduce its value, sometimes to the vanishing point, unless we are permitted to regard it only as a beginning, which is to find its fulfilment and ultimate justification in the life beyond. When Pliny nobly said: "Death is the end, not of life, but of our mortality," he struck the note which is absolutely essential to make life a reality, a significant reality. In youth and health there are full-blooded seasons of buoyant expectation and joyful achievement, which easily mislead us. For most men there have been days and weeks, if not months and years, in which to breathe, to eat, to move, to love, to labour, furnished all that seemed to be necessary. For a limited time we can live with a limited horizon. And it is certainly true that, with a definite object in view, a work to achieve, something to make or to finish, the mind may be so absorbed and concentrated that it is not conscious of any desire beyond. While Gibbon was engaged on his masterpiece, through those years of patient toil and brilliant performance, he desired no immortality, unless it were the immortality of his work. And a great part of mankind are at any given moment living under this restriction of view, the sails trimmed and taut before the steady gale of life. But this familiar fact does not alter the truth, that on the one hand these seasons are for all men exceptional, and on the other hand, even in the moment of deepest absorption, an hour's reflection would show that the effort and strain lacked a rational defence unless a draft might be drawn on the future. Sir Walter Scott was so absorbed in writing his novels, in order to pay off the huge obligations of Constable, that he lost sight of everything, except the money which the amazing stories brought in. But for that very reason the sight of that heroic toiler would become an anomaly and a pain, unless we might assume that not only were the works immortal, but the noble heart which conceived and executed them would continue in the universe of God, one of the noblest pieces of God's handiwork.

Scott's Melrose is a good place in which to work out this theme. In the burying-ground which surrounds the Abbey is an old gravestone, bearing a *Memento mori* and these satiric lines:

"Earth goeth on the earth, glistering as gold,
　The earth goes to the earth, sooner than it wold,
　The earth builds on the earth castles and towers,
　The earth says to the earth, 'All shall be ours.'"

It is a cryptic saying. Man is the earth walking on the earth. But when the earth says to him, All shall be ours, does it mean that earth claims for her offspring the future, the eternal? Or does it only express ungrammatically the idea that all, man included, shall return to dust?

But the question, however raised, is here surely answered. For under the south wall of the ruin is the grave of Sir David Brewster. There is a tragedy in that tomb. He left Tweedside in fear of the deep, swift rushing river, and yet afterwards his own son, at the age of thirteen, was drowned in it. There by the river lie his ashes, but on the tomb are the words: "The Lord is my light." The great searcher into the laws of light has found the Light. The earth goes to the earth, no doubt, but Sir David Brewster goes to the Light, that Lord in whose light we see light.

Those ruins thrill with spiritual and eternal meaning. From the keystone of an arch in a ruined passage looks down an exquisite carving of the face of Jesus. As one wanders and meditates among the rich memorials of the past, with the great names reverberating through the mind, the achievements of science and art, sure to remain while man remains on the earth, coming into review, the clear river lapsing by, the Eildon hills looking down, and the story of Border war and minstrelsy endowing the enchanted scene with spiritual glory, these monuments of mortality and decay are drenched with the light of immortality, and one is conscious that the great dead, known or unknown, have passed through these scenes and left the marks of their passage, because they are gone on to larger activities and to more enduring fame.

The instinct of the future life is too strong in great souls for us to know how they would have acted if it had not been there. The explanation of their greatness is so rooted in their everlastingness that we should hesitate to call them great if now they were dead or could die.

Even for ordinary men, with no works of genius to accomplish, but only the work of life to do, it would hardly be possible, when the few buoyant days of youth are over, to live worthily, if a doubt assailed them that life meant only the distance from birth to death. Within those cramping limits it is not possible to write anything great, or on a fine scale, were it only for this, that the ulterior limit is absolutely uncertain. How can one find heart to attempt nobly under the shadow of an impending sword? "Secure me my seventy years," a man might say at twenty, "and I will plan my life for a seventy years' achievement." But when the inexorable oracle answers, "I can secure you only to-day," the hand falters, the wings of desire are furled, and the heart finds its wisdom in the conclusion, "Let us eat and drink, for to-morrow we die."

We need the higher Oracle, which says credibly and convincingly: "You have for ever. The earthly life, it is true, is brief and uncertain, but conceive and work in the assurance of life continuing. You have plenty of time if your conception is worthy. Plan your life as part of eternity. Face death, but be not disconcerted by it, for it is only an incident, and not a disabling one."

Evidently some short lives are merely the exhibition of an activity destined for appreciation and achievement elsewhere:

> "Ostendent terris hunc tantum fata, neque ultra
> Esse sinent."

But all lives, even the longest, are of the same nature, brief manifestations in time of a persistent purpose and energy. The short earthly span has its purpose, for the world's life and for the soul's. When it is accomplished, the soul, like the work of the potter, is turned forth sufficiently impressed.

> "I count life just a stuff
> To try the soul's strength on, and educe the man."

With this wider range, not forgetting but ignoring death, we can approach our task in life undisturbed, unalarmed. We do not limit our undertakings to the permission of a future straitly defined though to us unknown. We draw our arc of the circle, be it long or short, by the foot of a compass planted in eternity. This gives the possibility of a high endeavour, of a noble achievement here, and the certainty of achievement, even the completest, elsewhere.

Herbert Coleridge, the grandson of the poet, was a great scholar at Oxford. He died at thirty. But when, eighteen months before the end, he was told that recovery was hopeless, his only reply was: "Then I must begin Sanscrit to-morrow." Yes, we must have large room and spiritual certainty to attempt or to achieve anything worthy. We must not waste time in fuming at its narrow limits, or refuse to use it because it is gone as soon as we begin. We want a reason for using each day with a reverent serenity, with a deliberate purpose, for using all the days without haste, without rest. This reason can only be found in a deep, unalterable conviction of the eternal value of time, and of the timeless life of the soul.

Unhappy and helpless is the soul that is haunted and paralyzed by a fear of death. Unhappy and decadent is a State which is composed of citizens thus under sentence of death. They will accomplish nothing great for themselves or for their country. The irony of things is too much for us, unless we are immortal.

Hazlitt says of Cavanagh, a famous fives player of the time: "The noisy shout of the ring happily stood him in stead of the unheard voice of posterity." Yes, for fives, for games, for trifles, the noisy shout of the moment suffices. But to do great things, long things and lasting, it is idle to depend on that noisy shout. What does the ring know of its benefactors and heroes? For a man to do greatly it is necessary to be independent of to-day's applause or of the evening's uncertain wage. Some holier voice must sound in his heart; not the ring of visible onlookers, but Eternity, like a great ring of pure and endless light, must be his tribunal. How else can life be nobly lived, or any worthy result be harvested? The limits of a man's life are not birth and death, but birth and Forever. Now, the failure to give worth to life apart from these regulative ideas, Love, God, and Eternity, is, if one rightly considers, the ratification of those ideas. For we can have no proof of anything stronger than the fact that it is necessary to the best and highest life. If it were conceivable that Love and God and Eternity were only ideas, destitute of reality or concrete existence, we should be justified in assuming them. These should be our postulates, because from them we can start to live serenely, joyously, and effectively.

If they should prove hereafter not to be; if we should plunge into forgetfulness at death and cease to be, defrauded of our dream — the very supposition becomes impious as we think more seriously about it — yet we should have done well, for we should have shaped and carried on our brief life on the grandest and noblest supposition which we could frame, we should have followed the instincts which verify themselves within us as the best we know.

For the march of life we must have some banner floating over us, some music to put vigour into our steps, some Leader who directs and inspires us. The conscious universe will not reproach us because, mortals, weak and limited, we marched, with love as the banner floating over us, to the music of eternity and under the leadership of God. On the other hand, what powers, seen or unseen, can greatly applaud the paltry march of the human atoms, each one selfish, living to himself and falling by the way into the unconscious dust, moving only to the dirge of death, led by nothing and no one but blind appetites and unverified surmise?

But when your life is thus conceived in the sweep of eternity, a moment in a succession which has a purpose and a progressive goal, when the length and the certainty of the years are subordinated to the assurance of the great Forever, you can fix your aims and adjust your activities on a noble scale. You can approach the task which harmonizes with your convictions and your capacities, you can set about it and continue in it serenely to the end. Meanwhile each day acquires its absolute value, and can be lived with an artistic completeness. The *now* has become significant precisely because it is eternal. Each day is a piece of the coloured glass to be fitted into the whole mosaic. It can be selected, cut, and adjusted with love and delight. The day, though one of an infinite series, is complete in itself, a pulse in the eternal music, beautiful and precious, not without its immortality in the growing sum of a soul's life and of the spiritual experience of the whole.

Therefore let each day be approached with insight and determination. This day is to be lived, not slipped through. Let it have its hours of devotion, its intercourse with God, its hallowing influences by which the Divine obtains free access to the springs of being. Let it have its hours of work, work necessary for the daily bread, work, if possible, serviceable in itself, to the world, a valid contribution to the whole life which is being lived under God's eye to-day. Let the recreation be joyful and clean, leaving no bitter dregs in the cup, no stains or strains on the soul. The day has its numerous points of contact with other souls. Here is the great opportunity. It was one of Scott's noblest characteristics, as it appears in his journal, that if he was depressed and miserable, he would take care to conceal it from all who were in the house, determined that the trouble should not be aggravated by making other people wretched.

In every encounter with others there is the possibility of honour and victory. A good day is often made up, not so much of its deep devotions, its strenuous activities, its planned recreations, as of the passing words and smiles, the spiritual emanations and radiations, which give to others the sense of joy, or beauty, or love. As a painter puts the colours on his canvas, eagerly, lovingly, so you may touch soul after soul throughout the day with some lasting colour from the palette of God which is in your hands. A picture is made by minute touches. A day is made by its details.

> "Count that day lost whose low descending sun
> Views from thy hand no worthy action done."

Often our worthiest action will be only a word, a peculiar intonation of the voice, a way of grasping a hand.

Sometimes the worthiest action will be a silent struggle in the breast and an inward victory. Frequently the worthiest action will be a prayer or an aspiration.

No day therefore need be lost. You may bear yourself in such a manner, you may so sit at the table of life, among the indiscriminate guests, you may employ your faculties, whatever they are, in such a spirit, that the day's life will be an achievement, another piece of coloured glass fitted into the mosaic. You may thank God for that day; and others may silently thank Him that you lived it.

CHAPTER XII

DEATH

LIFE is good, very good. Death also is good, though we hesitate to say very good, for there is a fear in it. Awe gathers around the name, and at times the King of Terrors seems the only suitable description of that shadow feared of man. How vague and unexplored it seems:

> "The other shape,
> If shape it might be called that shape had none
> Distinguishable in member, joint, or limb;
> Or substance might be called that shadow seemed,
> For each seemed either; black it stood as night,
> Fierce as ten furies, terrible as hell,
> And shook a dreadful dart; what seemed his head
> The likeness of a kingly crown had on."

And yet death is good, intrinsically good, good as life. There is only one fault which has invested the Angel Death with these grisly horrors: the fault is not in death, nor in God, but in us. The apostle uttered a deep and all-inclusive truth when he said, "The sting of death is sin." But for sin, death would be sweet and beautiful — beautiful as sleep, and as suggestive of the awaking. There is a misreading of the teaching of the Bible which makes death the result of sin, and commits Paul to the untenable and obviously untrue doctrine that before men sinned death was not in the world, nor, but for that sin, would it have entered. The rich records of the fossiliferous rocks, built up of dead organisms ages before man appeared on the earth, would in this case convict the Bible of error. But this is a misunderstanding, for Paul does not mean by death physical death. He knew well that death existed before and apart from human sin. But he means by death that horror — that vague possibility of hell and torture — which sin has introduced into the idea of death. A quotation from Professor Stevens, though long, may be welcome to the reader who has felt this difficulty in the New Testament conception of death: "Physiology regards death as the law to which all organisms are subject by their very nature. What standing ground can there be left for the view of Paul, that physical death is the consequence of sin? There is a measure of inconsistency here, though not of the sort which is sometimes asserted. Jewish religious thought, in which Paul's view was rooted, could not look at death from the standpoint of natural science. Death was viewed not as a law of all created organisms, but in its ethical aspects. That which constituted the essence of death to the Hebrew mind was not physical dissolution, but the weakness, sickness, and sorrow which are its accompaniments here, and especially the dread of the dark underworld, the land of shadows and forgetfulness into which death ushers the soul. The word 'death' had widely different associations for the Hebrew mind from what it has for the physiologist. The word 'life' has equally different meanings. Paul could say that Christ has abolished death,[1] although he knew perfectly well that physical dissolution is the lot of all bodily organisms. For the Christian death has been transformed by redemption into departure to be with Christ.[2] All things are his who belongs to Christ, including life and death,[3] because Christ has made death the gateway into His eternal joy. As a mere physiological fact — the fact of physical dissolution — death remains what it was before. But by a Jewish mind death is not regarded as a mere physiological phenomenon. When Paul says that death entered into the world and has continued to hold sway over mankind in consequence of sin, we should not, in order to resolve the difficulty in question, jump to the conclusion, as many expositors have done, that moral and not physical death is meant. We should rather remember what death connotes to the Jewish mind, which does not separate the physical from the moral after the manner of natural science, but finds the primary significance of the fact of death in its ethical aspects. It is sometimes said: On Paul's principles we should be required to suppose that, had sin never entered the world all the human beings that ever lived would still be living on earth. The

[1] 2 Tim. i. 10. [2] Phil. i. 23. [3] 1 Cor. iii. 22.

objection only shows how the real import of Paul's doctrine may be missed by making physical death mean in Paul just what it means in biology. Paul's thought would lead to the idea that, had there been no sin, death, with its accompaniments of sorrow, pain, and fear, would not have been. But some other transition or cessation of earthly existence (which would be death in the sense of biology) would not thereby be excluded. . . . Practically the religious motive of Paul's doctrine was that the sting of death is sin.[1] It is sin which makes death terrible; Redemption robs it of its terrors. Theoretically Paul held something more than this. But what was more than this was incidental to his thought in consequence of his Jewish training, and was not essential to his view of religion."[2]

Death in itself is good, a point in the wise and beneficent order of things. "After life's battle," says Arrian, "God, like a wise general, sounds a recall." Death has become suspect, terrible, the supreme enemy, only because sin has broken the connection with God and cast upon the unknown future the lurid fires of its passion and disorder. Directly sin is removed — or even so far as it is ignored — death assumes its unobtrusive place in the plan of organic evolution — an event not to be dreaded nor to be desired, but to be accepted with

---

[1] 1 Cor. xv. 56.
[2] "The Theology of the New Testament," p. 352. T. & T. Clark.

perfect equanimity, and, in the fulness of Christian hope, with triumphant joy.

They say that children have no fear of death.

> "'Tis the purblind
> Dim sense of after years that makes our monsters.
> The earth hath none to children and to angels.
> Eyes weak with vigil, seared with scalding tears,
> Betray us, and we start at death and phantoms
> Because they are pale." [1]

Like the animals, children suffer pain, and are restless in disease, but death does not trouble them. It comes to them unknowing, and has done with them before they are aware.

Something of the child element remains in all humanity, and a great proportion of mankind face death without any undue apprehensions. Perhaps most men pass the shadow with their eyes screened, and are unconscious that they are dying. Indeed, where death comes, not by disease, but by violence, the average man, though he be a criminal on the scaffold, maintains a brave show. Thus Clootz, who published "Evidences of the Mohammedan Religion," when brought to the guillotine, March 24, 1794, "still with an air of polished sarcasm endeavours to jest, to offer cheering arguments of materialism; he requested to be executed last 'in order to establish certain principles,' which hitherto I think," says Carlyle sardonically, "Philosophy has

---

[1] "The Roman," p. 81. Sidney Dobell.

got no good of."[1] And Danton at the foot of the scaffold was heard to ejaculate, "O my wife, my well beloved, I shall never see thee more then, but ——" interrupting himself — "Danton, no weakness!" And to Samson the headsman, "Thou wilt show my head to the people — it is worth seeing!" It is theatrical, we say, but yet it argues the strength of the human heart, or the shorn terrors of death, that one can keep up the miming under the stroke of such an execution.

There is a deep well of truth in the noble stoicism of Cleanthes, who, advised by the doctor not to eat, for an ulcer on the tongue, cured the ulcer by two days' fast, but then refused to eat, saying, "Since I have gone so far on the road it is a pity not to finish the journey." Nor can we deny fortitude and benignity to Petronius, the disciple of a very different school, who, having taken poison, talked gaily to the last of the current songs and epigrams.

Socrates showed for all time how serenely and unselfishly the man of high thoughts can die. "It is time to wash," he said, "for I think it better to wash before drinking the poison and not to give trouble to the women to wash the corpse."[2]

Hume should not, according to orthodox theories, have approached death with much alacrity; but when the sentence of its approach was passed, he took leave of life in these memorable words: "I now reckon

[1] Carlyle, "French Revolution," ii. 323.
[2] Phædo, 115. A.

upon a speedy dissolution. I have suffered very little pain from my disorder; and what is more strange, have, notwithstanding the great decline of my person, never suffered a moment's abatement of spirits; insomuch that were I to name the period of my life which I should most choose to pass over again, I might be tempted to point to this later period. I possess the same ardour as ever in study and the same gaiety in company; I consider besides that a man of sixty-five, by dying, cuts off only a few years of infirmities; and though I see many symptoms of my literary reputation's breaking out at last with additional lustre, I know that I could have but few years to enjoy it. It is difficult to be more detached from life than I am at present.

"To conclude historically with my own character, I am, or rather was (for that is the style I must now use in speaking of myself, which emboldens me the more to speak my sentiments); I was, I say, a man of mild dispositions, of command of temper, of an open, social, and cheerful humour, capable of attachment, but little susceptible of enmity, and of great moderation in all my passions. Even my love of literary fame, my ruling passion, never soured my temper, notwithstanding my frequent disappointments. My company was not unacceptable to the young and careless, as well as to the studious and literary; and as I took a particular pleasure in the company of modest women, I had no reason to be displeased with the reception I met with from them. In a word, though most men any wise eminent have found reason to complain of calumny, I never was touched or even attacked by her baleful tooth; and though I wantonly exposed myself to the rage of both civil and religious factions, they seemed to be disarmed in my behalf of their wonted fury. My friends never had occasion to vindicate any one circumstance of my character or conduct; not but that the zealots, we may well suppose, would have been glad to invent and propagate any story to my disadvantage, but they could never find any which they thought would wear the face of probability. I cannot say there is no vanity in making this funeral oration of myself, but I hope it is not a misplaced one; and this is a matter of fact which is easily cleared and ascertained." [1]

This is certainly the philosophical temper in perfection. As the sceptical philosopher enters the portals of the tomb "with no abatement of spirits," we may at least argue that death is not in itself, even apart from considerations of future life and felicity, anything but good.

But philosophy is no monopoly of the philosophers. Even Orsini, who had killed several people with the bomb which was intended to blow up Napoleon III., was perfectly calm as he mounted the scaffold, and said to Pierre, his companion in death, with a gentle tone of remonstrance, "Try to be calm, my friend; try to be calm."

[1] Huxley's "Life of Hume," p. 42.

The contemplation, therefore, of the exits made from life, even by persons who are unfortified by religious hope, and certainly unassured of a future felicity, is singularly calming. Death is seen to be, even at the lowest, a beneficent order of God, the necessary counterpart of earthly life, if not the transition to life of another kind.

Now, before passing to that irradiation of death which Christ has brought into the world by overcoming sin, let us take as a foil the manly and human consolation which could be addressed to the bereaved just before the advent of our Lord. Here is a letter from Servius Sulpicius to Cicero, on the occasion of the death of Tullia, Cicero's dearly-loved daughter. It is dated from Athens, in April, B.C. 45: "When I was informed of the demise of Tullia, your daughter, assuredly in proportion as I was bound to do I felt the burden and sorrow, and shared your trouble with you, as, if I had been on the spot, I would not have failed you, but would have shown you my grief face to face. Although this kind of consolation is poor and bitter, because the very people through whom it ought to be effected are themselves afflicted with the suffering, and only with many tears make the attempt, so that they seem rather to need the consolation of others than to be able to offer to others their services, yet I have resolved to write shortly to you the things which at present come into my mind, not that I think they will escape you, but that possibly you are hindered by grief from perceiving them. Why should your private grief so greatly move you? Consider how fortune has dealt with us up till now: that those things are snatched from us which ought to be no less dear than children, country, honour, dignity, and all our public offices. What could be added to our grief by this additional discomfort? Or ought not a mind trained in such experiences to be callous and set a lower value on everything? Or it is for her sake, I presume, you grieve? How often you, too, must have arrived at the conclusion — I have often reached it myself — that at such times as these they are not the worst off who have been permitted by a natural process to exchange life for death. But what was there which at this time could induce her to live? What possession? What hope? What mental comfort? That she might pass her life united to some young man of position? It was in your power, I presume, to choose a son-in-law, such as your position demanded from our present set of young men, one under whose protection you would think your child safe![1] Or that she might have children, in the sight of whose prosperity she might rejoice, who might hold independently the property they inherit? might seek public offices in due order? might enjoy their liberty in the State and in private life? Which of these has not been taken away before it was given?[2]

[1] She had been divorced by Dolabella.
[2] *Sc.* by Cæsar's usurpation, under which the republican malcontents were smarting.

"But it is an evil to lose our children! An evil, no doubt, were it not worse to bear and endure what we do. A circumstance which brought me considerable consolation I should like to tell you, if perchance it may lessen your grief. Returning from Asia, when I was sailing from Ægina towards Megara, I began to look round over the places; behind me was Ægina, before me Megara, to the right Piræus, to the left Corinth; towns which once were flourishing now lie fallen and in ruins before my eyes. I began to think within myself: 'Why, we small mortals are indignant if one of us dies or is killed, whose life ought to be shorter, when on one spot the corpses of so many towns lie exposed. Will you check yourself, Servius, and remember that you were born a man?' Believe me, I was comforted in no small measure by that thought. Set the same consideration, if you please, before your own eyes. Now at one time so many most illustrious men have perished; from the sovereignty of the Roman people so much has been taken; all the provinces have been convulsed. In the tiny soul of one little woman, if loss has been experienced, are you so greatly moved? who if she had not met her doom now, yet would have had to die a few years later, because she was born human!

"Do you, as well as I, call mind and thought from these things and rather remember those things which are worthy of your character, that she lived as long as she ought — lived as long as freedom — that she those bad doctors, who in the diseases of others profess that they hold the science of medicine, but cannot cure themselves, but rather present to yourself and keep before your mind the counsels which you are wont to give to others.

"There is no grief which time does not lessen and soften. That you should wait for this and not run to meet it by your wisdom is for you shameful. And if the departed have any consciousness — such was her love to you and her dutifulness to her friends — she certainly does not want you to incur that shame. Give your dead one this boon, give it to other friends and intimates who mourn in your grief, give it to your country, that where she needs it she may find your help and counsel.

"In fine, since we have come into such a pass that we must consult such considerations, do not give reason for the supposition that your sorrow is connected not with a daughter but with the political situation and the triumph of the other party. I am ashamed to write more on this subject lest I seem to doubt your prudence; therefore with one more consideration I will conclude. We have seen you

---

saw you her father prætor, consul, and augur, that she was married in the highest circles, that she ran the whole round of enjoyment, and when freedom died departed this life. What complaint have you or she with fortune on this score? Finally, do not forget that you are Cicero, he who has been wont to give precept and counsel to others, nor imitate

frequently support good fortune in the most admirable way, and win great fame from it. See to it now that we may find you equally able to bear adversity, and that it is not to you a greater burden than it ought to be, lest of all the virtues this alone be found wanting in you. As for me, when I know that you are more composed, I will tell you what is going on here and the state of the province. Farewell!"[1]

How frigid! How comfortless! She is gone, but the times are bad, and, besides, all things decay, and all men die. Her life was fortunate, notwithstanding three marriages and a divorce before thirty. If she knows, she would wish you to be calm and support your dignity. And then your grief may get you into political trouble; and if excessive it may damage your character for possessing all the virtues, fortitude included. How much better than all this rhetoric if he could have said, "She lives, and you will meet her in the world beyond!"

Nothing could show more clearly how the world needed a deeper consolation, a clearer hope. For that love must be tempered and chill indeed which can be consoled by these obvious moralizings about a ruined State and a decaying world. Nevertheless the peep into antiquity shows that death was not, to the dying or bereaved, by any means a chief calamity. Honour is more esteemed, and even political safety than prolonged life. Fear of death must be at the

[1] Ad Fam. iv. 5.

worst a weak passion, since every other passion can on occasion master it.

Christ brought life and immortality to light. He drew the sting of death, for He overcame sin and gave to men the possibility of a practical victory over it; in this way He opened the kingdom of heaven to all believers, for as sin disappears heaven appears, life for evermore. He delivered those who through fear of death were all their lifetime subject to bondage. A great voice sounded through the heavens, drowning the dirges and the funeral bells, "Blessed are the dead which die in the Lord from henceforth." Lecky brought out by a pithy contrast the change which was made in the thoughts of men. Anaxagoras, the philosopher, told that his son was dead, remarked, "I never supposed that I had begotten an immortal." But a Christian hermit, when his father's death was announced to him, exclaimed, "Cease your blasphemy; my father is immortal."[1] Even they who have but a taste of the Christian experience obtain a foretaste of this immortality, and they who have no taste of it yet share the conviction which has penetrated Christendom; some vague idea that death has become the gate of life, and that a better world opens out when this world is quitted, has become the common hope of all who inherit the Christian tradition. Men feel a solemn uplift of the heart, and catch glimpses of the visionary world at the tomb which has been proved incapable of retaining its occupant.

[1] "History of European Morals," i. 190–220.

Robert Louis Stevenson, who at no time surrendered, but in the experience of sickness and decline gradually held closer and closer, the Christian verities, wrote after an illness: "I am almost glad to have seen death so close with all my wits about me, and not in the customary lassitude and disenchantment of disease. Even thus clearly beheld, I find him not so terrible as we suppose. But, indeed, with the passing of years, the decay of strength, the loss of all my old active and pleasant habits, there grows more and more upon me that belief in the kindness of this scheme of things, and the goodness of our veiled God, which is an excellent and pacifying compensation." [1]

That is a frame of mind which comes to many through the diffused Christian hope which is in the air. A fuller faith gets fuller vision, and the prospect brightens. But the gleam of Christian faith, the experience, however partial, of the sinful habit overcome, and of the ineffable beauty of holiness, will send

". . . bright shoots of everlastingness"

through the soul, and invest with sudden meaning the resurrection of Him who gave the world this hope, and gives the heart this assurance. This Christian confidence has given to the closing days of men who have lived strenuously and believed firmly a transfiguring glory, making their end radiant like a splendid sunset, or shedding a flood of unearthly light

[1] Letters, vol. i. 357.

on the place of departure, and even on the body that is left behind. The heroic war-worn soul, like the pale, ethereal hulk of the old *Téméraire* in Turner's picture, drops quietly down on rippling, burnished waters, in the peaceful glow of the sinking sun, to its honourable resting-place, whispering immortality. Thus Sir Walter Raleigh ends his dazzling and heroic life — on the scaffold, it is true, but that scaffold rules the future. On the flyleaf of his Bible he writes:

> "Even such is time that takes on trust
>   Our youth, our joys, and all we have,
> And pays us but with age and dust
>   Who in the dark and silent grave,
> When we have wandered all our ways,
> Shut up the story of our days!
> But from this earth, this grave, this dust,
> The Lord shall raise me up, I trust."

How humble, penitent, and hopeful is the word which from the scaffold he addresses to men and to God! "And now I entreat that you all join with me in prayer to that great God of heaven whom I have so grievously offended, being a man full of all vanity, who has lived a sinful life in such callings as have been most inducing to it — for I have been a soldier, a sailor, and a courtier, which are courses of wickedness and vice — that His almighty goodness will forgive me, that He will cast away my sins from me, and that He will receive me into everlasting life. So I take my leave of you all, making my peace with God!"

On what easy terms has this far-travelled and chivalrous Christian come to be with death! The executioner, with all England, hesitated to behead King James's noblest subject, at the King's command. He held back the axe. "I prithee," said Raleigh, "let me see it; dost thou think I am afraid of it?" He felt the edge, and said to himself, "This is sharp medicine, but it is a sound cure for all diseases." As he knelt down some one said he should lay his face toward the east. "What matter," he replied, "how the head lie so the heart be right?" After he had prayed for a little he gave the signal, and as the headsman was reluctant to do his duty, he called on him to strike. So serenely, and carrying manifestly the banner of victory, did he go through the dreaded portal.[1]

These words of good and heroic spirits on the scaffold are among the surest encouragements of the fearful. Other men have not better served their kind by long and useful lives than these by their dauntless words under the gleam of the axe. Thus Sir Thomas More: "Pluck up thy spirits, man, and be not afraid to do thine office. My neck is very short; take heed therefore thou strike not awry, for saving of thine honesty." Bishop Fisher said to the executioner who knelt and asked his forgiveness: "I forgive thee with all my heart, and I trust thou shalt see me overcome this storm lustily." And so the Duke of Suffolk, in answer to the same request:

[1] History of England, S. R. Gardiner, iii. 151, 152.

"God forgive thee, and I do. And when thou dost thine office, I pray thee do it well, and bring me out of this world quickly, and God have mercy on thee!"[1]

Surely that must be a lighted way down which these brave souls step so cheerily — or at least it must open to the light.

Nor is it only on the scaffold, and in the pathos of premature and sudden departures, that the same heartening note sounds out. No scaffold gives a more commanding platform for addressing posterity than the life of a great and industrious man, who, like Gladstone, has wrought for many years in the eyes of men. Thus the words spoken calmly in the falling shadows pervade the world with reassurance and encouragement: "The attitude in which I endeavoured to fix myself was that of a soldier on parade in a line of men drawn up ready to march, and waiting for the word of command. I sought to be in preparation for prompt obedience, feeling no desire to go, but on the other hand without reluctance, because firmly convinced that whatever He ordains for us is best, best both for us and for all."[2]

The most English of these testaments of courage, however, is perhaps that of the only king who in England has earned the title Great. "So long as I have lived," said Alfred at the close, "I endeavoured to live worthily." That modest, unexcited estimate of life, in the shadow of death,

[1] See Hare's "Guesses at Truth," 124.
[2] Morley's "Life of Gladstone," iii. 320.

is the perfect expression of the Christian faith as it has embodied itself in the English character. Perhaps one other dying utterance of a great Englishman may be set beside it. The author of the "Ecclesiastical Polity," one of the masterpieces of the English genius, as the strenuous endeavour to find in matters spiritual the law and order which it is the Englishman's pride to secure in matters political, uttered in the confidence of faith what is the desire of every Englishman who is truly Christian, "I go to a world of order." There, with Hooker, may we who have striven unavailingly for truth and love in their combination be gathered!

In contrast with this spirit of English Christianity in the face of death, we may set the Italian spirit, expressed to perfection in the closing days of Leo IX. "On March 12, 1059, he left Benevento under the escort of the Norman Humfrey. He was obliged to rest twelve days at Capua. He arrived at Rome, but repressed the universal joy by melancholy intimations of his approaching death, too visibly confirmed by his helpless condition. His calm departure reaches sublimity. He ordered his coffin to be carried to St. Peter's; he reposed on a couch by its side. There he gave his last admonitions to the ecclesiastics around, entreating them to abstain from simony and the alienation of the estates of the Church; then he received the last Sacraments. He rose with difficulty and looked into his coffin. "Behold, my brethren, the mutability of human things.

The cell which was my dwelling when a monk expanded into yonder specious palace; it shrinks again into this narrow coffin." The next morning he was dead.[1]

In the closing verses of Leo's namesake, Leo XIII., this somewhat stoical resignation takes a more Christian turn. The aged Pope was most anxious to see his *Nocturna Ingemiscentis Animæ Meditatio* in print before he died. It is a human document of lasting interest, for Leo XIII. was the strongest and best man who occupied the Holy See in the nineteenth century. The elegiacs may be rendered in English:

"Leo, the fatal hour draws near; 'tis time for you to go,
  To take the endless road to bliss, or else to woe!
The gifts which God in bounty gave might bid you hope for heaven,
  The fatal keys, the weighty charge, for so long given.
But think of these with sighs, for he 'mong nations who shall be
  Exalted highest, miserable pays sharper penalty.
I tremble: then there comes a form sweet, and a sweeter voice of cheer,
  Which sounds along my heart and says: Why should you fear?
Why trace and mourn your vanished days? for Christ is near, and as you pray,
  He, pitying, at the cry of faith will wash your guilt away."[2]

---

[1] Milman's "Latin Christianity," iii. 408.

[2] "Fatalis ruit hora, Leo; jam tempus abire est
  Pro meritisque viam carpere perpetuam.

That is a truly human and infinitely pathetic exit. The Pope, who for so many years has held the keys of the kingdom, and spoken as the Vicar of Christ, steals at the last to the feet of Christ, and finds in Him, and Him alone, his peace.

But we have not yet touched that wellspring of holy joy which may be described as the more abundant entrance, that triumph in death which has been witnessed in certain Christians, whose lives have been a conscious recollection of the grace of Christ, or a whole-hearted service in making known that grace to others. If we could pass before our minds the closing scenes, and hear the dying testimonies, of the saints, apostles, martyrs, of the Christian faith, we should have a swelling chorus of the victory over death which was achieved by the passion and resurrection of our Lord.

These transactions on the bank of the dividing river, and the messengers sent from the other side to surprise, to cheer, and to enrapture those who are

> Quæ-te sors maneat? Cælum sperare jubebant
>   Largus contulerat quæ tibi dona Deus
> Et summæ claves, immenso pondere munus
>   Tot tibi gestum annos: hæc meditare gemens,
> Qui namque in populis excelso præstat honore
>   Hei misero! pœnas acrius inde luet.
> Hæc inter trepido. Dulcis succurrit imago
>   Dulcior atque animo vox sonat alloquii:
> Quid te tanta premit formido? Aevique peracti
>   Quid seriem repetens tristia corda foves?
> Christus adest miserans humili veniamque roganti
>   Erratum, ah fides, eluet omne tibi."

about to cross, are not, as some suppose, morbid creations of the sick fancy, or hysterical extravagances of the homiletic spirit. As it becomes more recognized to be a duty of the psychologist to examine the varieties of religious experience, so it might well be a recognized part of Christian apologetics to record and to appreciate those scenes in which the windows are thrown open and the light of eternity streams in.

Let us discard the morbid, the hysterical, and the unmanly. But let us also take note that, in such and such a way, Christians who have greatly lived greatly die, filling the long corridors of death with echoing songs of exultation and the light of a dawning glory.

Here, for instance, is the final bulletin concerning Jefferson, one of the most cultivated and most devoted of the early band of missionaries to the South Seas: "Death was not to him the king of terrors; he had been for a long time past awaiting for and desiring his dismission from a sinful and diseased body, yet often expressed a thankful acquiescence in the will of God; and though he did not experience any extraordinary raptures of joy, he, in general, for a considerable time past enjoyed a settled peace of conscience and a firm persuasion of his interest in Christ. Some of his last words were, 'Comfortable, comfortable; sweet, sweet; glory, glory be to Him!'"

Thus the much-toiling soul approaches its haven of rest, its Ithaca in the sea of eternity, with the sense that all is well and God is to be thanked.

Another veteran of the mission-field, Dr. Edkins, offered a rare glimpse into the unseen world as he approached the portal. He was eighty-three. The day before his death he suddenly exclaimed, "Wonderful! Wonderful!" "What is wonderful?" asked his wife, who was nursing him. "I cannot tell you," was the reply, "but you will know to-morrow." Evidently a scene opens before the soul in death, impressions are received, voices are heard — things which eye has not seen, nor ear heard, neither has it entered into the heart of man to conceive.

Thus the chamber and the article of death come to suggest immortality, and to be visited with wafts of the air from beyond. Look at that last letter written by John Stirling to his mother, only four days before she died; it is rich in the latent evidences of eternal life: "I felt myself walking with you in Greenwich Park, and on the sea-shore at Sandgate; almost even I seemed a baby with you bending over me. Dear mother, there is surely something uniting us that cannot perish. I seem so sure of a love which shall last and reunite us that even the remembrance, painful as that is, of all my own follies and ill-tempers cannot shake this faith. . . . Since you have been so ill everything has seemed to me holier, loftier, and more lasting, more full of hope and final joy. . . . The recollections of all you have been, and done, for me are now the most sacred and deepest as well as most beautiful thoughts that abide with me." [1]

[1] Carlyle's "Life of John Stirling," 216.

A few months later he was entering the unknown himself, ' without any thought of fear and with very much of hope." He wrote to his son: "Everything is so wonderful, great, and holy, so sad and yet not bitter, so full of Death and so bordering on Heaven. Can you understand anything of this? If you can you will begin to know what a serious matter our Life is."

What the Christian hope has done is to make the borderland between life and death a kind of holy country, where the leaves of the trees whisper, and the fruit of the trees is for healing, where the lapse of the waters has an undertone of music, and the air thrills with a great expectation. There is in that country a sacred and solemn joy, which is more satisfying than the festivities which attend our birth or our marriage. There is a suggestion of reunion and finality, the promise —

"And we shall sit at endless feast,
Enjoying each the other's good.'

The closing scenes of Sir David Brewster's life, in 1869, afford one of the most radiant examples on record of the illuminated, covered way which leads to eternal life. The famous man of science had reached the age of eighty-eight. A delightful conversation is recorded between him and Mr. Herdman, which gives an incomparable sense of security and triumph; but the following note of the last words seems to flood the grave with mellow light: "He was always peculiarly reverential and guarded in his way of speaking of Deity, habitually using the words 'God,' 'the Lord Jesus Christ,' 'our Saviour'; but on his death bed the sense of the nearness and the love of the Lord Jesus, at once his God, his Saviour, and his righteousness, overcame the habits of reserve of a lifetime, and he only spoke of Jesus as a personal, living, waiting Friend. Once, when a sense of difficulty seemed to cross his spirit, he said, 'Jesus will take me safe through' with restored confidence. Another time the seldom-spoken words came to my lips and I said, 'You will see Charlie,' but, gathering himself up after a pause, he answered, as if in gentle rebuke, 'I shall see Jesus who created all things, Jesus who made the worlds; I shall see Him as He is.' And he repeated, with that pathetic return to his native Scotch, which was not uncommon with him when greatly interested, 'I shall see Jesus, and that will be grand,' with an ineffably happy, cheerful look. 'You will understand everything then,' it was said. 'Oh, yes,' was the answer, which seemed to come from a very fulness of content. 'I wish all learned men had your simple faith,' it was said at another time; and again there was a pause and the gathering up, and the words dropped out, each with its own weight of feeling and of meaning, 'Yes, I have had the Light for many years, and oh, how bright it is! I feel *so safe, so satisfied*.'" [1]

[1] "The Home Life of Sir David Brewster," p. 415, by Mrs. Gordon.

It must be owned that death in such a cast has become beautiful as life, and even more beautiful, for it suggests a life which, unlike the earthly life, is permanent and satisfying.

In Dr. Rendell Harris's beautiful Life of Frank Crossley, the modern St. Francis, there are several instances of the victory over death which, it would seem, might be, and ought to be, the common experience of mankind. Major Crossley, the father, when he was dying, exclaimed, "Is this death? Why, this is nothing!" Fanny Crossley, the aunt, in her illness saw her departed sisters in the room: "How can any one call it a dark valley? It is all light and love!" Then, stretching out her hands to Christ, she whispered, "I could *run* to meet Him!" Frank Crossley himself said in dying that "he had come to the River, and *there was no River.*"

The secret of such a victory is faith in Christ, who has vanquished death, a mind occupied with Him, a life passed in His service. Brigadier Lee, one of the heroines of the Salvation Army in Norway, was dying, and when her husband said to her, "You are not afraid of death?" she looked at him with clear, surprised eyes and said, "But it's for this that I lived!"

And William Law, the non-juror, after twenty-one years of retirement at Kings Cliffe — years spent in prayer, meditation, writing, and charity — died at the age of seventy-five "in full, vigorous mind, and, in a rapture of joy, singing the angels' hymn."

And here I cannot but record the passing of my friend Lady Rogers, of Birmingham, for it is too beautiful to be locked up in the private records of those who loved her. Honoured and cherished, she lived the happiest of lives. She was always engaged in works of charity, especially among her fallen sisters; the girls of the city called her "the Mother of Birmingham." Happy in her husband and in her children, surrounded by everything that makes this present life dear, she received in the very midst of her years the "one clear call." The last evening that she was up she sang that song, "One more song . . . and then Eternity." An operation revealed that the disease was incurable and her days were numbered. When she knew, she showed no sign of grief, but proceeded to comfort her friends, telling them that she was eager to go. She had nothing but the liveliest interest in the life which was coming. Her minister called to see her, but she forestalled all consolation by saying, "I am not afraid." On the day when the end was near she called her relatives into the room and kissed them good-bye one by one. Then she called the nurses and kissed them, and thanked them for their kindness. Then she asked that the servants might come in; she kissed them and thanked them for their service. Then in a clear voice she prayed and commended them all to God. Presently, to every one's surprise, she began to sing. In a clear voice she sang through that matchless hymn which tells all the story of our need and our redemption:

"Eternal light, Eternal light,
  How pure the soul must be
When, placed within Thy burning sight,
It shrinks not, but with calm delight
  Can live and look on Thee.

The spirits that surround Thy throne
  May bear that burning bliss;
But that is surely theirs alone,
Since they have never, never known
  A fallen world like this.

But how shall I, whose native sphere
  Is dark, whose mind is dim,
Before the Ineffable appear,
And on my naked spirit bear
  The uncreated Beam?

There is a way for man to rise
  To that serene abode,
An offering and a sacrifice,
A Holy Spirit's energies,
  An Advocate with God:

These, these prepare me for the sight
  Of holiness above.
The sons of ignorance and night
May dwell in the eternal light
  Through the Eternal Love."

When she had finished this she sang with equal clearness:

"Rock of Ages, cleft for me."

Then her sister sang "Abide with me"; she could not do more than join in under her breath:

"Hold thou Thy cross before my closing eyes;
  Shine through the gloom and point me to the skies.

Heaven's morning breaks and earth's vain shadows flee:
In life, in death, O Lord, abide with me!"

"Now I am ready to go," she said, and, after a few hours of exhaustion, passed away.

I confess I frequently pray that my own death may be like this, a clear and ringing testimony to the power and sufficiency of Christ in the hour of death and in the day of judgment. But I recognize the wisdom which chooses for us, not only the time, but the mode of our departure. It is surely a high grace, which can be granted to but a few, to light up the gates of death with this ineffable and surviving glory. One thing, however, it is permitted to every Christian to receive by faith — that is, the abolition of death. For Christ has abolished death and brought life and immortality to light in the gospel.

INDEX

Abyssinian War, 175
Addison, 30
Æsop, 8
Æsthetes, 287
Alexander VI., 40
Alfred the Great, 369
Allingham, William, 268
Alva, 212
Apocalypse, 230
Aristotle, 93, 101, 103, 127, 134, 167, 171, 335
Arnold, Matthew, 268
Arrian, 354
Art, necessity of, 293
Art in worship, 315
Astronomy, 225
Athens, 313
Aurelius, Marcus, 39
Avignon, 71

Bacon, 192, 255
Ballard, Dr., 54
Baring Gould, Mr., 15
Bellamy, Edward, 150
Bellini, Giovanni, 309
Bentham, 166
Bible, the, 75, 211, 230, 285
Borrow, George, 265
Botticelli, 301
Bradley, 158, 162
Brewster, Sir David, 342, 374
Bright, John, 281
Bryce, 120
Buckle, 259
Buffon, 205
Bunyan, John, 280
Burns, 272
Burton, Abbot, 68
Butler, 169, 192
Byron, 272

Caird, 176
Calvin, 212
Carlyle, 37, 276, 289, 355, 373
Carruth, John, 324
Carruth, Professor, 28
Cartaphilus, 14
Catherine of Siena, 176
Cellini, Benvenuto, 297
Chemistry, 226
Chesterton, Mr., 156
Christ, a real Presence, 56
Christian Science, 185
Christianity best, 46
Christianity identified with morality, 64
Cicero, 359
Cities beautified, 312
Cleanthes, 356
Clement VI., 68
Clifford, Professor, 235
Clootz, 355
Cobden, 281
Coleridge, Herbert, 345
Comte, Auguste, 53
Conscience, 168, 169, 242
Corot, 303
Cosmas Indicopleustes, 189
Coulton, Mr., 63
Credi, Lorenzo di, 301
Crossley, Frank, 376

Dante, 136, 271
Danton, 356
Darwin, 122, 194, 247, 284
Death, fear of, 354
Defoe, 281
Democracy, 115
Dissent, 31
Dissent in Russia, 43
Dobell, Sidney, 355

381

INDEX

Dobson, 293
Donne, 272
Dowden, 293
Drama, the, 296
Drummond, Henry, 85, 246
Dualism, 251
Duel, 174
Duncan, Professor, 189
Dunlins, 322

ECCLESIASTES, 334
Edkins, Dr., 373
Emerson, 264
Ephesus, Council of, 23
Eucken, Professor, 291

FABIAUS, 125, 151
Fairbairn, Dr., 176
Fall, the, 6
Fiction, 274
Fitzgerald, Edward, 327
Florence, 313
Fourier, 128
Fox-hunter, the Tory, 30

GALILEO, 189
Gardiner, S. R., 367
Genesis, 190
George, Henry, 148
Gibbon, 341
Gladstone, 102, 119, 368
Gnus, 323
GOD revealed, 53, 250, 335, 338
Goethe, 272
Goldwin Smith, 198
Gospels, mythical, 21
Green, Thomas Hill, 97, 178
Gregory X., 71
Gregory XI., 70
Grenfell, George, 170
Guyan, 34

HAECKEL, 54, 159, 177, 190, 196
Harcourt, Sir W., 124
Hare's "Guesses at Truth," 368
Harnack, 46
Harris, Rendell, 376
Hazlitt, 346
Hegel, 158, 177, 295

Hell, 334
Hinduism, 181
Homer, 271
Hooker, 281, 369
Howard, John, 337
Hume, 281, 356
Hunt, Holman, 310
Huxley, 194, 202, 214, 329, 359

IMMORTALITY, 35, 330, 341, 364
Increment, unearned, 153
Italy, 301

J. B., 68
James, William, 158, 164, 179
Japan, 181
Jefferson, the missionary, 372
Jesuits, 44
JESUS, 50, 132, 183, 187, 375
Jew, Wandering, 13
Johnston, Sir Harry, 170
Journal Intime, 56
Journalism, 274
Jowett, Benjamin, 93, 205

KANT, the "Critique," 161-2, 197
Keller, Helen, 325
Kelvin, Lord, 196
Khayyam, Omar, 327
Kropotkin, Prince, 43, 246

LAND nationalisation, 150
Landor, Walter Savage, 270
Lanier, Sidney, 219
Law, William, 39, 376
Lecky, 36, 364
Leibnitz, 10
Leighton, Dr., 206
Lenzem, the holy well, 47
Leo IX., 369
Leo XIII., 370
Leviticus, 79
Life, its goodness, 326
Lightfoot, 39
Literature defined, 259
Lodge, Sir Oliver, 196, 201
Logos, 243
Luther, 138
Lyell, 194

INDEX

McCarthy, Justin, 287
Mæcenas, 319
Marlowe, 272
Melrose, 342
Meredith, George, 127, 308
Mill, John Stuart, 167, 240
Millet, 303
Milman, 370
Milton, 266, 294, 351
Mohammedanism, 77, 181
Monasticism, 98, 136, 166
Morley, John, 120, 274
Morris, William, 127
Municipalisation, 152
Murray, Prof. Gilbert, 267
Music, 295

Nero, 297
Nicholas III., 70
Nicoll, Dr. Robertson, 89
Nietzsche, 10

Obermann, 330
Orsini, 358
Owen, 128

Paley, 322
Pantheism, 241
Paris, Matthew, 13
Pastor, Prof. Ludwig, 42
Pater, Walter, 277
Paul, St., 352
Peace, 117, 174
Pearson, Karl, 247
Perugino, 300
Petrarch, 71
Petronius, 356
Phidias, 313
Plato, 1, 128, 157, 266, 289, 298
Pliny, 341
Plotinus, 24, 57, 204
Poetry, 266
Politics, defined, 92
Pragmatism, 158
Pre-Raphaelites, 287
Protestantism, 50
Psychology, 203, 236

Quincey, de, 277

Raleigh, Sir Walter, 366
Ray Lankester, Prof., 200
Reformation, The, 74, 138
Reid, 158
Religion, the *differentia* of man, 32
Religion and pragmatism, 180, 208
Renaissance, the, 301
Renunciation, 59
Revelation, 223
Réville, 33
Rhadamanthus, 2
Robertson, Dr., 255
Roumania, Charles of, 62
Rucellai, 41
Ruskin, 110, 276, 290, 306

Sand, George, 287
Saunderson, Col., 102
Schiller, F. C. S., 163
Schopenhauer, 178
Science and Religion, 25, 189
Scott, Sir Walter, 341, 348
Sectarianism, 32
Severus, 334
Simpson, Carnegie, 50, 66
Sin, 242
Slavery, 81-2, 172, 213
Smith, Adam, 281
Smyth, Newman, 76
Socialism, 124, 135
Socrates, 356
Sorrow, its use, 61
Spencer, Herbert, 53, 157, 223, 330
Spurgeon, 281
Stephen, James Fitzjames, 266
Stephen, R. K., 332
Stevens, Prof., 352
Stevenson, R. L., 279, 365
Stirling, John, 373
Stowe, Harriet Beecher, 172
Strauss, 16
Stubbs, Bishop, 283
Superstition, 209
Swinburne, 267, 269

Talleyrand, 233
Theology, a New, 232

Theology, Queen of sciences, 222
Thomson, Prof., 196, 239
Thurlow, 29
Thwackum, Parson, 29
Tithonus, 332
Titian, 312
Titus, 80
Tolstoi, 49
Tramps, 320
Trusts, 151
Tupper, 264
Turkey, resuscitated, 114
Tyler, 37
Tyrrell, George, 215

UNION, 39, 45
United States of Europe, 116

Utrecht, Treaty of, 172

VIRGIL, 302

WALKER, W. L., 140
Walker, the Puritan artist, 293
Ward, William George, 215
Wesley, 285
Whitman, 10, 328
Wilson, Richard, 309
Worcester, Ellwood, 250
Wordsworth, 271

YOUNG, EGERTON, 143

ZANGWILL, 15

By FRANCIS G. PEABODY
Plummer Professor of Christian Morals in Harvard University

Jesus Christ and the Christian Character
Cloth, $1.50 net

An examination of the teaching of Jesus in its relation to some of the moral problems of personal life.

"One of the most striking features of modern addresses and sermons is their practical character. . . . This is set forth very emphatically in one of the most remarkable books in the religious literature . . . a study of Christian ethics which is truly inspiring." — *Independent*.

Jesus Christ and the Social Question
Cloth, 12mo, $1.50 net

An examination of the teaching of Jesus in its relation to some problems of modern social life.

The Religion of an Educated Man
Cloth, 12mo, $1.00 net

Religion as education — Christ's message to the scholar — Knowledge and service.

The Approach to the Social Question
Cloth, 12mo, $1.25 net

By REV. WALTER RAUSCHENBUSCH
Professor of Church History in Rochester Theological Seminary

Christianity and the Social Crisis
Cloth, 12mo, $1.50 net

Mr. Ray Stannard Baker writes in the *American Magazine*:
"One of the questions I have asked most diligently as I have gone about among the more progressive religious leaders of the country is this:

"'What recent book, or what man, has given you the most light?'

"By all odds the book most frequently mentioned was 'Christianity and the Social Crisis,' by Walter Rauschenbusch. No recent religious book, perhaps, has had a more favorable reception among both church and secular journals, or a wider reading among religious leaders, than this."

PUBLISHED BY
THE MACMILLAN COMPANY
64-66 Fifth Avenue, New York

By DR. SHAILER MATHEWS
Professor of New Testament History and Interpretation in the University of Chicago

The Church and the Changing Order
Cloth, 12mo, $1.50 net

". . . a most interesting and valuable contribution to the literature of a subject that is growing in popular attention every day. This book is addressed much more, it seems, to the religious than to the scientific, possibly because the latter have the less need for repentance. Those who are troubled in any way at the seeming conflict between the demands of faith, on the one hand, and the experiences of their own reason and the problems of modern social and industrial life, will find here much sage, illuminating, and practical counsel." — *Evening Post*.

The Social Teachings of Jesus
An essay in Christian sociology.

Cloth, 12mo, $1.50 net

"The author is scholarly, devout, awake to all modern thought, and yet conservative and preëminently sane." — *The Congregationalist*.

By NEWELL DWIGHT HILLIS
Pastor of Plymouth Church, Brooklyn

The Influence of Christ in Modern Life
Cloth, 12mo, $1.50 net

A study of the new problems of the church in modern society.

"The new theology finds forceful utterance here. In Dr. Hillis's discourse one is often reminded of his predecessor in the Central Church at Chicago, the lamented David Swing. There is the same sparkle of imagination and wealth of illustration, the same sympathetic feeling and human warmth, the same light but firm touch, the same persuasiveness." — *The Outlook*.

By R. J. CAMPBELL
Minister of the City Temple, London

Christianity and the Social Order
Cloth, 12mo, $1.50 net

"There is a wonderful force of conviction felt pulsating in these clear and trenchant sentences." — *Standard*.

"Inspired by a sense of human need and a deep moral earnestness." — *The Congregationalist*.

By HENRY S. NASH
Ethics and Revelation
Cloth, 12mo, $1.50 net

"This is a great book. It is a poem in prose, a study in English. . . . Every word of the six lectures should be read by thoughtful men of the day, ministers and laymen, believers and sceptics." — JOHN H. VINCENT.

PUBLISHED BY

THE MACMILLAN COMPANY
64-66 Fifth Avenue, New York

By DR. LYMAN ABBOTT
The Great Companion *Cloth, 12mo, $1.00*
"In nothing that Dr. Abbott has ever published does his singularly lucid and felicitous power of statement appear to better advantage than here." — *Chicago Evening Post.*

The Other Room *Cloth, 12mo, $1.00*
"The beautiful faith expressed in this little volume cannot but uplift every Christian that reads it, whether he be Baptist, Catholic, Presbyterian, or Methodist." — *Christian Advocate.*

The Temple *Cloth, 12mo, $1.25 net*
"Dr. Abbott can always be depended upon to write something at once spiritually helpful and artistically satisfying. This combination freights his work with a double appeal, an appeal to the heart on the one hand, an appeal to the intellect on the other." — *Book News.*

By ROBERT M. WENLEY
Modern Thought and the Crisis in Belief
Cloth, 12mo, $1.50 net

A clear, compact, and reverent statement of precisely what conclusions have been reached in the application of scientific methods of research into the text of the Bible, the history of biblical times, and the bases of Christian religion.

By BISHOP CHARLES D. WILLIAMS
A Valid Christianity for To-day
Cloth, 12mo, $1.50 net

A welcome book to the man interested in bringing the church into living relations with the manifold life of the present age; a satisfactory book for the practical man who judges the vitality of the Christianity of to-day by its fruits rather than its roots.

By DR. ARTHUR S. HOYT
The Preacher: His Person, Message, and Method *By the author of "The Work of Preaching"*
Cloth, 12mo, $1.50 net

"Admirable in its matter and its style. Beginning as it does with 'The Personality' of the preacher . . . he carries his readers and students through a reverent study of 'The Message' and concludes with 'The Method.'" — *The Interior.*

PUBLISHED BY
THE MACMILLAN COMPANY
64-66 Fifth Avenue, New York

By HENRY C. KING *President of Oberlin College*

The Laws of Friendship, Human and Divine

Haverford Library Lectures *Cloth, 12mo, $1.25 net*

A summing up in brief compass and in a most winning manner of Dr. King's well-known philosophy of the end of life as the cultivation of friendship with God and man.

The Seeming Unreality of the Spiritual Life

Cloth, 12mo, $1.50 net

As more than one reader comments, this frank discussion of religious perplexities marks a notable and hopeful advance in recent years in rationality, in charity, in catholicity, in spirituality, and in real religious effectiveness.

Personal and Ideal Elements in Education

Cloth, 12mo, $1.50 net

"I am reading it with great profit. It is a magnificent utterance." — WILLIAM F. ANDERSON, Secretary Board of Education of the Methodist Episcopal Church.

Reconstruction in Theology

Cloth, 12mo, $1.50 net

"Its pages represent what is nearly, if not actually, the high-water mark of skill and success in blending a fearless yet discriminating progressiveness with a loyal conservatism in theology." — *The Congregationalist*.

Theology and the Social Consciousness

Cloth, crown 8vo, $1.25 net

"A valuable contribution to current discussion. . . . It is not scholastic; it is not phrased in the technical language of the schools; the thoughtful layman will readily understand it." — *The Outlook*.

Rational Living

Cloth, 12mo, $1.25 net

"As a constructive piece of work, making religiously available the results of contemporary researches in mind, the value of 'Rational Living' is tremendous. At this time particularly the religious teacher needs just what he finds in 'Rational Living' — a book sure, one thinks, to quicken the minister and his sermons and his people." — ARTHUR R. TAYLOR, Rector Trinity Memorial Church, Warren, Pennsylvania.

PUBLISHED BY
THE MACMILLAN COMPANY
64-66 Fifth Avenue, New York